PRECIOUS MOMENTS

by ENESCO

**Collector Handbook &
Secondary Market Price Guide**

THIRD EDITION

Managing Editor:	Jeff Mahony	Creative Director:	Joe T. Nguyen
Associate Editors:	Melissa A. Bennett	Production Supervisor:	Scott Sierakowski
	Jan Cronan	Senior Graphic Designers:	Lance Doyle
	Gia C. Manalio		Susannah C. Judd
	Paula Stuckart		David S. Maloney
Contributing Editor:	Mike Micciulla		Carole Mattia-Slater
Editorial Assistants:	Jennifer Filipek	Graphic Designers:	Jennifer J. Bennett
	Nicole LeGard Lenderking		Sean-Ryan Dudley
	Joan C. Wheal		Peter Dunbar
Research Assistants:	Timothy R. Affleck		Kimberly Eastman
	Priscilla Berthiaume		Jason C. Jasch
	Heather N. Carreiro		David Ten Eyck
	Beth Hackett	Web Graphic Designer:	Ryan Falis
	Victoria Puorro		
	Steven Shinkaruk		
Web Reporters:	Samantha Bouffard		
	Ren Messina		

ISBN 1-888-914-84-X

306 Industrial Park Road • Middletown, CT 06457
www.collectorbee.com

Contents

Foreword By Eugene Freedman

*T*he new millennium is finally here, and I, for one, feel very blessed to be alive to witness this "once in a millennium" occasion. I'm sure that you share my feelings in this regard. Another blessing that I trust we share are the 22 wonderful years that have passed since the PRECIOUS MOMENTS® collection began. I am very honored to have been a part of an endeavor that has touched so many lives and to have had the chance to meet so many collectors and club members along the way.

It has also been my great pleasure to work with two of the most talented and inspired people I know, artist Sam Butcher and Master Sculptor Yasuhei Fujioka. Working together, we developed a collection that now captures those special moments in everyone's lives . . . from birthdays and weddings to friendship and love . . . and more.

Since the introduction of the "Original 21" figurines in 1978, PRECIOUS MOMENTS has paved the way for us to touch other people's lives with beauty and emotion. We began a lasting relationship with Easter Seals and the Boys and Girls Clubs of America. In 1999, we formed an alliance with the National Alliance of Breast Cancer Organizations (NABCO) to help raise breast cancer awareness. Also in the past 22 years, we initiated the PRECIOUS MOMENTS *Collectors Club*® and have held 11 Local Club Chapter Conventions. More recently, we formed the PRECIOUS MOMENTS *Fun Club*SM for our younger collectors . . . and that's only the beginning of what's to come.

May I personally thank you, our valued collectors, for your ongoing support of this beloved collection. It is because of you that the PRECIOUS MOMENTS collection has become what it is today. Much more than a collection of figurines, the PRECIOUS MOMENTS message is a way of life. As we proceed into the 21st century, our greatest wish is that PRECIOUS MOMENTS will continue to bring loving, caring and sharing into the lives of so many around the world.

God Bless,

Eugene Freedman
Founding Chairman, Enesco Corporation

Welcome To The
Collector's Value Guide™

*O*ver the past 20 years, the PRECIOUS MOMENTS line has grown to become one of the largest and most popular collectible lines in the country, so it stands to reason that with over 1,600 pieces in the collection, it's no easy task to keep track of them all! Therefore, our Collector's Value Guide™ to PRECIOUS MOMENTS® by Enesco is the perfect resource to help you monitor the ever-popular line of inspirational pieces.

Within these pages you'll find the most up-to-date information on the PRECIOUS MOMENTS line, including color pictures and the current value of every piece, listed by its production mark. In addition, we'll give you information on the latest releases, retirements and suspensions, as well as an in-depth biography of the artist whose drawings brings each PRECIOUS MOMENTS piece to life. Inside our guide you'll also find:

💜 **A Look At The Upcoming Pieces For The Year 2000!**

💜 **The 10 Most Valuable PRECIOUS MOMENTS® PIECES!**

💜 A Tour Of The PRECIOUS MOMENTS® Chapel!

💜 **A Spotlight On Local PRECIOUS MOMENTS® Clubs!**

💜 **Easy Ways To Display Your PRECIOUS MOMENTS® Collection!**

💜 **Tips On How To Shop The Secondary Market!**

💜 **An Exclusive Interview With PRECIOUS MOMENTS® Artist, Sam Butcher, Plus Biographies Of Eugene Freedman And Yasuhei Fujioka!**

💜 **And So Much More!**

The PRECIOUS MOMENTS® Story

*F*or over 20 years, Sam Butcher and his PRECIOUS MOMENTS artwork have brought hope, comfort and joy to millions of people all over the world. It is hard to believe that this worldwide phenomenon, which encompasses figurines, plush animals, dolls, ornaments and giftware, originally started as a small greeting card business that was more of a hobby to its creator than a career.

THE TEAM IS FORMED!

The story behind the line's beginning is quite unique. While at a Los Angeles, California trade show in 1978, Eugene Freedman, then CEO and Chairman of Enesco Corporation, was struck by a young man named Sam Butcher and his series of greeting cards. The cards depicted a number of teardrop-eyed children, each portraying a different inspirational message of comfort and hope. Freedman immediately realized the potential within the artist. However, when he offered to turn the cards into a line of collectible figurines, Butcher initially refused, claiming that the illustrations would lose their messages in three-dimensional form.

Freedman, nonetheless, brought one of the cards to his longtime friend, Japanese sculptor Yasuhei Fujioka and asked him to create a porcelain bisque figurine of the drawing. Butcher was so overwhelmed when he saw how perfectly the outcome expressed his message, that, when he saw the piece, he began to weep with joy.

That piece, now known as "Love One Another," went on to become one of 21 PRECIOUS MOMENTS figurines to make their debut at a trade show in Chicago that fall. The "Original 21," as those first pieces are called, were highly successful and the line quickly began expanding as Sam Butcher, Eugene Freedman and Yasuhei Fujioka teamed up to bring more of Butcher's messages of "loving, caring and sharing" to the world. To date, the PRECIOUS MOMENTS collection includes over 1,600 pieces; including ornaments, bells, plates, hinged boxes, thimbles and more.

YEARS AND MARKS

The line's success is due in part to its variety of pieces, including a number of pieces which are limited by either time or production quantity. Annuals are pieces that are available for only one year and are marked with the year in which they were produced. A number of ornaments are featured as these "dated" pieces. Both limited and dated pieces are considered "closed" after their production run is complete. Store and catalog exclusives are some of the hardest pieces to obtain, as they are only available through a limited number of outlets and often sell out quickly. Retirements and suspensions also help to keep collectors excited about the line and eager to obtain each piece before it disappears. While a suspended piece is no longer being produced, it is possible that its reintroduction will occur in the future. On the other hand, if a piece is retired, Enesco will never produce that specific figurine again.

Enesco further fueled the excitement over the line by placing production marks on PRECIOUS MOMENTS collectibles since 1981. These marks serve as a classification system to help collectors determine the year in which their pieces were produced. For instance, "Seek Ye The Lord" was produced from 1983 until its suspension in 1986. Therefore, it can be found with four different production marks. A 1983 piece would be marked with a fish symbol, while a 1985 piece would be marked with a dove. Pieces created before 1981 are referred to as "no mark" pieces, while those pieces which were produced *after* 1981 without a mark are considered "unmarked." (See the *Production Mark Chart* on page 37 for more information on production marks.)

JOIN THE CLUB!

Also in 1981, collectors were given the opportunity to express their devotion to the PRECIOUS MOMENTS collection by joining the Enesco PRECIOUS MOMENTS *Collectors' Club.* Club members will receive a quarterly "GOODNEWSLETTER" publication, which details PRECIOUS MOMENTS news and events. Members are also given the opportunity to purchase exclusive pieces which are not made available to the general public. Club officials hoped that the club would have 10,000 members by the end of their charter year, but the success of the club surpassed everyone's expectations, with nearly 70,000 members joining in the first year! Since then, two other official PRECIOUS MOMENTS clubs have debuted. The Enesco PRECIOUS MOMENTS *Birthday Club®,* formed in 1985 for younger PRECIOUS MOMENTS collectors is no longer in existence. It was replaced by The PRECIOUS MOMENTS *Fun Club,* whose charter year was 1999.

CHAPEL OF LOVE . . .

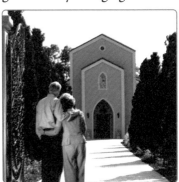

As the PRECIOUS MOMENTS collection grew, artist Sam Butcher decided he wanted to give something back to the collectors who had supported his work, and, in 1984, he decided to show his gratitude by bringing his art skills to a new medium. Butcher designed The PRECIOUS MOMENTS' Chapel as a place of worship for those who needed extra comfort or peace in their lives. The Chapel covers over 2,000 acres and includes a wedding chapel, a gallery museum and the magnificent Fountain of Angels'. The Chapel is also filled with Butcher's artwork, including a large mural entitled "Hallelujah Square" that is one of the most popular paintings on the grounds and generally thought to be one of the most inspirational works Butcher has created.

SHARING THE PRECIOUS MOMENTS®

Adding to the spirit of "loving, caring and sharing," in 1987, Enesco became a corporate sponsor of the National Easter Seals Society, beginning one of a series of relationships with several charities, many of which have continued to today. PRECIOUS MOMENTS dedicated a series of figurines to Easter Seals, releasing one 9" and one regular-sized piece each year. All of the proceeds from these limited edition pieces go to Easter Seals, which is dedicated to helping people with disabilities gain their independence. To date, Enesco has given approximately $30 million to the organization. In addition, Enesco sponsors the Boys And Girls Club Of America, St. Jude's Children's Research Hospital and C.A.U.S.E.S, an organization which supports the prevention of child abuse. Recently, Enesco also joined forces with the National Alliance of Breast Cancer Organizations to help raise money for their research efforts.

Through the years, the PRECIOUS MOMENTS line has continued to grow steadily in popularity, and by 1991 the Butcher family was overwhelmed with requests for licensing rights. At this point, PRECIOUS MOMENTS, Inc., a company designed specifically to handle licensing for PRECIOUS MOMENTS designs, was formed. Jon Butcher, Sam Butcher's son, runs the company today, which handles over 60 prestigious licensees.

The success of the line became even more evident in 1992, as Enesco was presented with both the National Association of Limited Edition Dealers' (NALED) "Collectible Of The Year" award and Sam Butcher won the "Artist of the Year" award, two of the most prestigious awards in the industry. The line continued to be just as successful in following years, and was awarded with NALED's "Figurine of the Year" award in 1994 and the "International Collectible Artist Award" in 1995. NALED's "Ornament of the Year" also went to PRECIOUS MOMENTS pieces in 1994, 1995 and 1996.

Within the past few years, excitement over the line has reached a new high as Enesco has begun adding new lines to the PRECIOUS MOMENTS collection. LITTLE MOMENTS, a collection of smaller sized teardrop eyed children, made their debut in 1996. This was soon followed by the cuddly plush TENDER TAILS who joined the line in 1997. COUNTRY LANE, a series of farm-themed pieces, followed in 1998.

ON THE ROAD WITH THE CARE-A-VAN

Also in 1998, PRECIOUS MOMENTS celebrated its 20th anniversary. The milestone was marked by several special activities, including the introduction of the PRECIOUS MOMENTS Care-A-Van, a promotional "Turn Back The Clock" event and the introduction of special limited edition pieces.

The PRECIOUS MOMENTS Care-A-Van is a colorfully decorated traveling museum filled with PRECIOUS MOMENTS pieces. After the van's debut in April of 1998, the Care-A-Van set out on a nationwide tour, visiting collectors in over 300 locations in the United States and Canada. Collectors could follow the progress of the van by logging on to the Enesco web site (*www.enesco.com*) where Nick, the van's driver, posted postcards and photographs detailing his adventures on the road. The Care-A-Van ended its official tour in November, but since many collectors did not get to see the Care-A-Van during its first tour, it has embarked on a second trip which will run through 1999, and is now called the Care-A-Van II.

DELIVERING THE MESSAGE

Also to commemorate the very special anniversary, a endearing limited edition anniversary figurine, titled "20 Years And The Vision's Still The Same" was introduced to the line. The piece portrays a little girl and a special friend being given an eye exam by a doctor in which she must read the words "loving, caring and sharing."

As the piece "20 Years And The Vision's Still The Same" symbolizes, Sam Butcher and his much loved PRECIOUS MOMENTS figurines have successfully delivered the message of "loving, caring and sharing" to the world for over twenty years now. And, as their success in the last two decades has shown, their contributions to the world have had an impact which is sure to last in the many years to come.

The Crystal Ball Says . . .

What's ahead for PRECIOUS MOMENTS artist Sam Butcher? In addition to continuing his successful line of PRECIOUS MOMENTS and his work on The Chapel, the artist has expressed the desire to market some of his contemporary art as prints; as well as write his autobiography (which he plans to have published posthumously).

Enesco And PRECIOUS MOMENTS®, Inc. Biographies

*E*nesco Corporation, the manufacturer of the PRE-CIOUS MOMENTS collection, was originally created as the import gifts division for the N. Shure Company, which was created in 1953. Upon disbanding from N. Shure, Enesco adopted the phonetic sound of its parent company's initials, (N. S. Co.). The young company was led by Eugene Freedman, who to this day serves as Founding Chairman of the multi-million dollar business. It was Freedman's discovery of the PRECIOUS MOMENTS artwork in 1978 that helped propel Enesco to the enormous success it is today.

In 1983, Enesco was purchased by Stanhome Inc., a move that helped Enesco to become an international power in the giftware industry. The company, which is now based in Itasca, Illinois, has 18 branches worldwide and handles over 12,000 collectible and giftware pieces from such lines as PRECIOUS MOMENTS, Cherished Teddies®, Mary's Moo Moos, Lilliput Lane® and David Winter Cottages®.

PRECIOUS MOMENTS, Inc. was formed in 1991 in response to an overwhelming amount of requests for licensing of PRECIOUS MOMENTS artwork. Today, the company works to oversee the licensing arrangements, making sure that only the highest quality products are released. In addition to handling a library which contains over 3,500 PRECIOUS MOMENTS images, PRECIOUS MOMENTS, Inc., commonly referred to as PMI, offers a full research and development center to its licensees. Jon Butcher, Sam Butcher's eldest son, is currently the C.E.O. and Sara Pilafas is President of PMI whose corporate offices are located in St. Charles, Illinois.

Eugene Freedman Biography

Over the past 45 years, Eugene Freedman has become one of the most well-known names in the collectibles business. Now the Founding Chairman of Enesco, Freedman has played a major role in making Enesco one of the top companies in the industry today.

Freedman had spent time all over the country by the time he reached his 20s. Born in Philadelphia and raised in Milwaukee, the young entrepreneur attended college at Northwestern University and the California Institute of Technology. Freedman also spent time in the South Pacific during World War II and received his naval officer's commission from Notre Dame University upon his return.

Eventually, Freedman returned to Milwaukee, where he accepted a job as a salesperson for a giftware company in the early 1950s. Although he enjoyed his work, Freedman felt the need to branch out on his own and left to open his own plastics and figurine company in 1958. Still not satisfied, Freedman sold his shares in the plastics business soon after and went in search of further adventure.

He found his calling soon after in Enesco, a new branch of the N. Shure Company that was responsible for gift importing. Freedman and six other men pooled their money and bought the branch, and Freedman took responsibility for buying giftware from Europe and the Orient. Since then, Freedman has introduced a number of popular lines for the company, including Enesco's best-selling line, PRECIOUS MOMENTS.

Freedman, who immediately saw the talent of young Sam Butcher upon their meeting in 1978, still holds the line very close to his heart and plays an active role in the line's development, as well as in following the tenets of "loving, caring and sharing."

Yasuhei Fujioka Biography

*W*ith over 50 years of experience, its no wonder that Yasuhei Fujioka is able to translate Sam Butcher's two-dimensional images of "loving, caring and sharing" into three-dimensional form so perfectly.

Born in Nagoya, Japan in 1921, Fujioka was trained from a very young age to learn and appreciate his family's profession of creating artwork. Fujioka studied design in college and set up his own Design Studio in 1955, after spending ten years in the ceramics industry. Through his studio, Fujioka set out on a mission to become a master porcelain and giftware sculptor and has spent years perfecting his sculpting techniques.

In 1960, Fujioka met Eugene Freedman and the two men began a personal and professional relationship that was very rewarding for both. Freedman was aware of Fujioka's talent, so it's no surprise that he trusted his good friend to "breathe life" into a drawing he brought over from America. The end result was "Love One Another," the very first PRECIOUS MOMENTS piece. When Sam Butcher saw Fujioka's translation, he was so awed that he insisted on meeting the sculptor, who has held the title of Master Sculptor ever since.

Although Fujioka has retired as President of the Design Studio, his son, Shuhei Fujioka, has been named as his successor. Yasuhei Fujioka still serves as Master Sculptor for the PRECIOUS MOMENTS line, overseeing a staff of 10 to 15 artisans and approving every figurine before it leaves the studio.

In his spare time, Fujioka has created two collectibles lines of his own, Coral Kingdom and Heavenly Kingdom. Both lines are manufactured by Enesco Corporation.

Sam Butcher
Biography

*I*t takes a very special man to be able to express sentiments and emotions as well as Sam Butcher does in his artwork. Butcher has touched collectors all over the world so deeply with his pieces, that many people who have never even met him consider him to be a close friend.

Butcher was born in Jackson, Michigan on New Year's Day in 1939 to an English-Irish mechanic and his Lebanese-Syrian wife. The third child out of five in the family, Butcher did not have a lot in common with his siblings as they adopted their parents' interest in race-car driving, while he preferred to spend his time writing and illustrating stories. While he was often very lonely as a child, Butcher does have fond memories of his grandmother, who would often tell him stories from the Bible. From a very early age, he was interested in these tales and often worked them into his paintings.

Butcher's passion for creating artwork grew as he entered school and the young boy knew that he wanted to be an artist by the time he entered kindergarten. At the age of 10, Sam and his family moved to northern California, where the Butcher children had to travel 60 miles to get to the nearest school. Butcher was a bright hard-working young man and his teachers encouraged him both in his schoolwork and his artwork. All the while, Butcher's father urged him to find a job rather than to pursue his dreams of becoming an artist.

When he reached his senior year of high school in 1957, Butcher's efforts paid off and he accepted a scholarship to the College Of Arts And Crafts in Berkeley, California. It was at the school where the young Butcher would meet Katie Cushman, who would become his wife two years later.

In 1962, the newly-married Sam and Katie Butcher celebrated the birth of their first son, Jon. Butcher left school and sacrificed his art in order to find a full-time job to support his family. In 1963, shortly after the birth of their second child, Philip, the Butchers began attending a small, local church. As his devotion to the Bible and its lessons grew Butcher began experiencing a number of changes in his outlook on life.

As his family continued to grow quickly, Butcher held numerous jobs over the years, including working as a janitor, a dishwasher and a short order cook. He eventually found a position where he could combine his spirituality with his talent for art, through working as a "chalkboard minister." In this position, Butcher used his illustrations to help teach children about the word of God and also helped to restore the faith of adults who were going through troubled times. Butcher's work on the street soon led to a position as a staff artist for the International Child Evangelism Fellowship in Grand Rapids, Michigan.

By 1974, Butcher's family had grown to include seven children and he supplemented his income by working as a janitor. In his spare time, he enjoyed creating inspirational cards featuring teardrop-eyed children for friends and family. Bill Biel, a close friend of Butcher's, encouraged the young artist to market these images in a line of inspirational greeting cards and the two formed a company called "Jonathan and David," named for the legendary friendship of Biblical figures David and Prince Jonathan.

In the late 1970s, Eugene Freedman, chairman and CEO of Enesco Corporation noticed the cards at a Los Angeles trade show and he approached Butcher about creating a line of three-dimensional

"Raindrops On Roses And Whiskers On Kittens ..."

Sam is often asked about his "favorite things." Here are a few of his responses which have been compiled over the years:

Favorite Color: The Rainbow
Favorite Coffee: McDonald's
Favorite Figurine: "To God Be The Glory"
Favorite Song: "I'll Meet You In The Morning"

figurines from the images. Butcher was initially hesitant to pursue the project, but once he saw how Freedman's friend, sculptor Yasuhei Fujioka, created a perfect translation of the piece's message, he was overcome with emotion and signed an agreement with Enesco to create a number of figurines for them.

Since then, Butcher has designed nearly 2,000 PRECIOUS MOMENTS pieces. As the fan base of the PRE-CIOUS MOMENTS collection has grown through the years, Butcher has won numerous awards, including NALED's prestigious "Artist of the Year" award in both 1992 and 1995. In 1989, he opened The PRE-CIOUS MOMENTS Chapel, a sanctuary for collectors who want to celebrate their love for PRE-CIOUS MOMENTS or who need a little extra comfort or peace in their lives.

With seven children of his own and 16 grandchildren, Butcher insists that his family is still (and always will be) the most important part of his life. Looking back through the years, the artist feels blessed to have been able to teach God's message of "loving, caring and sharing" to his family, as well as to the rest of the world through his beloved teardrop-eyed children.

Key MOMENTS

*C*an you believe that the PRECIOUS MOMENTS collection has been around for over 20 years? While the theme of "loving, caring and sharing" has remained a constant throughout its history, the line itself has undergone plenty of change. How many of these milestones are you aware of?

1978

• Eugene Freedman and Yasuhei Fujioka transform the "teardrop-eyed" children of Sam Butcher's greeting cards into figurines. The "Original 21" debut at a giftware show in Chicago in the fall.

1979

• Precious Moments figurines are first released into stores nationwide. Some of these "Original 21" pieces belong to the *Nativity* series, marking the first introduction of series into the line as well.

1980

• Enesco introduces five musical pieces to the growing line of figurines.

1981

• The Enesco PRECIOUS MOMENTS *Collectors' Club* debuts. Although Enesco anticipated an initial membership of 10,000, nearly 70,000 collectors joined the club in that first year!

• Production marks are used for the first time. These under-stamps are a handy way of distinguishing the year in which a piece was produced.

• Two of the "Original 21" pieces, "God Loveth A Cheerful Giver" and "Come Let Us Adore Him" are honored with retirement, thus forming a secondary market for the line.

• The first dressed, porcelain dolls are added to the PRECIOUS MOMENTS collection. Along with the two dolls, several ornaments, bells, plates, night lights and candle climbers also make their debut.

1982

• The first pieces from the *Mini Nativity* series make their way into stores, as well as the first frames and covered boxes.

1983

• The club figurine "Put On A Happy Face" is honored with the prestigious "Figurine Of The Year" award, just one of the many awards won by Sam Butcher and PRECIOUS MOMENTS through the years.

1984

• Sam Butcher sells his share of his greeting card business, "Jonathan and David," to partner and long-time friend Bill Biel.

• Sam Butcher begins a crusade to find the perfect setting for The PRECIOUS MOMENTS Chapel. After days of driving, he finds himself in Carthage, Missouri.

• Enesco announces the first PRECIOUS MOMENTS suspensions. Unlike retirements, suspended pieces may be reintroduced at a later date, although only a handful of suspended PRECIOUS MOMENTS pieces have been reissued thus far.

• Ornaments, bells and musicals begin to retire.

1985

• Enesco introduces the Enesco PRECIOUS MOMENTS *Birthday Club* to attract younger PRECIOUS MOMENTS collectors.

• The first PRECIOUS MOMENTS thimble is released and the first doll retirement is announced.

• The first eight pieces in the popular *Birthday Train* series are introduced. Unlike other PRECIOUS MOMENTS products, these figurines come in train-shaped boxes.

1986

• The *Birthday Series* is introduced featuring dated ornaments for each year. In 1987, the *Birthday Series* expanded to include figurines.

1987

• Enesco becomes a corporate sponsor of the Easter Seals Society in an effort to give back to the community. To this day, Enesco has raised funds somewhere in the range of $30 million for the organization.

1988

• PRECIOUS MOMENTS celebrates ten years of collectible success.

• Butcher is honored with NALED's "Special Recognition Award."

• The first special event piece "You Are My Main Event," is available at retailers. These exclusive pieces are only available to collectors who attend retailer events.

1989

• The PRECIOUS MOMENTS Chapel opens to the public. The Chapel, Sam Butcher's self-proclaimed "life's work" features over 50 spectacular murals and 30 stained glass windows.

• The *Collectors' Club* holds its first national convention of Local Club Chapters.

1990

• The first PRECIOUS MOMENTS treetoppers and jack-in-the-boxes join the many accessories available to collectors.

1991

• PRECIOUS MOMENTS, Inc., is founded to oversee the licensing of PRECIOUS MOMENTS images and products.

1992

• The *Sugar Town* series, which depicts life in a small town, is introduced and becomes a collectors' favorite.

• Butcher is named "Artist of the Year" by NALED for the first time.

• PRECIOUS MOMENTS introduces its "Distinguished Service Retailer" program, which allows retailers priority status in ordering new and retired pieces in exchange for hosting an annual PRECIOUS MOMENTS event for collectors.

1993

• The first piece in the Noah's Ark" themed series, *Two By Two*, is introduced.

1994

• The circus comes to town with the new *Sammy's Circus* series.

1995

• Enesco launches its "Century Circle" recognition program for PRECIOUS MOMENTS retailers who demonstrate the values of "loving, caring and sharing" through special collector events, as well as community and charitable activities.

• The "A King is Born" figurine and ornament become the first Chapel exclusives to be retired.

1996

• The LITTLE MOMENTS line, a series of smaller PRECIOUS MOMENTS figurines, makes its debut.

1997

• The Fountain of Angels, a spectacular water, light and music show, opens in The PRECIOUS MOMENTS Chapel.

• A Collector Advisory Board is instituted by Enesco and 1997 PRECIOUS MOMENTS, Inc. The board, which consists of seven PRECIOUS MOMENTS "experts," meets twice a year to discuss collector concerns and recommendations.

• The TENDER TAILS line of stuffed plush animals begins to appear in retail stores.

1998

• PRECIOUS MOMENTS celebrates two decades of "loving, caring and sharing." The celebration kicks off with two "Turn Back the Clock" events where collectors can purchase two of the "Original 21" figurines for the original 1978 price.

• The final *Sugar Town* piece, "Sugar Town Post Office Collector's Set," is both released and retired.

• The PRECIOUS MOMENTS Care-A-Van, a 53-foot-long RV that doubles as a traveling PRECIOUS MOMENTS museum, begins to travel U.S. highways.

1999

• Enesco disbands the PRECIOUS MOMENTS *Birthday Club* and launches a new family club, the PRECIOUS MOMENTS *Fun Club*.

2000

• PRECIOUS MOMENTS collectible plush, *Hugs For The Soul*, are welcomed to store shelves. These bears come with porcelain hearts and are named after popular figurines in the PRECIOUS MOMENTS collection.

On The Road To Success

The Precious Moments Care-A-Van toured from April to November as part of the 20th Anniversary Celebration. During that time, the Care-A-Van:

+ Traveled 22,000 miles through 44 states and Canada

+ Drew 91,652 visitors in 149 stops

+ Collected 56,618 pounds of food for Second Harvest

The tour was so successful that Enesco decided to extend the trip into 1999.

What's New For 2000

*E*nesco recently announced their first releases for the year 2000. Among the numerous pieces released were an addition to the *Two By Two* series, 28 general figurines and new COUNTRY LANE pieces. The LITTLE MOMENTS collection saw several new additions this year as well. A collection of plush bears called *Hugs For The Soul* made their way into the PRECIOUS MOMENTS family and 53 new TENDER TAILS (several of which are from series) also made their debut. Most pieces are expected to debut early in the year, so be sure to check with your PRECIOUS MOMENTS retailer for a firsthand look at what's new.

GENERAL FIGURINES

ALLELUIA, HE IS RISEN . . . A girl carries a white lily in remembrance of the Lord in this touching figurine.

BE FRUITFUL AND MULTIPLY . . . Every parent can relate to the love and pride this mom and dad feel for their newborns.

BLESS BE THE TIE THAT BINDS . . . A wife playfully "helps" her husband get dressed for work in this adorable piece.

BLESS YOU . . . Armed with a box of tissues and a hot water bottle, this young lady is ready to fight off the worst of colds!

A Collection Of Precious Moments . . . Nostalgia touches this mom as she looks through an album of old family photos.

Dedicated To God . . . The miracle of new life is expressed in this sweet baptismal figurine.

Friendship's A Slice Of Life . . . This young lady has learned that the best pizza is the kind that's shared with friends!

God Knows Our Ups And Downs . . . This girl and her yo-yo expresses the thought that God is always there to guide us through thick and thin.

God Loves A Happy Camper . . . With a knapsack full of supplies and a flashlight to help guide him, this young boy is prepared for whatever crosses his path!

Good Advice Has No Price . . . While it's important to do well in school, the most important lessons are the ones found in the Bible.

Happy Birthday To Ewe . . . A little lamb celebrates its one year anniversary of life on Earth in the best way possible – with cake and a good friend!

HAY GOOD LOOKIN' (COUNTRY LANE) . . . This little farmgirl takes a break to get lost in her daydreams – and in the hay as well!

HE SHALL LEAD THE CHILDREN INTO THE 21ST CENTURY . . . Children gather around the Lord in this set found in Enesco's "Time Capsule."

ICE SEE IN YOU A CHAMPION . . . This Canadian exclusive depicts a sweetie on skates who has the determination and drive to make her a star!

LET FREEDOM RING . . . A junior Uncle Sam waits by the phone, eagerly anticipating an extra-special call!

THE LORD BLESS YOU AND KEEP YOU . . . Proudly clutching her diploma, this proud little girl beams from ear to ear!

THE LORD BLESS YOU AND KEEP YOU . . . This figurine is the perfect memento to help graduates remember their special day.

THE LORD IS THE HOPE OF THE FUTURE . . . A young graduate looks eagerly towards the future in this touching piece.

THE LORD IS THE HOPE OF THE FUTURE ... As this graduate's special day comes to a close, this adorable girl cherishes her memories.

LORD, I'M IN IT AGAIN ... Tippy proves that dogs really are "man's best friend" by sharing his home with a friend.

A LOVE LIKE NO OTHER ... This special Mother's Day piece captures the unbreakable bond between every mother and child.

LOVINGCARINGSHARING.COM ... You can find nearly anything on the Internet these days – even loving, caring and sharing!

PEACE IN THE VALLEY ... This girl and her horse symbolize a world where all god's creatures can get along in perfect harmony.

PEACE ON EARTH ... Helping to restore peace and happiness across the planet, this pair feel like they are "on top of the world!"

PRECIOUS MOMENTS WILL LAST FOREVER ... Eugene Freedman, Founding Chairman of Enesco, is the star of this exclusive piece.

SCOOTIN' YOUR WAY TO A PERFECT DAY . . . This motorcycle rider is all revved up and ready to go on his new scooter!

A TAIL OF LOVE (TWO BY TWO) . . . This king and queen of the jungle let their tails do the talking as they express their "jungle love" for one another!

THIS DAY HAS BEEN MADE IN HEAVEN . . . Dressed in his Sunday best, this little gentleman makes his way to church.

WE KNEAD YOU GRANDMA . . . This little girl especially needs her Grandma to get her out of a "sticky" situation!

WISHING YOU A BLOW OUT BIRTHDAY . . . This adorable little birthday girl closes her eyes and gets ready to make a wish!

YES DEAR, YOU'RE ALWAYS RIGHT . . . This young man learns the hard way that sometimes the path of least resistance is the best road to take.

YOU COMPLETE MY HEART . . . It's easy to see that this starry-eyed little girl has just been hit by Cupid's arrow!

YOU HAVE THE SWEETEST HEART . . . The only thing sweeter than this shy little girl is the heart-shaped candy that she offers!

FIGURINE SERIES

I'M PROUD TO BE AN AMERICAN . . . A new series of figurines pays respect to the millions of men and women who faithfully serve our country through the armed forces. The Army, Navy and Air Force are just some of the armed forces represented in this release of 20 pieces.

LITTLE MOMENTS
BIBLE STORIES

BABY MOSES . . . Baby Moses is rescued from the river in this depiction of the well-known Biblical tale.

THE GOOD SAMARITAN . . . The Samaritan showed compassion to a stranger who had been beaten and robbed by a group of thieves.

THE GREAT PEARL . . . This piece symbolizes a Biblical verse in which heaven is compared to a merchant who sells everything he has to buy one pearl.

HUGS FOR THE SOUL

FRIENDSHIP HITS THE SPOT . . . This sunshine-colored bear tempts you to settle in for a cup of tea and some afternoon chit-chat!

GOD LOVETH A CHEERFUL GIVER . . . This purple teddy comes with her very own best friend – her puppy!

LORD KEEP ME ON MY TOES . . . All ready for the big performance, this bear looks adorable in her pink bow and tutu!

LOVE ONE ANOTHER . . . This set of bears is offered through select *Century Circle* retailers.

PUT ON A HAPPY FACE . . . No frowns are allowed when this comical clown is around! He is sure to brighten up even the worst day!

TELL IT TO JESUS . . . This teddy is hoping Jesus can help him with his problems – so he decides to call him!

YOU HAVE TOUCHED SO MANY HEARTS . . . This precious teddy bear has enough heart for everyone around her!

TENDER TAILS GENERAL

46 new TENDER TAILS pieces were introduced to the regular line this season. The new pieces span a wide variety of creatures, including bugs and dinosaurs.

BUG SERIES

Six not-so-creepy creatures make their debut in the TENDER TAILS *Bug Series*. Much more lovable-looking than their real life counterparts, the first series consists of an ant, a beetle, a caterpillar, a dragonfly, a grasshopper and a snail.

COLLECT YOUR OWN FAMILY SERIES

The first four TENDER TAILS families make their debut in 2000. Collectors can choose from a bear, a bunny, a cat and a kangaroo, and add as few or as many babies they want to make their ideal animal family.

BIBLE STORIES

ASCENSION OF JESUS . . . This dove serves as a reminder of the miracle of Jesus' ascension and the lessons which he taught while on Earth.

GOD MADE THE WORLD . . . God created everyone and everything in this world, from the smallest bug to the tallest giraffe!

JESUS FEEDS THE 5,000 PEOPLE . . . This fish comes in a decorated box, which tells the Biblical story of Jesus feeding his people.

JESUS AND THE CHILDREN . . . Children are the lamb of God and Jesus dedicated his life to teaching them right from wrong.

NOAH'S ARK ... Two of each animal, even the hefty elephant, were invited into the Ark to survive savage floods.

THE TEN COMMANDMENTS ... This bluebird serves as a reminder of the Ten Commandments which God gave us to follow.

HUGS FOR YOU

TENDER TAILS *Hugs For You*, is a series of larger TENDER TAILS pieces who wear inspiring messages on their T-shirts and come equipped with Velcro paws, which make them even better huggers!

ORNAMENTS

One set of new ornaments has been added to the collection this year. The set of "Bunny Mini Ornaments" includes six adorable colored bunnies, who are perfect for wiping away those "winter blues."

Recent Retirements

*A*s part of their "A Toast to 2000" event, which was broadcast live over the Enesco website on October 29, 1999, Enesco announced the immediate retirement of 21 pieces. These pieces, which include 18 figurines, two ornaments and one tree topper, are listed below, along with five retirements that were announced on the QVC Shopping Network on November 9, 1999.

Figurines

- ❏ Can't Be Without You (*Birthday Series*) . . . (#524492, 1991)
- ❏ God Is Love, Dear Valentine . . . . (#523518, 1990)
- ❏ Hallelujah For The Cross . . . . (#532022, 1995)
- ❏ Happy Birthday Jesus (*Miniature Nativity*). . (#530492, 1993)
- ❏ Have I Got News For You
  (*Miniature Nativity*) . . . . (#528137, 1994)
- ❏ Hoppy Easter, Friend . . . . (#521906, 1991)
- ❏ I Can't Bear To Let You Go . . . . (#532037, 1995)
- ❏ It's A Perfect Boy (*Miniature Nativity*) . . . . (#525286, 1991)
- ❏ Just Poppin' In To Say Halo! . . . . (#523755, 1994)
- ❏ Lettuce Pray. . . . . (#261122, 1997)
- ❏ Mornin' Pumpkin . . . . (#455687, 1998)
- ❏ Nobody Likes To Be Dumped
  (COUNTRY LANE) . . . . (#307041, 1998)
- ❏ Our Friendship Is Soda-licious . . . . (#524336, 1993)
- ❏ Sharing Sweet Moments Together. . . . . . . (#526487, 1994)
- ❏ This Too Shall Pass. . . . . (#114014, 1988)
- ❏ To A Special Mum . . . . (#521965, 1991)
- ❏ What The World Needs Is Love . . . . (#531065, 1995)
- ❏ Wishing You A Basket Full Of Blessings . (#109924, 1988)
- ❏ Wishing You A Happy Easter . . . . (#109886, 1988)

❏ You Suit Me To A Tee . . . . (#526193, 1994)

Ornaments

❏ He Cleansed My Soul . . . . (#112380, 1987)
❏ Waddle I Do Without You . . . . (#112364, 1987)
❏ Joy To The World . . . . (#150320, 1995)
❏ Joy To The World . . . . (#153338, 1996)
❏ Joy To The World . . . . (#272566, 1997)

Tree Toppers

❏ Sing In Excelsis Deo . . . . (#183830, 1996)

PRECIOUS MOMENTS® Top Ten

*T*his section highlights the ten most valuable PRECIOUS MOMENTS pieces as determined by their secondary market values. In order to qualify for this list, pieces must have top dollar value and show a significant percentage increase in value from their original retail price. You will notice that several of the pieces are either from the early years of the collection or are limited editions.

God Loveth A Cheerful Giver
Figurine • #E1378
Issued: 1979 • Retired: 1981
Issue Price: $9.50 • Value: NM – $1,000

But Love Goes On Forever
Retailer's Dome • #E7350
Issued: 1984 • Closed: 1984
Issue Price: N/A
Value: ✝ – $855

Good Friends Are Forever
Special Event Figurine • #525049
Issued: 1990 • Closed: 1990
Issue Price: N/A • Value: 🎐 – $760

Friends Never Drift Apart (LE-1993)
Medallion • #529079
Issued: 1993 • Closed: 1993
Issue Price: N/A • Value: UM – $645

Tammy (LE-5,000)
Doll • #E7267G
Issued: 1982 • Closed: 1982
Issue Price: $300 • Value: UM – $565

Nobody's Perfect
Figurine • #E9268
Issued: 1983 • Retired: 1990
Issue Price: $21
Value: Smile Variation – $557

Sailabration Cruise (LE-1995)
Figurine • #150061
Issued: 1995 • Closed: 1995
Issue Price: N/A • Value: ◁ – $550

Cubby (LE-5,000)
Doll • #E7267B
Issued: 1982 • Closed: 1982
Issue Price: $200 • Value: UM – $480

Hello Lord, It's Me Again
Members Only Figurine • #PM811
Issued: 1981 • Closed: 1981
Issue Price: $25 • Value: ▲ – $455

Jesus Is Born
Figurine • #E2801
Issued: 1980 • Suspended: 1984
Issue Price: $37 • Value: NM – $405

PRECIOUS MOMENTS®
Production Marks

*S*ince 1981, each of the porcelain bisque pieces from the Enesco PRECIOUS MOMENTS line has been given a production mark to denote the year the piece was produced. For instance, a piece that was issued in 1990 and retired in 1992 can be found with the following marks: a flame, a vessel and a clef. Often times, pieces can be found with a mark from the year before its release or a year following its retirement or suspension.

Pre-1981		**1990**		**2000**	
NM	No Mark	🕯	Flame	🥚	Egg
1981		**1991**		**Other**	
▲	Triangle	🏺	Vessel	UM	Unmarked
1982		**1992**		**Other**	
⧗	Hourglass	𝄞	Clef	◆	Diamond[1]
1983		**1993**		**Other**	
🐟	Fish	🦋	Butterfly	⚑	Flag[2]
1984		**1994**		**Other**	
✝	Cross	🎺	Trumpet	⚑★	Flag with Star[3]
1985		**1995**		**Other**	
🕊	Dove	⛵	Ship	🌹	Rosebud[4]
1986		**1996**			
🌿	Olive Branch	♡	Heart		
1987		**1997**			
🌲	Cedar Tree	🗡	Sword		
1988		**1998**			
⚓	Flower	👓	Eyeglasses		
1989		**1999**			
⤙	Bow and Arrow	★	Star		

[1] appears only on piece #103004

[2] appears only on "Bless Those Who Serve Their Country" figurines produced in 1991

[3] appears only on "Bless Those Who Serve Their Country" figurines produced in 1992

[4] appears only on piece #525049

How To Use Your Collector's Value Guide™

1. Locate your piece in the Value Guide. Figurine series are listed first, followed by general figurines, COUNTRY LANE and LITTLE MOMENTS. Listed next are the series and general ornaments, then other PRECIOUS MOMENTS collectibles (bells, boxes, dolls, musicals, etc.). TENDER TAILS, *Chapel Exclusives* and *Club* pieces conclude the Value Guide. Pieces are

VALUES: ↑ $46
♦ $43

Wishing You A Merry
Christmas (Dated 1984)
#E5383
Issued: 1984 • Closed: 1984
Retail Price: $17

listed alphabetically by inspirational title within most sections; however, in annual groupings pieces are listed in chronological order. To help you locate your pieces we have provided numerical and alphabetical indexes in the back of the book.

2. Find the market value of your piece. To do this, look at the bottom or back of your piece to find the production marking. Next, find your piece's production mark in the "Values" chart on the right side of the picture box.

3. Record the retail price you paid and the secondary market value in the corresponding boxes at the bottom of the page. Each piece's picture box contains a "Retail Price" line which shows the price at the

Annual Christmas Figurines	
Price Paid	Value
1. $17.00	$46.00
2.	
3.	
4.	
5.	
6.	
7.	
$17.00	$46.00
Totals	

time of issue. If there is a second price, that is the piece's current retail price, or the last suggested retail price (if the piece is no longer available).

4. Calculate the value for the page by adding all of the boxes in each column. Use a pencil so you can change the totals as your collection grows.

5. Transfer each page's totals to the "Total Value Of My Collection" worksheets found in the back of the book.

6. Add all of the totals from the Value Guide pages together to determine the overall value of your collection.

Figurine Series

For the beginning of the year 2000, "A Tail Of Love" from the *Two By Two* series and the *Easter Seals Commemorative Figurine*, "Jesus Loves Me," were the only two new pieces introduced into an existing series. A brand new series, *I'm Proud To Be An American* has also been introduced, featuring 20 new military-themed pieces, which make the perfect gift for friends and family in the service.

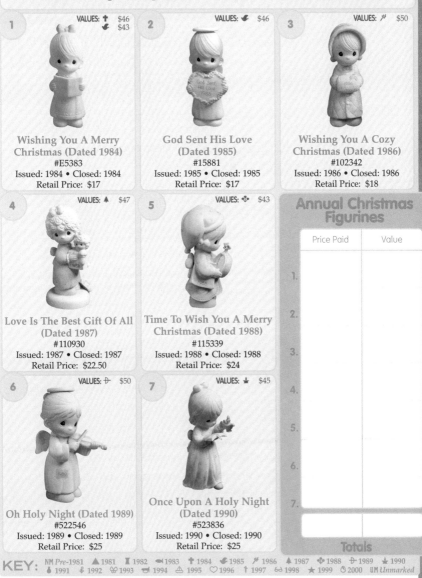

1 — VALUES: † $46 ↩ $43
Wishing You A Merry Christmas (Dated 1984)
#E5383
Issued: 1984 • Closed: 1984
Retail Price: $17

2 — VALUES: ↩ $46
God Sent His Love (Dated 1985)
#15881
Issued: 1985 • Closed: 1985
Retail Price: $17

3 — VALUES: ⚞ $50
Wishing You A Cozy Christmas (Dated 1986)
#102342
Issued: 1986 • Closed: 1986
Retail Price: $18

4 — VALUES: ▲ $47
Love Is The Best Gift Of All (Dated 1987)
#110930
Issued: 1987 • Closed: 1987
Retail Price: $22.50

5 — VALUES: ⚜ $43
Time To Wish You A Merry Christmas (Dated 1988)
#115339
Issued: 1988 • Closed: 1988
Retail Price: $24

6 — VALUES: Ð $50
Oh Holy Night (Dated 1989)
#522546
Issued: 1989 • Closed: 1989
Retail Price: $25

7 — VALUES: ★ $45
Once Upon A Holy Night (Dated 1990)
#523836
Issued: 1990 • Closed: 1990
Retail Price: $25

Annual Christmas Figurines

	Price Paid	Value
1.		
2.		
3.		
4.		
5.		
6.		
7.		
Totals		

KEY: NM *Pre-1981* ▲1981 ℤ1982 ↩1983 †1984 ↩1985 ⚞1986 ▲1987 ⚜1988 Ð1989 ★1990
🌢1991 ⚶1992 ⚘1993 ⚞1994 ⬥1995 ♡1996 †1997 ᢏ1998 ★1999 ◔2000 UM *Unmarked*

Figurine Series

1 VALUES: 🌢 $37

May Your Christmas Be
Merry (Dated 1991)
#524166
Issued: 1991 • Closed: 1991
Retail Price: $27.50

2 VALUES: 🖋 $35
     UM $40

But The Greatest Of These
Is Love (Dated 1992)
#527688
Issued: 1992 • Closed: 1992
Retail Price: $27.50

3 VALUES: 🎗 $48

Wishing You The Sweetest
Christmas (Dated 1993)
#530166
Issued: 1993 • Closed: 1993
Retail Price: $27.50

4 VALUES: 🛷 $42

You're As Pretty As A
Christmas Tree (Dated 1994)
#530425
Issued: 1994 • Closed: 1994
Retail Price: $27.50

5 VALUES: ⛺ $42

He Covers The Earth With
His Beauty (Dated 1995)
#142654
Issued: 1995 • Closed: 1995
Retail Price: $30

6 VALUES: ♡ $36

Peace On Earth . . . Anyway
(Dated 1996)
#183342
Issued: 1996 • Closed: 1996
Retail Price: $32.50

Annual Christmas Figurines

	Price Paid	Value
1.		
2.		
3.		
4.		
5.		
6.		
7.		
8.		
9.		
Totals		

7 VALUES: ✝ $33

Cane You Join Us For A Merry
Christmas (Dated 1997)
#272671
Issued: 1997 • Closed: 1997
Retail Price: $30

8 VALUES: 👓 $32

I'm Sending You A Merry
Christmas (Dated 1998)
#455601
Issued: 1998 • Closed: 1998
Retail Price: $30

9 VALUES: ★ N/E

Slide Into The Next
Millennium With Joy
(Dated 1999)
#587761
Issued: 1999 • Closed: 1999
Retail Price: $35

KEY: NM *Pre-1981* ▲ 1981 ▩ 1982 ◀ 1983 ✝ 1984 ✦ 1985 ✗ 1986 ▲ 1987 ✤ 1988 ⊕ 1989 ★ 1990
🌢 1991 🖋 1992 🎗 1993 🛷 1994 ⛺ 1995 ♡ 1996 ✝ 1997 👓 1998 ★ 1999 🌑 2000 UM *Unmarked*

Value Guide — PRECIOUS MOMENTS®

Figurine Series

1 — VALUES: † $32 / 6ð $32 / ★ $32 / ⊙ $30

Friendship Hits The Spot
#306916
Issued: 1998 • Open
Retail Price: $30

2 — VALUES: ♡ $26 / † $26 / 6ð $26

God Loveth A Cheerful Giver
#272477
Issued: 1997 • Retired: 1998
Retail Price: $25

3 — VALUES: ♡ $32 / † $32 / 6ð $32 / ★ $32 / ⊙ $30

Good Friends Are Forever
#272422
Issued: 1997 • Open
Retail Price: $30

4 — VALUES: † $25 / 6ð $25 / ★ $25 / ⊙ $25

He Cleansed My Soul
#306940
Issued: 1998 • Open
Retail Price: $25

5 — VALUES: ♡ $26 / † $26 / 6ð $26 / ★ $26 / ⊙ $25

I Believe In Miracles
#272469
Issued: 1997 • Open
Retail Price: $25

6 — VALUES: ♡ $26 / † $26 / 6ð $26 / ★ $26 / ⊙ $25

Love Is Sharing
#272493
Issued: 1997 • Open
Retail Price: $25

7 — VALUES: ♡ $32 / † $32 / 6ð $32 / ★ $32 / ⊙ $30

Love One Another
#272507
Issued: 1997 • Open
Retail Price: $30

8 — VALUES: † $27 / 6ð $27 / ★ $27 / ⊙ $25

Loving You Dear Valentine
#306932
Issued: 1998 • Open
Retail Price: $25

9 — VALUES: ♡ $30 / † $30 / 6ð $30 / ★ $30 / ⊙ $30

Make A Joyful Noise
#272450
Issued: 1997 • Open
Retail Price: $30

10 — VALUES: ♡ $25 / † $25 / 6ð $25 / ★ $25 / ⊙ $25

We Are God's Workmanship
#272434
Issued: 1997 • Open
Retail Price: $25

Baby Classics

	Price Paid	Value
1.		
2.		
3.		
4.		
5.		
6.		
7.		
8.		
9.		
10.		

Totals

KEY: NM *Pre-1981* ▲1981 ⅠⅠ 1982 ◄1983 † 1984 ✦1985 ✗ 1986 ▲ 1987 ✿1988 ⊕1989 ✦1990 ♦ 1991 ♪ 1992 ⍟1993 ➤1994 ⌂ 1995 ♡1996 † 1997 6ð 1998 ★ 1999 ⊙2000 UM *Unmarked*

41

Value Guide — PRECIOUS MOMENTS®

1 VALUES: ♡ $26 / † $26 / 6♉ $26 / ★ $26 / �఩ $25

You Have Touched So Many Hearts
#272485
Issued: 1997 • Open
Retail Price: $25

2 VALUES: ♠ $49 / ♣ $45 / ♭ $43 / ♩ $39 / ♦ $36 / ♧ $34 / ♈ $32

Brighten Someone's Day
#105953
Issued: 1987 • Susp.: 1993
Retail Price: $12.50 – $15

3 VALUES: ♦ $27 / ♧ $24 / ♈ $22 / ♉ $19 / △ $18 / ♡ $18 / † $18 / 6♉ $18 / ★ $18

Can't Be Without You
#524492
Issued: 1991 • Retired: 1999
Retail Price: $16 – $17.50

4 VALUES: ♣ $46 / ♭ $40 / ♩ $38 / ♦ $35 / ♧ $33 / ♈ $30 / UM $65

Friends To The End
#104418
Issued: 1988 • Susp.: 1993
Retail Price: $15 – $18.50

5 VALUES: ♡ $27 / † $22 / 6♉ $22 / ★ $22 / �఩ $20

From The First Time I Spotted You I Knew We'd Be Friends
#260940
Issued: 1997 • Open
Retail Price: $20

6 VALUES: ♧ $35 / ♈ $32 / ♉ $30 / △ $27 / ♡ $25

Happy Birdie
#527343
Issued: 1992 • Susp.: 1996
Retail Price: $16 – $17.50

Price Paid	Value
1.	

2.
3.
4.
5.
6.
7.
8.
9.
10.

Totals

7 VALUES: ♣ $30 / ♭ $25 / ♩ $22 / ♦ $20 / ♧ $20 / ♈ $18 / ♉ $18 / △ $18 / ♡ $17.50 / † $17.50 / 6♉ $17.50 / ★ $17.50

Hello World
#521175
Issued: 1989 • Retired: 1999
Retail Price: $13.50 – $17.50

8 VALUES: ♈ $33 / ♉ $30 / △ $26

Hope You're Over The Hump
#521671
Issued: 1993 • Susp.: 1996
Retail Price: $17.50 – $18.50

9 VALUES: ♦ $28 / ♧ $22 / ♈ $20 / ♉ $18 / △ $18 / ♡ $17.50 / † $17.50 / 6♉ $17.50 / ★ $17.50 / ♉ $17.50

How Can I Ever Forget You
#526924
Issued: 1991 • Open
Retail Price: $15 – $17.50

10 VALUES: △ $18 / ♡ $14 / † $14 / 6♉ $13.50 / ★ $13.50 / ♉ $13.50

I Haven't Seen Much Of You Lately
#531057
Issued: 1996 • Open
Retail Price: $13.50

KEY: NM Pre-1981 ▲1981 ✠1982 ◄1983 †1984 ✿1985 ♪1986 ♠1987 ♣1988 ♭1989 ♩1990 ♦1991 ♧1992 ♈1993 ♉1994 △1995 ♡1996 †1997 6♉1998 ★1999 ♉2000 UM Unmarked

Figurine Series

1

VALUES:
- 🐚 $27
- ♀ $22
- △ $20
- ⚠ $18
- ✝ $18
- ✝ $18
- 🔭 $18

I Only Have Arms For You
#527769
Issued: 1993 • Retired: 1998
Retail Price: $15 – $17.50

2

VALUES:
- 🐚 $39
- ♀ $35
- 🔭 $33
- 🍴 $30
- △ $28
- ♡ $26

Let's Be Friends
#527270
Issued: 1992 • Retired: 1996
Retail Price: $15 – $17.50

3

VALUES:
- ✝ $20
- 🔭 $17
- ★ $15
- 🕐 $15

My World's Upside Down Without You
#531014
Issued: 1998 • Open
Retail Price: $15

4

VALUES:
- ★ $42
- ♦ $38
- ♀ $36
- 🔭 $33
- 🔭 $32

Not A Creature Was Stirring (set/2)
#524484
Issued: 1990 • Susp.: 1994
Retail Price: $17

5

VALUES:
- 🔭 $20
- △ $17
- △ $16
- ✝ $16
- ✝ $15
- 🔭 $15
- ★ $15
- 🕐 $15

Oinky Birthday
#524506
Issued: 1994 • Open
Retail Price: $13.50 – $15

6

VALUES:
- ▲ $62
- 🔭 $55
- ⊕ $50
- ★ $46
- ♦ $44
- ♀ $42
- 🔭 $40

Showers Of Blessings
#105945
Issued: 1987 • Retired: 1993
Retail Price: $16 – $20

7

VALUES:
- ⊕ $58
- ★ $52
- ♦ $50
- ♀ $46
- 🔭 $44
- 🍴 $42

To Be With You Is Uplifting
#522260
Issued: 1989 • Retired: 1994
Retail Price: $20 – $22.50

8

VALUES:
- ⊕ $56
- ★ $42
- ♦ $38
- ♀ $36
- 🔭 $35

To My Favorite Fan
#521043
Issued: 1990 • Susp.: 1993
Retail Price: $16

9

VALUES:
- 🍴 $48
- △ $43
- ♡ $40

Wishing You A Happy Bear Hug
#520659
Issued: 1995 • Susp.: 1996
Retail Price: $27.50

10

VALUES:
- 🍓 $43
- ⚘ $30
- ▲ $28
- ⊕ $26
- ⊕ $26
- ★ $25
- ♦ $25
- ♀ $24
- 🔭 $23
- 🍴 $23
- △ $23
- ♡ $22.50
- ✝ $22.50
- 🔭 $22.50
- ★ $22.50
- 🕐 $22.50

Bless The Days Of Our Youth
#16004
Issued: 1985 • Open
Retail Price: $15 – $22.50

Birthday Series

	Price Paid	Value
1.		
2.		
3.		
4.		
5.		
6.		
7.		
8.		
9.		

Birthday Train

10.		

Totals

KEY: NM *Pre-1981* ▲ 1981 𝕀 1982 ◀ 1983 𝟙 1984 🍓 1985 ⚘ 1986 ▲ 1987 ⊕ 1988 ⊕ 1989 ★ 1990 ♦ 1991 ♀ 1992 🔭 1993 🍴 1994 △ 1995 ♡ 1996 ✝ 1997 🔭 1998 ★ 1999 🕐 2000 UM *Unmarked*

43

Figurine Series

VALUES:
- 🦋 $43
- ♬ $27
- ♠ $23
- ⚓ $20
- ✦ $20
- 🔔 $18
- ✿ $16
- 🐝 $16
- ⚵ $15
- ♡ $15
- ✝ $15
- ★ $15
- ☉ $15

May Your Birthday Be Warm (Baby)
#15938
Issued: 1985 • Open
Retail Price: $10 – $15

VALUES:
- 🦋 $46
- ♬ $30
- ♠ $26
- ⚓ $23
- ✦ $20
- 🔔 $20
- 🔔 $20
- ✿ $18
- 🐝 $18
- ⚵ $15
- ♡ $15
- ✝ $15
- ★ $15
- ☉ $15

Happy Birthday Little Lamb (Age 1)
#15946
Issued: 1985 • Open
Retail Price: $10 – $15

VALUES:
- 🦋 $48
- ♬ $34
- ♠ $32
- ⚓ $29
- ✦ $29
- ✦ $26
- 🔔 $24
- ✿ $22
- 🐝 $20
- ⚵ $20
- ⚵ $18
- ♡ $18
- ✝ $17.50
- ★ $17.50
- ☉ $17.50

God Bless You On Your Birthday (Age 2)
#15962
Issued: 1985 • Open
Retail Price: $11 – $17.50

VALUES:
- 🦋 $43
- ♬ $30
- ♠ $27
- ⚓ $25
- ✦ $22
- 🔔 $22
- 🔔 $22
- ✿ $20
- 🐝 $19
- ⚵ $18
- ⚵ $17.50
- ♡ $17.50
- ✝ $17.50
- ★ $17.50
- ☉ $17.50

Heaven Bless Your Special Day (Age 3)
#15954
Issued: 1985 • Open
Retail Price: $11 – $17.50

VALUES:
- 🦋 $47
- ♬ $36
- ♠ $30
- ⚓ $26
- ✦ $25
- 🔔 $25
- ✦ $24
- ✿ $22
- 🐝 $20
- ⚵ $20
- ⚵ $20
- ♡ $20
- ✝ $20
- ★ $20
- ☉ $20

May Your Birthday Be Gigantic (Age 4)
#15970
Issued: 1985 • Open
Retail Price: $12.50 – $20

VALUES:
- 🦋 $42
- ♬ $32
- ♠ $28
- ⚓ $27
- ✦ $27
- ✦ $25
- 🔔 $25
- ✿ $25
- 🐝 $22.50
- ⚵ $22.50
- ⚵ $22.50
- ♡ $22.50
- ✝ $22.50
- ★ $22.50
- ☉ $22.50

This Day Is Something To Roar About (Age 5)
#15989
Issued: 1985 • Open
Retail Price: $13.50 – $22.50

Birthday Train

	Price Paid	Value
1.		
2.		
3.		
4.		
5.		
6.		
7.		
8.		
9.		
10.		

Totals

VALUES:
- 🦋 $42
- ♠ $34
- ⚓ $29
- ✦ $29
- ⚓ $29
- ✦ $26
- 🔔 $26
- ✿ $24
- 🐝 $23
- ⚵ $22.50
- ⚵ $22.50
- ♡ $22.50
- ✝ $22.50
- ⚵ $22.50
- ★ $22.50
- ☉ $22.50

Keep Looking Up (Age 6)
#15997
Issued: 1985 • Open
Retail Price: $13.50 – $22.50

VALUES:
- ♠ $40
- ⚓ $32
- ✦ $30
- ✦ $28
- 🔔 $26
- ✿ $24
- 🐝 $24
- ⚵ $24
- ⚵ $22.50
- ♡ $22.50
- ✝ $22.50
- ⚵ $22.50
- ★ $22.50
- ☉ $22.50

Wishing You Grr-eatness (Age 7)
#109479
Issued: 1988 • Open
Retail Price: $18.50 – $22.50

VALUES:
- ♠ $38
- ⚓ $34
- ⚓ $32
- ✦ $29
- 🔔 $27
- ✿ $25
- 🐝 $22.50
- ⚵ $22.50
- ⚵ $22.50
- ♡ $22.50
- ✝ $22.50
- ⚵ $22.50
- ★ $22.50
- ☉ $22.50

Isn't Eight Just Great (Age 8)
#109460
Issued: 1988 • Open
Retail Price: $18.50 – $22.50

VALUES:
- 🐝 $35
- ⚵ $31
- ⚵ $29
- ⚵ $26
- ♡ $25
- ✝ $25
- ⚵ $25
- ★ $25
- ☉ $25

Being Nine Is Just Divine (Age 9)
#521833
Issued: 1992 • Open
Retail Price: $25

44

1 VALUES: 🐚 $35 / 🐌 $31 / 🛁 $29 / 🔺 $26 / ♡ $25 / ✝ $25 / 👣 $25 / ★ $25 / 🕐 $25

May Your Birthday Be Mammoth (Age 10)
#521825
Issued: 1992 • Open
Retail Price: $25

2 VALUES: 6∂ $25 / ★ $25 / 🕐 $25

Take Your Time It's Your Birthday (Age 11)
#488003
Issued: 1999 • Open
Retail Price: $25

3 VALUES: 🎵 $65 / 🔺 $52

He Walks With Me (LE-1987)
#107999
Issued: 1987 • Closed: 1987
Retail Price: $25

4 VALUES: 🔺 $40 / 🔹 $33

Blessed Are They That Overcome (LE-1988)
#115479
Issued: 1988 • Closed: 1988
Retail Price: $27.50

5 VALUES: 🔹 $64 / ∂ $54

His Love Will Shine On You (LE-1989)
#522376
Issued: 1989 • Closed: 1989
Retail Price: $30

6 VALUES: ∂ $52 / ⚓ $46

Always In His Care (LE-1990)
#524522
Issued: 1990 • Closed: 1990
Retail Price: $30

7 VALUES: ⚓ $70 / 🔴 $62

Sharing A Gift Of Love (LE-1991)
#527114
Issued: 1991 • Closed: 1991
Retail Price: $30

8 VALUES: 🔴 $115 / 🐚 $105

A Universal Love (LE-1992)
#527173
Issued: 1992 • Closed: 1992
Retail Price: $32.50

9 VALUES: 🐚 $60 / 🐌 $52

You're My Number One Friend (LE-1993)
#530026
Issued: 1993 • Closed: 1993
Retail Price: $30

10 VALUES: 🐌 $53 / 🍴 $46

It Is No Secret What God Can Do (LE-1994)
#531111
Issued: 1994 • Closed: 1994
Retail Price: $30

Birthday Train

	Price Paid	Value
1.		
2.		

Easter Seals Commemorative Figurines

3.		
4.		
5.		
6.		
7.		
8.		
9.		
10.		

Totals

KEY: NM Pre-1981 ▲1981 ▮1982 ◀1983 ✝1984 🍀1985 🎵1986 ▲1987 ✛1988 ∂1989 ⚓1990 🔴1991 🐚1992 🐌1993 🍴1994 △1995 ♡1996 ✝1997 6∂1998 ★1999 🕐2000 ◻M Unmarked

45

Figurine Series

1
VALUES: ⊖ $45
        ⚠ $40

Take Time To Smell The Flowers (LE-1995)
#524387
Issued: 1995 • Closed: 1995
Retail Price: $30

2
VALUES: △ $38
        ♡ $35

You Can Always Count On Me (1996 Limited Edition)
#526827
Issued: 1995 • Closed: 1996
Retail Price: $30

3
VALUES: ♡ $37
        † $35

Give Ability A Chance (1997 Limited Edition)
#192368
Issued: 1996 • Closed: 1997
Retail Price: $30

4
VALUES: † $45
        6∂ $42

Somebody Cares (1998 Limited Edition)
#522325
Issued: 1997 • Closed: 1998
Retail Price: $40

5
VALUES: 6∂ $37
        ★ $37

Heaven Bless You Easter Seal (1999 Limited Edition)
#456314
Issued: 1998 • Closed: 1999
Retail Price: $35

6
VALUES: ★ $30
        ⧖ $30

Give Your Whole Heart (2000 Limited Edition)
#490245
Issued: 1999 • To Be Closed: 2000
Retail Price: $30

Easter Seals Commemorative Figurines

	Price Paid	Value
1.		
2.		
3.		
4.		
5.		
6.		
7.		

Limited Edition 9" Easter Seals Figurines

8.		
9.		
10.		

Totals

7
VALUES: ⧖ N/E

New!

Jesus Loves Me (2001 Limited Edition)
#745766
Issued: 2000 • To Be Closed: 2001
Retail Price: N/A

8
VALUES: ♣ $1800
        ✥ $1550

Jesus Loves Me (LE-1,000)
#104531
Issued: 1988 • Closed: 1988
Retail Price: $500

9
VALUES: Ð $950

Make A Joyful Noise (LE-1,500)
#520322
Issued: 1989 • Closed: 1989
Retail Price: $500

10
VALUES: Ð $650
        ⚓ $585

You Have Touched So Many Hearts (LE-2,000)
#523283
Issued: 1990 • Closed: 1990
Retail Price: $500

KEY: NM *Pre-1981* ▲ 1981 Ⅱ 1982 ◄ 1983 † 1984 ❀ 1985 ♪ 1986 ▲ 1987 ✥ 1988 Ð 1989 ⚓ 1990
     ♦ 1991 ⧉ 1992 ꙮ 1993 ⊖ 1994 △ 1995 ♡ 1996 † 1997 6∂ 1998 ★ 1999 ⧖ 2000 UM *Unmarked*

Value Guide — PRECIOUS MOMENTS®

1
VALUES: ★ $710
      ▲ $675

We Are God's
Workmanship (LE-2,000)
#523879
Issued: 1991 • Closed: 1991
Retail Price: $500

2
VALUES: ▲ $650
      ▲ $600

You Are Such A Purr-fect
Friend (LE-2,000)
#526010
Issued: 1992 • Closed: 1992
Retail Price: $500

3
VALUES: ▲ $630
      ∞ $585

Gather Your Dreams
(LE-2,000)
#529680
Issued: 1993 • Closed: 1993
Retail Price: $500

4
VALUES: ∞ $560
      ▬ $525

You Are The Rose Of His
Creation (LE-2,000)
#531243
Issued: 1994 • Closed: 1994
Retail Price: $500

5
VALUES: ▬ $600
      △ $580

He's Got The Whole World
In His Hands (LE-2,000)
#526886
Issued: 1995 • Closed: 1995
Retail Price: $500

6
VALUES: △ $560
      ♡ $560

HE Loves Me (LE-2,000)
#152277
Issued: 1995 • Closed: 1996
Retail Price: $500

7
VALUES: ♡ $530
      † $530

Love Is Universal (LE-2,000)
#192376
Issued: 1996 • Closed: 1997
Retail Price: $500

8
VALUES: † $520
      ∞ $520

Love Grows Here (LE-2,000)
#272981
Issued: 1997 • Closed: 1998
Retail Price: $500

Limited Edition 9" Easter Seals Figurines

	Price Paid	Value
1.		
2.		
3.		
4.		
5.		
6.		
7.		
8.		
9.		
10.		
Totals		

9
VALUES: ∞ $520
      ★ $520

We Are All Precious In
His Sight (LE-2,000)
#475068
Issued: 1998 • Closed: 1999
Retail Price: $500

10
VALUES: ★ $500
      ◐ $500

Jesus Loves Me (LE-1,500)
#634735
Issued: 1999 • To Be Closed: 2000
Retail Price: $500

KEY: NM *Pre-1981* ▲ 1981 ✕ 1982 ◄ 1983 † 1984 ◄ 1985 ✗ 1986 ▲ 1987 ◆ 1988 ᵹ 1989 ★ 1990 ▲ 1991 ▲ 1992 ∞ 1993 ▬ 1994 △ 1995 ♡ 1996 † 1997 ∞ 1998 ★ 1999 ◐ 2000 UM *Unmarked*

47

It's A Girl
#136204
Issued: 1995 • Open
Retail Price: $22.50

VALUES: ⚜ $30 / ♡ $24 / † $22.50 / 😀 $22.50 / ★ $22.50 / 🕐 $22.50

Age 1
#136190
Issued: 1995 • Open
Retail Price: $25

VALUES: ⚜ $33 / ♡ $25 / † $25 / 😀 $25 / ★ $25 / 🕐 $25

Age 2
#136212
Issued: 1995 • Open
Retail Price: $25

VALUES: ⚜ $32 / ♡ $25 / † $25 / 😀 $25 / ★ $25 / 🕐 $25

Age 3
#136220
Issued: 1995 • Open
Retail Price: $25

VALUES: ⚜ $32 / ♡ $25 / † $25 / 😀 $25 / ★ $25 / 🕐 $25

Age 4
#136239
Issued: 1995 • Open
Retail Price: $27.50

VALUES: ⚜ $36 / ♡ $28 / † $27.50 / 😀 $27.50 / ★ $27.50 / 🕐 $27.50

Age 5
#136247
Issued: 1995 • Open
Retail Price: $27.50

VALUES: ⚜ $35 / ♡ $28 / † $27.50 / 😀 $27.50 / ★ $27.50 / 🕐 $27.50

Growing In Grace

	Price Paid	Value
1.		
2.		
3.		
4.		
5.		
6.		
7.		
8.		
9.		
10.		
Totals		

Age 6
#136255
Issued: 1995 • Open
Retail Price: $30

VALUES: ⚜ $37 / ♡ $32 / † $32 / 😀 $30 / ★ $30 / 🕐 $30

Age 7
#163740
Issued: 1996 • Open
Retail Price: $32.50

VALUES: ⚜ $38 / ♡ $33 / † $32.50 / 😀 $32.50 / ★ $32.50 / 🕐 $32.50

Age 8
#163759
Issued: 1996 • Open
Retail Price: $32.50

VALUES: ⚜ $38 / ♡ $33 / † $32.50 / 😀 $32.50 / ★ $32.50 / 🕐 $32.50

Age 9
#183865
Issued: 1996 • Open
Retail Price: $30

VALUES: ♡ $33 / † $30 / 😀 $30 / ★ $30 / 🕐 $30

KEY: NM *Pre-1981* ▲ 1981 Ⅱ 1982 ◀ 1983 † 1984 🍀 1985 1986 ♣ 1987 🔷 1988 🕊 1989 ⚖ 1990 ♦ 1991 🔥 1992 🎯 1993 🎀 1994 ⚜ 1995 ♡ 1996 † 1997 😀 1998 ★ 1999 🕐 2000 UM *Unmarked*

Value Guide — PRECIOUS MOMENTS®

1

VALUES: ♡ $41
† $37.50
6∂ $37.50
★ $37.50
◌ $37.50

Age 10
#183873
Issued: 1996 • Open
Retail Price: $37.50

2

VALUES: ♡ $42
† $38
6∂ $37.50
★ $37.50
◌ $37.50

Age 11
#260924
Issued: 1997 • Open
Retail Price: $37.50

3

VALUES: ♡ $42
† $38
6∂ $37.50
★ $37.50
◌ $37.50

Age 12
#260932
Issued: 1997 • Open
Retail Price: $37.50

4

VALUES: † $42
6∂ $42
★ $42
◌ $40

Age 13
#272647
Issued: 1997 • Open
Retail Price: $40

5

VALUES: † $36
6∂ $36
★ $36
◌ $35

Age 14
#272655
Issued: 1997 • Open
Retail Price: $35

6

VALUES: † $42
6∂ $42
★ $42
◌ $40

Age 15
#272663
Issued: 1997 • Open
Retail Price: $40

7

VALUES: △ $53
♡ $48
6∂ $45
★ $45
◌ $45

Age 16
#136263
Issued: 1995 • Open
Retail Price: $45

8

New!

VALUES: ◌ $32.50

I'm Proud To Be An American
#588105
Issued: 2000 • Open
Retail Price: $32.50

9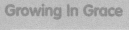

New!

VALUES: ◌ $32.50

I'm Proud To Be An American
#588113
Issued: 2000 • Open
Retail Price: $32.50

10

New!

VALUES: ◌ $32.50

I'm Proud To Be An American
#588121
Issued: 2000 • Open
Retail Price: $32.50

Growing In Grace

	Price Paid	Value
1.		
2.		
3.		
4.		
5.		
6.		
7.		

Proud To Be An American

8.		
9.		
10.		

Totals

Figurine Series

KEY: NM Pre-1981 ▲1981 ▮1982 ◄1983 †1984 ♥1985 ✐1986 ▲1987 ✤1988 ✦1989 ★1990 ♣1991 ♣1992 ❀1993 ♒1994 △1995 ♡1996 †1997 6∂1998 ♣1999 ◌2000 UM Unmarked

49

Figurine Series

VALUES: ⏱ $32.50

New!

I'm Proud To Be An
American
#588148
Issued: 2000 • Open
Retail Price: $32.50

VALUES: ⏱ $32.50

New!

I'm Proud To Be An
American
#588156
Issued: 2000 • Open
Retail Price: $32.50

VALUES: ⏱ $32.50

New!

I'm Proud To Be An
American
#729876
Issued: 2000 • Open
Retail Price: $32.50

VALUES: ⏱ $32.50

New!

I'm Proud To Be An
American
#729884
Issued: 2000 • Open
Retail Price: $32.50

VALUES: ⏱ $32.50

New!

I'm Proud To Be An
American
#729892
Issued: 2000 • Open
Retail Price: $32.50

VALUES: ⏱ $32.50

New!

I'm Proud To Be An
American
#729906
Issued: 2000 • Open
Retail Price: $32.50

VALUES: ⏱ $32.50

New!

I'm Proud To Be An
American
#729914
Issued: 2000 • Open
Retail Price: $32.50

VALUES: ⏱ $32.50

New!

I'm Proud To Be An
American
#729922
Issued: 2000 • Open
Retail Price: $32.50

VALUES: ⏱ $32.50

New!

I'm Proud To Be An
American
#729930
Issued: 2000 • Open
Retail Price: $32.50

VALUES: ⏱ $32.50

New!

I'm Proud To Be An
American
#729949
Issued: 2000 • Open
Retail Price: $32.50

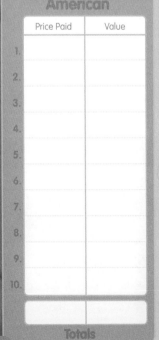

I'm Proud To Be An American

	Price Paid	Value
1.		
2.		
3.		
4.		
5.		
6.		
7.		
8.		
9.		
10.		
Totals		

KEY: NM *Pre-1981* ▲ 1981 ✠ 1982 ◄ 1983 † 1984 ✦ 1985 ♪ 1986 ♣ 1987 ✥ 1988 ♱ 1989 ♦ 1990 ♠ 1991 ♒ 1992 ♉ 1993 ♒ 1994 ⌂ 1995 ♡ 1996 ↑ 1997 ๘ 1998 ★ 1999 ⏱ 2000 UM *Unmarked*

Value Guide — PRECIOUS MOMENTS®

1 VALUES: ○ $32.50

New!

I'm Proud To Be An
American
#729957
Issued: 2000 • Open
Retail Price: $32.50

2 VALUES: ○ $32.50

New!

I'm Proud To Be An
American
#729965
Issued: 2000 • Open
Retail Price: $32.50

3 VALUES: ○ $32.50

New!

I'm Proud To Be An
American
#729973
Issued: 2000 • Open
Retail Price: $32.50

4 VALUES: ○ $32.50

New!

I'm Proud To Be An
American
#730009
Issued: 2000 • Open
Retail Price: $32.50

5 VALUES: ○ $32.50

New!

I'm Proud To Be An
American
#730017
Issued: 2000 • Open
Retail Price: $32.50

6 VALUES: ○ $32.50

New!

I'm Proud To Be An
American
#730025
Issued: 2000 • Open
Retail Price: $32.50

7 VALUES: ○ $32.50

New!

I'm Proud To Be An
American
#730033
Issued: 2000 • Open
Retail Price: $32.50

8 VALUES: † $19
        ∞ $18.50
        ★ $18.50
        ○ $18.50

Cats With Kitten
#291293
Issued: 1997 • Open
Retail Price: $18.50

9 *Variation* VALUES: see list

Come Let Us Adore Him (set/11)
#E2395
Issued: 1982 • Open
Retail Price: $80 – $140
Variation: Shepherd w/turban set – $240

VALUES: ⅃ $175, † $160, ⚘ $155, ⚘ $150, ♫ $150, ▲ $145, ⬥ $142, ⬥ $142, ♦ $142, ♣ $140, ♣ $140, ❀ $140, ⚊ $140, △ $140, ♡ $140, † $140, ∞ $140, ★ $140, ○ $140

I'm Proud To Be An American

	Price Paid	Value
1.		
2.		
3.		
4.		
5.		
6.		
7.		

Miniature Nativity

8.		
9.		

Totals

KEY: NM *Pre-1981* ▲ 1981 ⅃ 1982 ◁ 1983 † 1984 ⚘ 1985 ♫ 1986 ▲ 1987 ⬥ 1988 ⊕ 1989 ★ 1990 ♣ 1991 ♦ 1992 ❀ 1993 ⚊ 1994 △ 1995 ♡ 1996 † 1997 ∞ 1998 ★ 1999 ○ 2000 UM *Unmarked*

51

Figurine Series

1

VALUES: ⚜ $40
♡ $35
† $35
∞ $35
★ $35
⊘ $35

Come Let Us Adore Him (set/3)
#142743
Issued: 1995 • Open
Retail Price: $35

2

VALUES: † $30
∞ $30
★ $30
⊘ $30

Donkey, Camel And Cow (set/3)
#279323
Issued: 1997 • Open
Retail Price: $30

3

VALUES: † $17.50
∞ $17.50
★ $17.50
⊘ $17.50

For An Angel You're So Down To Earth
#283444
Issued: 1997 • Open
Retail Price: $17.50

4

VALUES: ∞ $17.50
★ $17.50
⊘ $17.50

Hang On To That Holiday Feeling
#455962
Issued: 1998 • Open
Retail Price: $17.50

5

VALUES: ♀ $27
⚘ $23
⚜ $20
♡ $20
† $20
∞ $20
★ $20

Happy Birthday Jesus
#530492
Issued: 1993 • Retired: 1999
Retail Price: $20

6

VALUES: ⚒ $22
⚜ $18.50
♡ $18.50
† $18.50
∞ $18.50
★ $18.50

Have I Got News For You
#528137
Issued: 1994 • Retired: 1999
Retail Price: $16 – $18.50

7

VALUES: † $35
✝ $32
♪ $28
⚓ $28
❥ $26
⊅ $24
☆ $22
♣ $20
⚘ $18.50
♀ $18.50
⊶ $18.50
⚜ $18.50
⊘ $18.50
† $18.50
∞ $18.50
★ $18.50
⊘ $18.50
ℳ $38

I'll Play My Drum For Him
#E5384
Issued: 1984 • Open
Retail Price: $10 – $18.50

8

VALUES: ⊅ $38
☆ $35
♣ $33
♪ $33
♀ $30

Isn't He Precious
#522988
Issued: 1989 • Susp.: 1993
Retail Price: $15 – $16.50

9

VALUES: ♣ $28
⚘ $22
♀ $20
⊶ $18.50
⚜ $18.50
♡ $18.50
† $18.50
∞ $18.50
★ $18.50

It's A Perfect Boy
#525286
Issued: 1991 • Retired: 1999
Retail Price: $16.50 – $18.50

10

VALUES: ♡ $22
† $18.50
∞ $18.50
★ $18.50
⊘ $18.50

Making A Trail To Bethlehem
#184004
Issued: 1996 • Open
Retail Price: $18.50

Miniature Nativity

	Price Paid	Value
1.		
2.		
3.		
4.		
5.		
6.		
7.		
8.		
9.		
10.		
Totals		

KEY: NM *Pre-1981* ▲ 1981 ℤ 1982 ◄ 1983 † 1984 ⬥ 1985 ♪ 1986 ♠ 1987 ⬧ 1988 ⊅ 1989 ☆ 1990 ♣ 1991 ⚘ 1992 ♀ 1993 ⊶ 1994 ⚜ 1995 ♡ 1996 † 1997 ∞ 1998 ★ 1999 ⊘ 2000 ℳ *Unmarked*

Value Guide — PRECIOUS MOMENTS®

1
VALUES: ❧ $40
▲ $35
❖ $35
Ð $35
▲ $33
♣ $33
𝄞 $33

Mini Animals (set/3)
#102296
Issued: 1986 • Susp.: 1992
Retail Price: $13.50 – $19

2
VALUES: I $135
$115
† $110
Ð $102
❧ $102
▲ $95
Ð $90
▲ $80
▲ $80
♣ $80
𝄞 $77
☙ $77
△ $77
♡ $77
† $75
66 $75
★ $75
☉ $75

**Nativity Buildings
And Tree (set/4)**
#E2387
Issued: 1982 • Open
Retail Price: $45 – $75

3
VALUES: † $40
66 $40
★ $40
☉ $40

Nativity Wall
#283436
Issued: 1997 • Open
Retail Price: $40

4
VALUES: † $64
♣ $57
❧ $52

Oh Worship The Lord
#E5385
Issued: 1984 • Susp.: 1986
Retail Price: $10

5
VALUES: † $70
♣ $62
❧ $57

Oh Worship The Lord
#E5386
Issued: 1984 • Susp.: 1986
Retail Price: $10

6
VALUES: ❖ $35
Ð $27
▲ $24
▲ $22
𝄞 $20
❀ $18.50
🍴 $18.50
△ $18.50
♡ $18.50
† $18.50
66 $18.50
★ $18.50
☉ $18.50

Rejoice O Earth
#520268
Issued: 1988 • Open
Retail Price: $13 – $18.50

7
VALUES: † $22.50
66 $22.50
★ $22.50
☉ $22.50

Shepherd And Sheep (set/2)
#213616
Issued: 1997 • Open
Retail Price: $22.50

8
VALUES: ❧ $33
▲ $23
Ð $20
Ð $20
▲ $20
▲ $20
𝄞 $18.50
❀ $18.50
🍴 $18.50
△ $18.50
♡ $18.50
† $18.50
66 $18.50
★ $18.50
☉ $18.50

Shepherd Of Love
#102261
Issued: 1986 • Open
Retail Price: $10 – $18.50

9
VALUES: ⚓ $40
$37
𝄞 $33
❀ $30

Some Bunny's Sleeping
#522996
Issued: 1990 • Susp.: 1993
Retail Price: $12

10
VALUES: ▲ $140
❖ $125
Ð $120
▲ $120
▲ $120
𝄞 $120
❀ $120
🍴 $120
△ $120
♡ $120
† $120
66 $120
★ $120
☉ $120

**They Followed
The Star (set/3)**
#108243
Issued: 1987 • Open
Retail Price: $75 – $120

Minature Nativity

	Price Paid	Value
1.		
2.		
3.		
4.		
5.		
6.		
7.		
8.		
9.		
10.		
Totals		

KEY: NM *Pre-1981* ▲ 1981 I 1982 ◄ 1983 † 1984 ◄ 1985 ❧ 1986 ▲ 1987 ❖ 1988 Ð 1989 ⚓ 1990 ▲ 1991 𝄞 1992 ❀ 1993 🍴 1994 △ 1995 ♡ 1996 † 1997 66 1998 ★ 1999 ☉ 2000 UM *Unmarked*

Figurine Series

VALUES: 🕯 $18
⚙ $14
🔔 $12
△ $10
♡ $10
† $10
6ð $10
★ $10

Tubby's First Christmas
#525278
Issued: 1992 • Retired: 1999
Retail Price: $10

VALUES: △ $16
♡ $12
† $12
6ð $12
★ $12
🕐 $12

We Have Come From Afar
#530913
Issued: 1995 • Open
Retail Price: $12

VALUES: ♡ $55
† $55
6ð $55
★ $55
🕐 $55

Wee Three Kings (set/3)
#213624
Issued: 1996 • Open
Retail Price: $55

VALUES: ♡ $32.50
† $32.50
6ð $32.50
★ $32.50
🕐 $32.50

All Sing His Praises
#184012
Issued: 1996 • Open
Retail Price: $32.50

VALUES: † $32.50
6ð $32.50
★ $32.50
🕐 $32.50

And You Shall See A Star
#272787
Issued: 1997 • Open
Retail Price: $32.50

VALUES: ★ $45
🕐 $45

Behold The Lamb Of God
#588164
Issued: 1999 • Open
Retail Price: $45

Miniature Nativity

	Price Paid	Value
1.		
2.		
3.		

Nativity

4.		
5.		
6.		
7.		
8.		
9.		

Totals

VALUES: 🪱 $100
† $90
🔔 $90
🎗 $82
♠ $80

Bringing God's Blessing To You
#E0509
Issued: 1983 • Susp.: 1987
Retail Price: $35 – $38.50

VALUES: NM $112
▲ $100
I $92
◄ $86
† $79
🔔 $77

Christmas Is A Time To Share
#E2802
Issued: 1980 • Susp.: 1984
Retail Price: $20 – $27.50

VALUES: I $60
† $52
🔔 $47
🎗 $45
♠ $43
🎗 $43
Ꝺ $37
★ $37
🕯 $37
⚙ $37
🔔 $35
🪱 $35
♡ $35
† $35
6ð $35
★ $35
🕐 $35

Camel
#E2363
Issued: 1982 • Open
Retail Price: $20 – $35

KEY: NM *Pre-1981* ▲ 1981 I 1982 ◄ 1983 † 1984 🔔 1985 🎗 1986 ♠ 1987 🎗 1988 Ꝺ 1989 ★ 1990 🕯 1991 & 1992 ⚙ 1993 ◄ 1994 △ 1995 ♡ 1996 † 1997 6ð 1998 ★ 1999 🕐 2000 UM *Unmarked*

Value Guide — PRECIOUS MOMENTS®

Figurine Series

1

VALUES: NM $220
▲ $180
Ⅱ $170
◄ $162
† $154
◄ $148

Come Let Us Adore Him (set/9)
#E2800
Issued: 1980 • Susp.: 1986
Retail Price: $60 – $90

2

VALUES: NM $52
▲ $45
Ⅱ $40
◄ $38
† $35
◄ $35

Come Let Us Adore Him
#E5619
Issued: 1981 • Susp.: 1985
Retail Price: $10 – $11

3

VALUES: ◄ $150
⅊ $145
▲ $140
✧ $140
Ð $140
✦ $140
♦ $140
⅌ $140
♋ $140
〓 $140
△ $140
♡ $140
† $140
∞ $140
★ $140
◔ $140

Come Let Us Adore Him (set/9)
#104000
Issued: 1986 • Open
Retail Price: $95 – $140

4

VALUES: △ $57
♡ $50
† $50
∞ $50
★ $50
◔ $50

Come Let Us Adore Him (set/3)
#142735
Issued: 1995 • Open
Retail Price: $50

5

VALUES: † $47
⅊ $45
▲ $42
✧ $42
✧ $40
Ð $36
✦ $36
♦ $32.50
⅌ $32.50
♋ $32.50
〓 $32.50
△ $32.50
♡ $32.50
† $32.50
∞ $32.50
★ $32.50
◔ $32.50
UM $55

Cow With Bell
#E5638
Issued: 1981 • Open
Retail Price: $16 – $32.50

6

VALUES: NM $115
▲ $110
Ⅱ $90
† $83
† $82
◄ $78

Crown Him Lord Of All
#E2803
Issued: 1980 • Susp.: 1984
Retail Price: $20 – $27.50

7

VALUES: † $25
⅊ $23
▲ $20
✧ $20
✧ $20
Ð $18
✦ $15
♦ $15
⅌ $15
♋ $15
△ $15
♡ $15
† $15
∞ $15
★ $15
◔ $15
UM $35

Donkey
#E5621
Issued: 1981 • Open
Retail Price: $6 – $15

8

VALUES: Ⅱ $80
▲ $75
† $72
UM $75

The First Noël
#E2365
Issued: 1982 • Susp.: 1984
Retail Price: $16 – $17

Nativity

	Price Paid	Value
1.		
2.		
3.		
4.		
5.		
6.		
7.		
8.		

Totals

KEY: NM *Pre-1981* ▲ 1981 Ⅱ 1982 ◄ 1983 † 1984 ◄ 1985 ⅊ 1986 ♦ 1987 ✧ 1988 Ð 1989 ★ 1990 ♦ 1991 ✦ 1992 ♋ 1993 〓 1994 △ 1995 ♡ 1996 † 1997 ∞ 1998 ★ 1999 ◔ 2000 UM *Unmarked*

55

Figurine Series

Value Guide — PRECIOUS MOMENTS®

1

VALUES: Ⅰ $82
🖌 $77
✝ $70
UM $75

The First Noël
#E2366
Issued: 1982 • Susp.: 1984
Retail Price: $16 – $17

2

VALUES: ✝ $150
🖌 $130
✳ $122

For God So Loved The World (set/4)
#E5382
Issued: 1984 • Susp.: 1986
Retail Price: $70

3

VALUES: Ⅰ $72
✝ $68
✝ $65
✳ $62
✳ $55
▲ $55
🔷 $52
🔶 $48
UM $76

Goat
#E2364
Issued: 1982 • Susp.: 1989
Retail Price: $10 – $15

4

VALUES: ⚲ $39
⚱ $32
⚚ $26
🌸 $25

Happy Birthday Dear Jesus
#524875
Issued: 1990 • Susp.: 1993
Retail Price: $13.50

5

VALUES: ▲ $68
✝ $60
🔶 $53
⚱ $49
⚚ $49

Have I Got News For You
#105635
Issued: 1987 • Susp.: 1991
Retail Price: $22.50 – $30

6

VALUES: NM $160
▲ $135
Ⅰ $125
◀ $115
✝ $108

He Careth For You
#E1377B
Issued: 1979 • Susp.: 1984
Retail Price: $9 – $20

Nativity

	Price Paid	Value
1.		
2.		
3.		
4.		
5.		
6.		
7.		
8.		
9.		
10.		

Totals

7

VALUES: NM $150
▲ $130
Ⅰ $115
◀ $105
✝ $98

He Leadeth Me
#E1377A
Issued: 1979 • Susp.: 1984
Retail Price: $9 – $20

8

VALUES: 6ᗺ $24

He Leadeth Me
Special Event Figurine
#E1377R
Issued: 1998 • Closed: 1998
Retail Price: $9

9

VALUES: NM $85
▲ $75
Ⅰ $62
🔶 $53
✝ $48
✦ $42
✳ $42
▲ $40
🔷 $37
🔶 $37
⚲ $34
⚱ $34
⚚ $34
🌸 $32.50
⌇ $32.50
⚠ $32.50
♡ $32.50
✝ $32.50
6ᗺ $32.50
★ $32.50
◌ $32.50

The Heavenly Light
#E5637
Issued: 1981 • Open
Retail Price: $15 – $32.50

10

VALUES: ✝ $127
✦ $116
✳ $105
▲ $105

His Name Is Jesus
#E5381
Issued: 1984 • Susp.: 1987
Retail Price: $45 – $50

56

KEY: NM *Pre-1981* ▲ 1981 Ⅰ 1982 ◀ 1983 ✝ 1984 ✦ 1985 ✳ 1986 ▲ 1987 🔷 1988 🔶 1989 ⚲ 1990 ⚱ 1991 ⚚ 1992 🌸 1993 ⌇ 1994 ⚠ 1995 ♡ 1996 ✝ 1997 6ᗺ 1998 ★ 1999 ◌ 2000 UM *Unmarked*

Value Guide — PRECIOUS MOMENTS®

1

VALUES: 𝕀 $84
🐟 $79
✝ $74
UM $116

His Sheep Am I
#E7161
Issued: 1982 • Susp.: 1984
Retail Price: $25 – $27.50

2

VALUES: 🍂 $38
〃 $33
▲ $30
🔷 $30
🦋 $27
⚓ $27
🔔 $25
🎂 $25
🎀 $23
♥ $20
❤ $20
🔆 $20
★ $20
🕊 $20

Honk If You Love Jesus (set/2)
#15490
Issued: 1985 • Open
Retail Price: $13 – $20

3

VALUES: 𝕀 $120
🐟 $95
✝ $88
🍂 $82

I'll Play My Drum For Him
#E2356
Issued: 1982 • Susp.: 1985
Retail Price: $30 – $33

4

VALUES: 𝕀 $53
🐟 $46
✝ $40
〃 $40
〃 $37
▲ $34
🔷 $34
⚓ $34
🔔 $32
🎂 $32
🎀 $30
🎀 $30
⚓ $27.50
△ $27.50
♥ $27.50
✝ $27.50
🔆 $27.50
★ $27.50
🕊 $27.50

I'll Play My Drum For Him
#E2360
Issued: 1982 • Open
Retail Price: $16 – $27.50

5

VALUES: ✝ $53
🍂 $45
▲ $45
🔷 $40
🦋 $37
⚓ $37
🔔 $34
🎂 $34
🎀 $34
🎀 $32.50
🛷 $32.50
△ $32.50
♥ $32.50
✝ $32.50
🔆 $32.50
★ $32.50
🕊 $32.50

Isn't He Precious
#E5379
Issued: 1984 • Open
Retail Price: $20 – $32.50

6

VALUES: NM $85
▲ $75
𝕀 $70
✝ $65
✝ $62
🍂 $60

Isn't He Wonderful
#E5639
Issued: 1981 • Susp.: 1985
Retail Price: $12 – $17

7

VALUES: NM $85
▲ $80
𝕀 $73
✝ $70
✝ $68
🍂 $65

Isn't He Wonderful
#E5640
Issued: 1981 • Susp.: 1985
Retail Price: $12 – $17

8

VALUES: 🍂 $82
✝ $76
🍂 $70
〃 $70
▲ $67
🔷 $67
⚓ $67
🔔 $67

It's A Perfect Boy
#E0512
Issued: 1983 • Susp.: 1990
Retail Price: $18.50 – $27.50

9

VALUES: 〃 $57
▲ $52
🔷 $52
⚓ $50

It's The Birthday Of A King
#102962
Issued: 1986 • Susp.: 1989
Retail Price: $19 – $25

10
VALUES: NM $155
▲ $148
𝕀 $140
🍂 $124
✝ $120

Jesus Is Born
#E2012
Issued: 1979 • Susp.: 1984
Retail Price: $12 – $25

Nativity

	Price Paid	Value
1.		
2.		
3.		
4.		
5.		
6.		
7.		
8.		
9.		
10.		

Totals

KEY: NM *Pre-1981* ▲ 1981 𝕀 1982 ◀ 1983 ✝ 1984 🍂 1985 〃 1986 ▲ 1987 🔷 1988 🔆 1989 ★ 1990 🔔 1991 🎂 1992 🎀 1993 🛷 1994 △ 1995 ♥ 1996 ✝ 1997 🕊 1998 ★ 1999 ○ 2000 UM *Unmarked*

57

Figurine Series

1 VALUES: NM $405
▲ $370
✕ $345
✦ $330
✝ $310

Jesus Is Born
#E2801
Issued: 1980 • Susp.: 1984
Retail Price: $37 – $55

2 VALUES: ❧ $52
☘ $48
♦ $44
⚘ $40
♘ $38

Jesus Is The Sweetest Name I Know
#523097
Issued: 1989 • Susp.: 1993
Retail Price: $22.50 – $25

3 VALUES: ❀ $68
❧ $57
☘ $52
♦ $48
⚘ $46
♘ $45

Jesus The Savior Is Born
#520357
Issued: 1988 • Susp.: 1993
Retail Price: $25 – $32.50

4 VALUES: ✝ $63
✦ $60
✎ $56
♦ $56
❀ $54
♘ $52

Joy To The World
#E5378
Issued: 1984 • Susp.: 1989
Retail Price: $18 – $25

5 VALUES: 68 $30
★ $30
◐ $30

The Light Of The World Is Jesus
#455954
Issued: 1998 • Open
Retail Price: $30

6 VALUES: ✝ $100
68 $100
★ $100
◐ $100

Lighted Inn
#283428
Issued: 1997 • Open
Retail Price: $100

Nativity

	Price Paid	Value
1.		
2.		
3.		
4.		
5.		
6.		
7.		
8.		
9.		
10.		

Totals

7 VALUES: △ $37
♡ $34
✝ $34
68 $34

Making A Trail To Bethlehem
#142751
Issued: 1995 • Retired: 1998
Retail Price: $30 – $32.50

8 VALUES: ✝ $92
✦ $86
✎ $82

A Monarch Is Born
#E5380
Issued: 1984 • Susp.: 1986
Retail Price: $33

9 VALUES: ◄ $22
△ $18.50
♡ $18.50
✝ $18.50
68 $18.50
★ $18.50
◐ $18.50

Nativity Cart
#528072
Issued: 1994 • Open
Retail Price: $18.50

10 VALUES: UM $24

Nativity Displayer
#PMA077
Issued: 1993 • Open
Retail Price: $18 – $24

KEY: NM *Pre*-1981 ▲ 1981 ✕ 1982 ◄ 1983 ✝ 1984 ✦ 1985 ✎ 1986 ▲ 1987 ❀ 1988 ♘ 1989 ★ 1990
♦ 1991 ⚘ 1992 ♘ 1993 ◄ 1994 △ 1995 ♡ 1996 ✝ 1997 68 1998 ★ 1999 ◐ 2000 UM *Unmarked*

Value Guide — PRECIOUS MOMENTS®

1
VALUES: NM $165 / ▲ $160 / ✗ $148 / ◄ $140 / † $135 / ✦ $132 / ♪ $130 / ▲ $130 / ✦ $125 / ♦ $125 / ✦ $125 / ♦ $125 / ✦ $120 / ✦ $120 / ✦ $120 / ◄ $120 / △ $120 / ♡ $120 / † $120 / ★ $120 / ⊙ $120
Nativity Wall (set/2)
#E5644
Issued: 1981 • Open
Retail Price: $60 – $120

2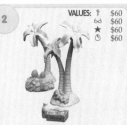
VALUES: † $60 / 6d $60 / ★ $60 / ⊙ $60
Palm Trees, Hay Bale And Baby Food (set/4)
#272582
Issued: 1997 • Open
Retail Price: $60

3
VALUES: ◄ $180 / † $160 / ✦ $152 / ♪ $147
Prepare Ye The Way Of The Lord (set/6)
#E0508
Issued: 1983 • Susp.: 1986
Retail Price: $75

4
VALUES: NM $85 / ▲ $77 / ✗ $62 / ◄ $54 / † $50 / ✦ $45 / ♪ $42 / ▲ $42 / ✦ $37 / ♦ $35 / ♦ $35 / ● $32.50 / ♦ $32.50 / ♀ $32.50 / ◄ $32.50 / △ $32.50 / ♡ $32.50 / † $32.50 / 6d $32.50 / ★ $32.50
Rejoice O Earth
#E5636
Issued: 1981 • Retired: 1999
Retail Price: $15 – $32.50

5
VALUES: ♀ $58 / ◄ $48 / △ $35 / ♡ $32 / † $32
Ring Out The Good News
#529966
Issued: 1993 • Retired: 1997
Retail Price: $27.50 – $30

6
VALUES: ♡ $40 / † $40 / 6d $40 / ★ $40 / ⊙ $40
Shepherd With Lambs (set/3)
#183954
Issued: 1996 • Open
Retail Price: $40

7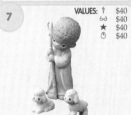
VALUES: † $40 / ★ $40 / ★ $40 / ⊙ $40
Shepherd With Two Lambs (set/3)
#183962
Issued: 1997 • Open
Retail Price: $40

8
VALUES: ✦ $46 / ♦ $39 / ♦ $36 / ● $36 / ♦ $34 / ♀ $33 / ◄ $30 / △ $30 / ♡ $30
Some Bunny's Sleeping
#115274
Issued: 1988 • Susp.: 1996
Retail Price: $15 – $18.50

9
VALUES: NM $350 / ▲ $305 / ✗ $265 / ◄ $250 / † $240 / ✦ $240 / ♪ $240 / ▲ $240 / ✦ $240 / ♦ $240 / ♦ $235 / ● $235 / ♦ $230 / ♀ $225 / ◄ $225 / △ $225 / ♡ $225 / † $225 / ★ $225 / ⊙ $225
They Followed The Star (set/3)
#E5624
Issued: 1981 • Open
Retail Price: $130 – $225

10
VALUES: NM $260 / ▲ $250 / ✗ $235 / ◄ $215 / † $200 / ✦ $195
They Followed The Star
#E5641
Issued: 1981 • Susp.: 1985
Retail Price: $75 – $100

Nativity

Price Paid	Value
1.	
2.	
3.	
4.	
5.	
6.	
7.	
8.	
9.	
10.	

Totals

Figurine Series

VALUES: ⤙ $53
† $42
🦋 $40
▲ $40
⚓ $38
✚ $38
𝄐 $38
✝ $35
🔔 $35
📿 $32
♈ $30

Tubby's First Christmas
#E0511
Issued: 1983 • Susp.: 1993
Retail Price: $12 – $16.50

VALUES: 🔔 $34
🔥 $30
♈ $26
🎺 $22

We Have Come From Afar
#526959
Issued: 1991 • Susp.: 1994
Retail Price: $17.50

VALUES: NM $123
▲ $115
✕ $96
⤙ $92
✝ $86

We Have Seen His Star
#E2010
Issued: 1979 • Susp.: 1984
Retail Price: $8 – $19

VALUES: NM $160
▲ $138
✕ $118
⤙ $100
✚ $97
🦋 $92
✝ $85
✝ $85
⚓ $83
✝ $83
🌾 $80
♈ $77
🔥 $77
♈ $75
△ $75
♡ $75
† $75
📿 $75
★ $75
🕐 $75

We Three Kings
(set/3)
#E5635
Issued: 1981 • Open
Retail Price: $40 – $75

VALUES: † $30
📿 $30
★ $30
🕐 $30

Wishing Well
#292753
Issued: 1997 • Open
Retail Price: $30

VALUES: 🔥 $42
♈ $35
♈ $32
△ $30
♡ $30
† $30
📿 $30
★ $30

Wishing You A Comfy Christmas
#527750
Issued: 1992 • Retired: 1999
Retail Price: $27.50 – $30

	Price Paid	Value
1.		
2.		
3.		
4.		
5.		
6.		
7.		
8.		
Totals		

7

VALUES: 🦋 $530

Come Let Us Adore Him (Dealers' Only, set/9)
#104523
Issued: 1986 • Closed: 1986
Retail Price: $400

8

VALUES: ▲ $260
⚓ $235
🅳 $230
★ $230
🔔 $230

O Come Let Us Adore Him (set/4)
#111333
Issued: 1987 • Susp.: 1991
Retail Price: $200 – $220

KEY: NM *Pre-1981* ▲ 1981 ✕ 1982 ⤙ 1983 † 1984 ✓ 1985 🦋 1986 ▲ 1987 ⚓ 1988 🅳 1989 ★ 1990
🔔 1991 🔥 1992 ♈ 1993 🎺 1994 △ 1995 ♡ 1996 † 1997 📿 1998 ★ 1999 🕐 2000 UM *Unmarked*

1 VALUES: ✿ $115
🔔 $105
⚖ $96
♡ $96

Circus Tent Night-Light
#528196
Issued: 1994 • Susp.: 1996
Retail Price: $90

2 VALUES: ✿ $32
🔔 $28
⚖ $24
♡ $22

Collin
#529214
Issued: 1994 • Susp.: 1996
Retail Price: $20

3 VALUES: ✿ $32
🔔 $28
⚖ $25
♡ $25

Dusty
#529176
Issued: 1994 • Susp.: 1996
Retail Price: $22.50

4 VALUES: ⚖ $30
♡ $25

Jennifer (set/2)
#163708
Issued: 1996 • Susp.: 1996
Retail Price: $20

5 VALUES: 🔔 $32
⚖ $26
♡ $23

Jordan (set/2)
#529168
Issued: 1995 • Susp.: 1996
Retail Price: $20

6 VALUES: ✿ $33
🔔 $26
⚖ $22
♡ $19

Katie
#529184
Issued: 1994 • Susp.: 1996
Retail Price: $17

7 VALUES: ✿ $30
🔔 $24
⚖ $22
♡ $20

Markie
#528099
Issued: 1994 • Susp.: 1996
Retail Price: $18.50

8 VALUES: ✿ $52
🔔 $35

Sammy (LE-1994)
#529222
Issued: 1994 • Closed: 1994
Retail Price: $20

9 VALUES: UM $24

Sammy's Circus Displayer
#PMB015
Issued: 1994 • Discontinued: 1997
Retail Price: $18 – $24

Sammy's Circus

	Price Paid	Value
1.		
2.		
3.		
4.		
5.		
6.		
7.		
8.		
9.		

Totals

KEY: NM *Pre-1981* ▲1981 Ⅱ1982 ◄1983 ✝1984 ✦1985 ♫1986 ♣1987 ✿1988 ✢1989 ✦1990 ❀1991 $1992 ✿1993 🔔1994 ⚖1995 ♡1996 ✝1997 ∞1998 ★1999 ◔2000 UM *Unmarked*

61

Figurine Series

1
VALUES: 🐝 $22
🐚 $19
△ $15
♡ $14

Tippy
#529192
Issued: 1994 • Susp.: 1996
Retail Price: $12

2
VALUES: 🐝 $300
🐚 $260

Sammy's Circus (set/7, *includes* 528099, 528196, 529176, 529184, 529192, 529214 & 529222)
#604070
Issued: 1994 • Closed: 1994
Retail Price: $200

3
VALUES: UM $22

Accessories (set/8)
#212725
Issued: 1997 • Retired: 1997
Retail Price: $20

4
VALUES: † $34

Aunt Bulah And Uncle Sam
#272825
Issued: 1997 • Retired: 1997
Retail Price: $22.50

Sammy's Circus

	Price Paid	Value
1.		
2.		

Sugar Town

3.		
4.		
5.		
6.		
7.		
8.		

Totals

5
VALUES: † $26

Aunt Cleo
#272817
Issued: 1997 • Retired: 1997
Retail Price: $18.50

6
VALUES: 💰 $50
🐝 $42
🐚 $36

Aunt Ruth And Aunt Dorothy
#529486
Issued: 1992 • Retired: 1994
Retail Price: $20

7
VALUES: † $18

Bike Rack
#272906
Issued: 1997 • Retired: 1997
Retail Price: $15

8
VALUES: △ $18
♡ $14
† $12

Bird Bath
#150223
Issued: 1995 • Retired: 1997
Retail Price: $8.50

KEY: NM *Pre-1981* ▲ 1981 ▋ 1982 ◄ 1983 † 1984 ✦ 1985 ✗ 1986 ▲ 1987 ✤ 1988 ♫ 1989 ✦ 1990 ● 1991 💰 1992 🐝 1993 🐚 1994 △ 1995 ♡ 1996 † 1997 ⬡ 1998 ★ 1999 ○ 2000 UM *Unmarked*

Value Guide — PRECIOUS MOMENTS®

1 VALUES: ♡ $20 / † $16

Bonfire
#184152
Issued: 1996 • Retired: 1997
Retail Price: $10

2 VALUES: † $13

Bunnies
#531804
Issued: 1997 • Retired: 1997
Retail Price: $10

3 VALUES: ⌂ $18 / ♡ $13 / † $13

Bus Stop
#150207
Issued: 1995 • Retired: 1997
Retail Price: $8.50

4 VALUES: † $34

Chuck (LE-1997)
#272809
Issued: 1997 • Closed: 1997
Retail Price: $22.50

5 VALUES: ⊐ $33 / ⌂ $24 / ♡ $24 / † $22

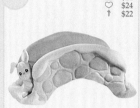

Cobblestone Bridge
#533203
Issued: 1994 • Retired: 1997
Retail Price: $17

6 VALUES: ♡ $20 / † $13

Cocoa
#184063
Issued: 1996 • Retired: 1997
Retail Price: $7.50

7 VALUES: ⊐ $23 / ⌂ $17 / ♡ $15 / † $15

Curved Sidewalk
#533149
Issued: 1994 • Retired: 1997
Retail Price: $10

8 VALUES: ⊐ $108 / ⌂ $100 / ♡ $95 / † $95

Doctor's Office Night-Light
#529869
Issued: 1994 • Retired: 1997
Retail Price: $80 – $85

9 VALUES: ⌂ $37 / ♡ $33 / † $29

Donny
#531871
Issued: 1995 • Retired: 1997
Retail Price: $22.50

10 VALUES: ⊐ $25 / ⊿ $16 / ♡ $16 / † $16

Double Tree
#533181
Issued: 1994 • Retired: 1997
Retail Price: $10

Sugar Town

	Price Paid	Value
1.		
2.		
3.		
4.		
5.		
6.		
7.		
8.		
9.		
10.		

Totals

KEY: NM *Pre-1981* ▲ 1981 ✕ 1982 ◀1983 † 1984 ◆1985 ✒ 1986 ▲ 1987 ✤ 1988 ✿ 1989 ★ 1990 ♦ 1991 ✦ 1992 ♈ 1993 ⊐ 1994 ⌂ 1995 ♡ 1996 † 1997 ∞ 1998 ★ 1999 ○ 2000 UM *Unmarked*

63

Figurine Series

VALUES: 🥨 $38
△ $26
♡ $23
✝ $20

1

Dr. Sam Sugar
#529850
Issued: 1994 • Retired: 1997
Retail Price: $17

VALUES: 🎀 $35
🥨 $30
△ $26
♡ $23
✝ $23

2

Dusty
#529435
Issued: 1993 • Retired: 1997
Retail Price: $17

VALUES: 🍬 $42
🎀 $36
🥨 $33

3

Evergreen Tree
#528684
Issued: 1992 • Retired: 1994
Retail Price: $15

VALUES: △ $13
♡ $8
✝ $8

4

Fire Hydrant
#150215
Issued: 1995 • Retired: 1997
Retail Price: $5

VALUES: ♡ $22
✝ $19

5

Flag Pole
#184136
Issued: 1996 • Retired: 1997
Retail Price: $15

VALUES: 🥨 $30
△ $25
♡ $22
✝ $20

6

Free Christmas Puppies
#528064
Issued: 1994 • Retired: 1997
Retail Price: $12.50

Sugar Town

	Price Paid	Value
1.		
2.		
3.		
4.		
5.		
6.		
7.		
8.		
9.		
10.		

Totals

VALUES: ✝ $26

7

Garbage Can
#272914
Issued: 1997 • Retired: 1997
Retail Price: $20

VALUES: 🍬 $42
🥨 $33
🎀 $30

8

Grandfather
#529516
Issued: 1992 • Retired: 1994
Retail Price: $15

VALUES: ♡ $35
✝ $30

9

Hank And Sharon
#184098
Issued: 1996 • Retired: 1997
Retail Price: $25

VALUES: ✝ $28

10

Heather
#272833
Issued: 1997 • Retired: 1997
Retail Price: $20

KEY: NM Pre-1981 ▲1981 𝕀1982 ◀1983 ✝1984 🍃1985 ♪1986 ▲1987 🌸1988 ☝1989 ⚖1990 ♦1991 🍬1992 🎀1993 🥨1994 △1995 ♡1996 ✝1997 ∞1998 ★1999 ○2000 UM Unmarked

Value Guide — PRECIOUS MOMENTS®

1

VALUES: ♡ $21
† $18

Hot Cocoa Stand
#184144
Issued: 1996 • Retired: 1997
Retail Price: $15

2

VALUES: ⛟ $33
△ $28
♡ $24
† $20

Jan
#529826
Issued: 1994 • Retired: 1997
Retail Price: $17

3

VALUES: ⚘ $42
⛟ $34
△ $33
♡ $27
† $26

Katy Lynne
#529524
Issued: 1993 • Retired: 1997
Retail Price: $20

4

VALUES: ⛟ $17
△ $14
♡ $12
† $12

Lamp Post
#529559
Issued: 1994 • Retired: 1997
Retail Price: $8

5

VALUES: ⛟ $37
△ $30
♡ $30
† $25

Leon And Evelyn Mae
#529818
Issued: 1994 • Retired: 1997
Retail Price: $20

6

VALUES: ♡ $28
† $24

Leroy
#184071
Issued: 1996 • Retired: 1997
Retail Price: $18.50

7

VALUES: ♡ $62
† $54

Lighted Tree
#184039
Issued: 1996 • Retired: 1997
Retail Price: $45

8

VALUES: △ $24
♡ $18
† $17

Luggage Cart
#150185
Issued: 1995 • Retired: 1997
Retail Price: $13

9

VALUES: ⛟ $15
△ $11
♡ $8
† $8

Mailbox
#531847
Issued: 1994 • Retired: 1997
Retail Price: $5

10

VALUES: ♡ $33
† $27

Mazie
#184055
Issued: 1996 • Retired: 1997
Retail Price: $18.50

Sugar Town

	Price Paid	Value
1.		
2.		
3.		
4.		
5.		
6.		
7.		
8.		
9.		
10.		

Totals

KEY: NM *Pre-1981* ▲ 1981 Ⅺ 1982 ◀1983 † 1984 ◀1985 ✸ 1986 ▲ 1987 ✤ 1988 ✛ 1989 ★ 1990
⚬ 1991 ⚘ 1992 ⚘ 1993 ⛟ 1994 △ 1995 ♡ 1996 † 1997 ⚭ 1998 ★ 1999 ○ 2000 UM *Unmarked*

Value Guide — PRECIOUS MOMENTS®

Figurine Series

1 VALUES: † $28

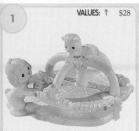

Merry Go Round
#272841
Issued: 1997 • Retired: 1997
Retail Price: $20

2 VALUES: ☖ $55
☗ $47
☷ $43

Nativity
#529508
Issued: 1992 • Retired: 1994
Retail Price: $20

3 VALUES: ☖ $24
♡ $18
† $18

Park Bench
#529540
Issued: 1995 • Retired: 1997
Retail Price: $13

4 VALUES: ☖ $45
☗ $40
☷ $33

Philip
#529494
Issued: 1992 • Retired: 1994
Retail Price: $17

5 VALUES: ☖ $22
♡ $17
† $17

Railroad Crossing Sign
#150177
Issued: 1995 • Retired: 1997
Retail Price: $12

6 VALUES: ☖ $50
♡ $35

Sam (LE-1995)
#150169
Issued: 1995 • Closed: 1995
Retail Price: $20

Sugar Town

	Price Paid	Value
1.		
2.		
3.		
4.		
5.		
6.		
7.		
8.		
9.		
10.		
Totals		

7 VALUES: ☖ $200

Sam Butcher (LE-1992)
#529567
Issued: 1992 • Closed: 1992
Retail Price: $22.50

8 VALUES: ☗ $68

Sam Butcher With Sugar Town Population Sign (LE-1993)
#529842
Issued: 1993 • Closed: 1993
Retail Price: $22.50

9 VALUES: ☗ $38
☷ $33
☖ $33
♡ $30
† $27

Sam's Car
#529443
Issued: 1993 • Retired: 1997
Retail Price: $22.50

10 VALUES: ☗ $110
☷ $95
☖ $95
♡ $90
† $90

Sam's House Night-Light
#529605
Issued: 1993 • Retired: 1997
Retail Price: $80 – $85

66

KEY: NM *Pre-*1981 ▲1981 ▮1982 ◀1983 ✝1984 ✦1985 ✱1986 ♣1987 ✧1988 ✛1989 ★1990 ☗1991 ☖1992 ☗1993 ☷1994 ☖1995 ♡1996 †1997 ᭺1998 ★1999 ○2000 UM *Unmarked*

Value Guide — PRECIOUS MOMENTS®

Figurine Series

1 VALUES: 🐾 $40 · ⚜ $32 · △ $25 · ♡ $23 · † $23

Sammy
#528668
Issued: 1993 • Retired: 1997
Retail Price: $17

2 VALUES: † $105

School House Night-Light
(also available with
Canadian flag)
#272795
Issued: 1997 • Retired: 1997
Retail Price: $80

3 VALUES: 🖌 $22 · △ $14 · ♡ $12 · † $12

Single Tree
#533173
Issued: 1994 • Retired: 1997
Retail Price: $10

4 VALUES: 🖌 $55

Stork With Baby Sam
(LE-1994)
#529788
Issued: 1994 • Closed: 1994
Retail Price: $22.50

5 VALUES: 🖌 $20 · △ $16 · ♡ $13 · † $13

Straight Sidewalk
#533157
Issued: 1994 • Retired: 1997
Retail Price: $10

6 VALUES: △ $21 · ♡ $15 · † $15

Street Sign
#532185
Issued: 1995 • Retired: 1997
Retail Price: $10

7 VALUES: △ $35 · △ $32 · ♡ $30 · † $27

Sugar And Her
Doghouse (set/2)
#533165
Issued: 1994 • Retired: 1997
Retail Price: $20

8 VALUES: UM $32

Sugar Town Cargo Car
(LE-1997)
#273007
Issued: 1997 • Closed: 1997
Retail Price: $27.50

9 VALUES: 🖋 $160 · 🐾 $145 · 🖌 $135

Sugar Town Chapel
Night-Light
#529621
Issued: 1992 • Retired: 1994
Retail Price: $85

10 VALUES: 🐾 $35

Sugar Town Chapel
Ornament (LE-1993)
#530484
Issued: 1993 • Closed: 1993
Retail Price: $17.50

Sugar Town

	Price Paid	Value
1.		
2.		
3.		
4.		
5.		
6.		
7.		
8.		
9.		
10.		

Totals

KEY:: NM *Pre-1981* ▲ 1981 I 1982 ◀ 1983 † 1984 🍃 1985 ⚘ 1986 ▲ 1987 ✤ 1988 ⊕ 1989 ★ 1990 🖋 1991 🖌 1992 🐾 1993 🖌 1994 △ 1995 ♡ 1996 † 1997 ⬡ 1998 ★ 1999 ◌ 2000 UM *Unmarked*

67

1 VALUES: UM $24

Sugar Town Displayer
#PMB007
Issued: 1993 • Retired: 1997
Retail Price: $18 – $24

2 VALUES: △ $30

Sugar Town Doctor's Office Ornament (LE-1995)
#530441
Issued: 1995 • Closed: 1995
Retail Price: $17.50 – $20

3 VALUES: UM $90

Sugar Town Express (set/3)
♪ *Christmas Medley*
#152595
Issued: 1995 • Retired: 1997
Retail Price: $75

4 VALUES: ♈ $20
　　　　　🍷 $15
　　　　　△ $15
　　　　　♡ $12
　　　　　† $12

Sugar Town Fence
#529796
Issued: 1993 • Retired: 1997
Retail Price: $10

5 VALUES: UM $30

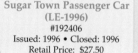

Sugar Town Passenger Car (LE-1996)
#192406
Issued: 1996 • Closed: 1996
Retail Price: $27.50

6 VALUES: △ $30
　　　　　△ $22

Sugar Town Sam's House Ornament (LE-1994)
#530468
Issued: 1994 • Closed: 1994
Retail Price: $17.50

7 VALUES: ♡ $56
　　　　　† $50

Sugar Town Skating Pond
#184047
Issued: 1996 • Retired: 1997
Retail Price: $40

8 VALUES: ♡ $35
　　　　　† $27

Sugar Town Skating Sign (LE-1996)
#184020
Issued: 1996 • Closed: 1996
Retail Price: $15

9 VALUES: 🍷 $115
　　　　　△ $95
　　　　　♡ $90
　　　　　† $90

Sugar Town Square Clock
#532908
Issued: 1994 • Retired: 1997
Retail Price: $80 – $85

Sugar Town

	Price Paid	Value
1.		
2.		
3.		
4.		
5.		
6.		
7.		
8.		
9.		
Totals		

KEY: NM *Pre-1981* ▲1981 Ⅱ1982 ◄1983 † 1984 ✔1985 ♪ 1986 ♠ 1987 ♣ 1988 ♫ 1989 ★ 1990 ♦ 1991 ♒ 1992 ♈ 1993 🍷 1994 △ 1995 ♡ 1996 † 1997 ∞ 1998 ★ 1999 ◔ 2000 UM *Unmarked*

Value Guide — PRECIOUS MOMENTS®

1 VALUES: ♡ $27   † $22

Sugar Town Train Station Ornament (LE-1996)
#184101
Issued: 1996 • Closed: 1996
Retail Price: $18.50

2 VALUES: △ $35   ♡ $32   ♡ $28

Tammy And Debbie
#531812
Issued: 1995 • Retired: 1997
Retail Price: $22.50

3 VALUES: △ $130   ♡ $120   † $110

Train Station Night-Light
#150150
Issued: 1995 • Retired: 1997
Retail Price: $100

4 VALUES: ♡ $72   † $66

Warming Hut Night-Light
#192341
Issued: 1996 • Retired: 1997
Retail Price: $60

5 VALUES: 🛏 $290   △ $251   ♡ $231   † $214

Sugar Town Doctor's Office Collector's Set (set/6,
includes 528064, 529818, 529826, 529850, 529869 & 533165)
#184187
Issued: 1996 • Retired: 1997
Retail Price: $170

6 VALUES: 🛏 $343

Sugar Town Doctor's Office Collector's Set
(set/7, LE-1994, *includes* 528064, 529788, 529818, 529826,
529850, 529869 & 533165)
#529281
Issued: 1994 • Closed: 1994
Retail Price: $189

7 VALUES: △ $90   ♡ $61   † $61

Sugar Town Enhancement Set (set/5, *includes* 150207,
150215, 150223, 529540 & 532185)
#152269
Issued: 1995 • Retired: 1997
Retail Price: $45

8 VALUES: ♡ $59   † $51

Sugar Town Enhancement Set (set/3, *includes*
184136, 184144 & 184152)
#184160
Issued: 1996 • Retired: 1997
Retail Price: $40

Sugar Town

	Price Paid	Value
1.		
2.		
3.		
4.		
5.		
6.		
7.		
8.		

Totals

KEY: NM *Pre*-1981 ▲ 1981 ▮ 1982 ◀ 1983 † 1984 ♡ 1985 ♪ 1986 ♠ 1987 ♦ 1988 ♫ 1989 ± 1990
♦ 1991 ♣ 1992 ♈ 1993 🛏 1994 △ 1995 ♡ 1996 † 1997 ∞ 1998 ★ 1999 🕭 2000 UM *Unmarked*

69

Figurine Series

1 VALUES: † $53

**Sugar Town Enhancement
Set (set/3, *includes*
272906, 272914 & 531804)**
#273015
Issued: 1997 • Retired: 1997
Retail Price: $45

2 VALUES: 6ə $260

Sugar Town Post Office Collector's Set (set/8, LE-1998)
#456217
Issued: 1998 • Closed: 1998
Retail Price: $250

3 VALUES: ♉ $283
◥ $242
⚠ $223
♡ $209
† $203

**Sugar Town Sam's House Collector's Set
(set/6, *includes* 528668, 529435, 529443, 529524, 529605 & 529796)**
#184195
Issued: 1996 • Retired: 1997
Retail Price: $170

4 VALUES: ♉ $351

**Sugar Town Sam's House Collector's Set
(set/7, LE-1993, *includes* 528668, 529435, 529443, 529524,
529605, 529796 & 529842)**
#531774
Issued: 1993 • Closed: 1993
Retail Price: $189

Sugar Town

	Price Paid	Value
1.		
2.		
3.		
4.		
5.		
Totals		

5 VALUES: † $249

**Sugar Town School House Collector's Set
(set/6, LE-1997, *includes* 272795, 272809, 272817, 272825,
272833 & 272841, also available with Canadian flag)**
#272876
Issued: 1997 • Closed: 1997
Retail Price: $183.50

KEY: NM *Pre*-1981 ▲1981 Ⅱ1982 ◄1983 †1984 ✿1985 ✦1986 ✦1987 ✦1988 ⅌1989 ★1990
● 1991 ⑤ 1992 ♉1993 ⬬1994 ⚠1995 ♡1996 †1997 6ə1998 ★1999 ⚪2000 UM *Unmarked*

Value Guide — PRECIOUS MOMENTS®

1

VALUES: ♡ $263
† $231

Sugar Town Skating Pond Collector's Set
(set/7, LE-1996, *includes* 184020, 184047, 184055, 184063, 184071, 184098 & 192341)
#184128
Issued: 1996 • Closed: 1996
Retail Price: $184.50

2

VALUES: ♡ $231
† $204

Sugar Town Skating Pond Collector's Set
(set/6, *includes* 184047, 184055, 184063, 184071, 184098 & 192341)
#272930
Issued: 1997 • Retired: 1997
Retail Price: $169.50

3

VALUES: ⌂ $275
♡ $241

Sugar Town Train Station Collector's Set (set/6, LE-1995,
includes 150150, 150169, 150177, 150185, 531812 & 531871)
#150193
Issued: 1995 • Closed: 1995
Retail Price: $190

4

VALUES: ⌂ $230
♡ $208
† $193

Sugar Town Train Station Collector's Set
(set/5, *includes* 150150, 150177, 150185, 531812 & 531871)
#184179
Issued: 1996 • Retired: 1997
Retail Price: $170

Sugar Town

Price Paid	Value
1.	
2.	
3.	
4.	

Totals

Figurine Series

VALUES:	🐾	$18
	🦋	$12
	⚜	$10
	♡	$9
	†	$9
	👓	$9
	★	$9
	🕐	$9

1

Bunnies
#530123
Issued: 1993 • Open
Retail Price: $9

VALUES:	⚜	$22
	♡	$15
	†	$15
	👓	$15
	★	$15
	🕐	$15

2

**Congratulations, You
Earned Your Stripes**
#127809
Issued: 1995 • Open
Retail Price: $15

VALUES:	🐾	$27
	🦋	$20
	⚜	$18
	♡	$18
	†	$18
	👓	$18
	★	$18
	🕐	$18

3

Elephants
#530131
Issued: 1993 • Open
Retail Price: $18

VALUES:	🐾	$24
	🦋	$19
	⚜	$16
	♡	$16
	†	$16
	👓	$16
	★	$16
	🕐	$16

4

Giraffes
#530115
Issued: 1993 • Open
Retail Price: $16

VALUES:	⚜	$16
	♡	$10
	†	$10
	👓	$10
	★	$10
	🕐	$10

5

**I'd Goat Anywhere
With You**
#163694
Issued: 1996 • Open
Retail Price: $10

VALUES:	🦋	$22
	⚜	$17
	♡	$15
	†	$15
	👓	$15
	★	$15
	🕐	$15

6

Llamas
#531375
Issued: 1994 • Open
Retail Price: $15

Two By Two

	Price Paid	Value
1.		
2.		
3.		
4.		
5.		
6.		
7.		
8.		
9.		
10.		
Totals		

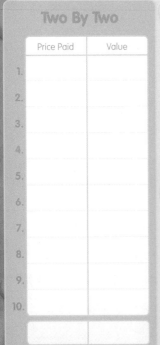

VALUES:	🐾	$145
	🦋	$134
	⚜	$125
	♡	$125
	†	$125
	👓	$125
	★	$125
	🕐	$125

7

**Noah's Ark Night-Light
(set/3)**
#530042
Issued: 1993 • Open
Retail Price: $125

VALUES:	🐾	$20
	🦋	$16
	⚜	$14
	♡	$12
	†	$12
	👓	$12
	★	$12
	🕐	$12

8

Pigs
#530085
Issued: 1993 • Open
Retail Price: $12

VALUES:	🐾	$18
	🦋	$15
	⚜	$12
	♡	$10
	†	$10
	👓	$10
	★	$10
	🕐	$10

9

Sheep
#530077
Issued: 1993 • Open
Retail Price: $10

VALUES:	★	$20
	🕐	$20

10

New!

A Tail Of Love
#679976
Issued: 2000 • Open
Retail Price: $20

KEY: NM *Pre-1981* ▲ *1981* Ⅱ *1982* ◄ *1983* † *1984* ✦ *1985* ✗ *1986* ▲ *1987* ✦ *1988* ✦ *1989* ★ *1990* ⬥ *1991* ⬧ *1992* 🐾 *1993* 🦋 *1994* ⚜ *1995* ♡ *1996* † *1997* 👓 *1998* ★ *1999* 🕐 *2000* UM *Unmarked*

1 VALUES: UM $24

2 VALUES: ✻ $245
⛢ $212
△ $195
♡ $190
✝ $190
👓 $190
★ $190
🕐 $190

Two By Two Displayer
#PMA022
Issued: 1993 • Discontinued: 1993
Retail Price: $24

Two By Two Collector's Set
(set/8, *includes* 530042, 530077, 530085,
530115, 530123 & 530131)
#530948
Issued: 1993 • Open
Retail Price: $190

Two By Two

	Price Paid	Value
1.		
2		

Totals

KEY: NM *Pre-1981* ▲ 1981 ✖ 1982 ◀ 1983 ✝ 1984 🍃 1985 ✹ 1986 ▲ 1987 ✤ 1988 ✤ 1989 ✦ 1990 ♦ 1991 ♪ 1992 ✻ 1993 ⬳ 1994 △ 1995 ♡ 1996 ✝ 1997 👓 1998 ★ 1999 🕐 2000 UM *Unmarked*

General Figurines

The original PRECIOUS MOMENTS collection that debuted in 1978 consisted of 21 figurines from both the series and general lines. While the collection has grown to include many other products, general figurines are the mainstay of the line, making up nearly a third of the approximately 1,800 pieces. In 1999, several old favorites retired, making way for new pieces to take their place and ensuring many more PRECIOUS MOMENTS to come.

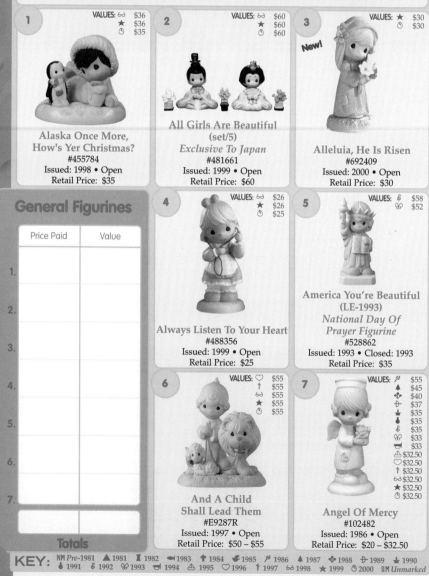

1 VALUES: 6ᵔ $36 ★ $36 ○ $35

**Alaska Once More,
How's Yer Christmas?**
#455784
Issued: 1998 • Open
Retail Price: $35

2 VALUES: 6ᵔ $60 ★ $60 ○ $60

**All Girls Are Beautiful
(set/5)**
Exclusive To Japan
#481661
Issued: 1999 • Open
Retail Price: $60

3 New! VALUES: ★ $30 ○ $30

Alleluia, He Is Risen
#692409
Issued: 2000 • Open
Retail Price: $30

4 VALUES: 6ᵔ $26 ★ $26 ○ $25

Always Listen To Your Heart
#488356
Issued: 1999 • Open
Retail Price: $25

5 VALUES: ⚘ $58 ♀♀ $52

**America You're Beautiful
(LE-1993)**
*National Day Of
Prayer Figurine*
#528862
Issued: 1993 • Closed: 1993
Retail Price: $35

6 VALUES: ♡ $55 † $55 6ᵔ $55 ★ $55 ○ $55

**And A Child
Shall Lead Them**
#E9287R
Issued: 1997 • Open
Retail Price: $50 – $55

7 VALUES: ℱ $55 ▲ $45 ⬥ $40 ⊕ $37 ★ $35 ● $35 ⚘ $35 ♀♀ $33 ⊟ $33 ⬠ $32.50 ♡ $32.50 † $32.50 6ᵔ $32.50 ★ $32.50 ○ $32.50

Angel Of Mercy
#102482
Issued: 1986 • Open
Retail Price: $20 – $32.50

General Figurines

	Price Paid	Value
1.		
2.		
3.		
4.		
5.		
6.		
7.		
Totals		

KEY: NM *Pre-1981* ▲ 1981 𝕀 1982 ◀1983 † 1984 🍃1985 ℱ 1986 ▲ 1987 ⬥1988 ⊕ 1989 ★ 1990 ● 1991 ⚘ 1992 ♀♀1993 ⊟ 1994 ⬠ 1995 ♡ 1996 † 1997 6ᵔ 1998 ★ 1999 ○2000 UM *Unmarked*

Value Guide — PRECIOUS MOMENTS®

1

VALUES: ♡ $45 / † $45 / 6ð $45 / ★ $45 / ☾ $45

Angels On Earth
#183776
Issued: 1996 • Open
Retail Price: $40 – $45

2

VALUES: ♦ $98 / ♒ $90 / ♦ $86 / ☖ $82 / ☖ $80 / ♡ $80

Angels We Have Heard On High
#524921
Issued: 1991 • Retired: 1996
Retail Price: $60 – $70

3

VALUES: ◄ $32 / † $29 / ☘ $29 / ♪ $25 / ♠ $24 / ♣ $24 / Đ $24 / ♨ $22 / ♦ $22 / UM $34

Animal Collection – Bunny
#E9267C
Issued: 1983 • Susp.: 1991
Retail Price: $6.50 – $11

4

VALUES: ◄ $32 / † $29 / ☘ $29 / ♪ $25 / ♠ $24 / ♣ $24 / Đ $24 / ♨ $22 / ♦ $22 / UM $34

Animal Collection – Dog
#E9267B
Issued: 1983 • Susp.: 1991
Retail Price: $6.50 – $11

5

VALUES: † $32 / ☘ $29 / ♪ $29 / ♠ $25 / ♣ $24 / Đ $24 / ♨ $24 / ♦ $22 / ☾ $22 / UM $34

Animal Collection – Kitten
#E9267D
Issued: 1983 • Susp.: 1991
Retail Price: $6.50 – $11

6

VALUES: ◄ $32 / † $29 / ☘ $29 / ♪ $25 / ♠ $24 / ♣ $24 / Đ $24 / ♨ $22 / ♦ $22 / UM $34

Animal Collection – Lamb
#E9267E
Issued: 1983 • Susp.: 1991
Retail Price: $6.50 – $11

7

VALUES: ◄ $32 / † $29 / ☘ $29 / ♪ $25 / ♠ $24 / ♣ $24 / Đ $24 / ♨ $22 / ♦ $22 / UM $34

Animal Collection – Pig
#E9267F
Issued: 1983 • Susp.: 1991
Retail Price: $6.50 – $11

8

VALUES: † $32 / ☘ $29 / ♪ $29 / ♠ $25 / ♣ $24 / Đ $24 / ♨ $24 / ♦ $22 / ☾ $22 / UM $34

Animal Collection – Teddy
#E9267A
Issued: 1983 • Susp.: 1991
Retail Price: $6.50 – $11

9

VALUES: ☖ $28 / ☖ $21 / ♡ $18.50 / † $18.50 / 6ð $18.50 / ★ $18.50 / ☾ $18.50

Another Year And More Grey Hares
#128686
Issued: 1995 • Open
Retail Price: $17.50 – $18.50

10

VALUES: ♠ $115 / ♣ $57 / Đ $48 / ♨ $45 / ♦ $42 / ♒ $42 / ♒ $42 / ☖ $40 / ☖ $40 / ♡ $40 / † $40 / 6ð $40 / ★ $40 / ☾ $40

April
Calendar Girl Series
#110027
Issued: 1988 • Open
Retail Price: $30 – $40

General Figurines

	Price Paid	Value
1.		
2.		
3.		
4.		
5.		
6.		
7.		
8.		
9.		
10.		

Totals

KEY: NM *Pre-1981* ▲1981 ☒1982 ◄1983 †1984 ☘1985 ♪1986 ♠1987 ♣1988 Đ1989 ♨1990 ♦1991 ♒1992 ☖1993 ☖1994 ☖1995 ♡1996 †1997 6ð1998 ★1999 ☾2000 UM *Unmarked*

75

1 VALUES: ✿ $73
⊕ $62
✝ $58
🕯 $54
🐚 $52
🎄 $52
△ $50
♡ $50
✝ $50
🕯 $50
★ $50
🕐 $50

August
Calendar Girl Series
#110078
Issued: 1988 • Open
Retail Price: $40 – $50

2 VALUES: 🍂 $86
🍁 $65

Autumn's Praise (LE-1986)
The Four Seasons
Figurine Series
#12084
Issued: 1986 • Closed: 1986
Retail Price: $30

3 VALUES: 6ᴣ $30
★ $30
🕐 $25

Baby Figurine (personalized)
#163651B
Issued: 1998 • Open
Retail Price: $25

4 VALUES: 6ᴣ $30
★ $30
🕐 $25

Baby Figurine (personalized)
#163651G
Issued: 1998 • Open
Retail Price: $25

5 VALUES: ✝ $42
🍁 $37
🍂 $35
▲ $35
⚓ $33
⊕ $32
🕯 $32
🐚 $32
🎄 $27
♀ $27
△ $23
△ $23
♡ $23

Baby Figurines – Baby Boy
Crawling
#E2852E
Issued: 1984 • Susp.: 1996
Retail Price: $12 – $18.50

6 VALUES: ✝ $42
🍁 $37
🍂 $35
▲ $35
⚓ $33
⊕ $32
🕯 $32
🐚 $32
🎄 $27
♀ $27
△ $23
△ $23
♡ $23

Baby Figurines – Baby Boy
Sitting
#E2852C
Issued: 1984 • Susp.: 1996
Retail Price: $12 – $18.50

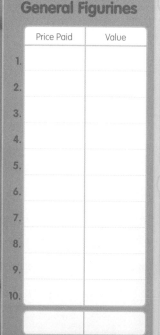

7 VALUES: ✝ $42
🍁 $37
🍂 $35
▲ $35
⚓ $33
⊕ $32
🕯 $32
🐚 $32
🎄 $27
♀ $27
△ $23
♡ $23

Baby Figurines – Baby Boy
Standing
#E2852A
Issued: 1984 • Susp.: 1996
Retail Price: $12 – $18.50

8 VALUES: ✝ $42
🍁 $37
🍂 $35
▲ $35
⚓ $33
⊕ $32
🕯 $32
🐚 $32
🎄 $27
♀ $27
△ $23
△ $23
♡ $23

Baby Figurines – Baby Girl
Clapping
#E2852D
Issued: 1984 • Susp.: 1996
Retail Price: $12 – $18.50

9 VALUES: ✝ $42
🍁 $37
🍂 $35
▲ $35
⊕ $33
⊕ $32
🕯 $32
🐚 $32
🎄 $27
♀ $27
△ $23
△ $23
♡ $23

Baby Figurines – Baby Girl
Lying Down
#E2852F
Issued: 1984 • Susp.: 1996
Retail Price: $12 – $18.50

10 VALUES: ✝ $42
🍁 $37
🍂 $35
▲ $35
✿ $33
⊕ $32
🕯 $32
🐚 $32
🎄 $27
♀ $27
△ $23
△ $23
♡ $23

Baby Figurines – Baby Girl
Standing With Bow
#E2852B
Issued: 1984 • Susp.: 1996
Retail Price: $12 – $18.50

General Figurines

	Price Paid	Value
1.		
2.		
3.		
4.		
5.		
6.		
7.		
8.		
9.		
10.		
Totals		

KEY: NM *Pre-1981* ▲ 1981 ☒ 1982 ◖1983 ✝ 1984 🍂 1985 🍁 1986 ▲ 1987 ✿ 1988 ⊕ 1989 ★ 1990 🕯 1991 🐚 1992 ♀ 1993 ◄ 1994 △ 1995 ♡ 1996 ✝ 1997 6ᴣ 1998 ★ 1999 🕐 2000 UM *Unmarked*

1 VALUES:
🍸	$37
♀	$29
⊟	$26
△	$25
♡	$25
†	$25
👓	$25
★	$25
⏰	$25

Baby's First Birthday
Baby's First Series
#524069
Issued: 1993 • Open
Retail Price: $25

2 VALUES: 🍂 $40

Baby's First Christmas
(Dated 1985)
#15539
Issued: 1985 • Closed: 1985
Retail Price: $13

3 VALUES: 🍂 $40

Baby's First Christmas
(Dated 1985)
#15547
Issued: 1985 • Closed: 1985
Retail Price: $13

4 VALUES:
🍂	$190
♪	$175
♣	$168

Baby's First Haircut
Baby's First Series
#12211
Issued: 1985 • Susp.: 1987
Retail Price: $32.50 – $40

5 VALUES:
🍸	$55
🍸	$47
♀	$44
⊟	$42
△	$42
♡	$42
†	$42
👓	$42
★	$42

Baby's First Meal
Baby's First Series
#524077
Issued: 1991 • Retired: 1999
Retail Price: $35 – $40

6 VALUES:
✤	$90
⊕	$82
★	$78
🍸	$72
🍸	$70
♀	$67
⊟	$65

Baby's First Pet
Baby's First Series
#520705
Issued: 1989 • Susp.: 1994
Retail Price: $45 – $50

7 VALUES:
†	$195
🍂	$176
♪	$170

Baby's First Picture
Baby's First Series
#E2841
Issued: 1984 • Retired: 1986
Retail Price: $45

8 VALUES:
†	$106
🍂	$102
♪	$100
♣	$95
✤	$95

Baby's First Step
Baby's First Series
#E2840
Issued: 1984 • Susp.: 1988
Retail Price: $35 – $40

9 VALUES:
🍂	$320
♪	$315
♣	$300
✤	$290
⊕	$285

Baby's First Trip
Baby's First Series
#16012
Issued: 1986 • Susp.: 1989
Retail Price: $32.50 – $45

10 VALUES:
🍸	$36
♀	$30
⊟	$28
△	$26
♡	$26
†	$26
👓	$26
★	$26

Baby's First Word
Baby's First Series
#527238
Issued: 1992 • Retired: 1999
Retail Price: $25

General Figurines

	Price Paid	Value
1.		
2.		
3.		
4.		
5.		
6.		
7.		
8.		
9.		
10.		
Totals		

KEY: NM *Pre-1981* ▲ 1981 ✠ 1982 ◁ 1983 † 1984 🍂 1985 ♪ 1986 ♣ 1987 ✤ 1988 ⊕ 1989 ★ 1990 🍸 1991 🍸 1992 ♀ 1993 ⊟ 1994 △ 1995 ♡ 1996 † 1997 👓 1998 ★ 1999 ⏰ 2000 UM *Unmarked*

77

General Figurines

1

New!

VALUES: ★ $50
⊙ $50

Be Fruitful And Multiply
#524409
Issued: 2000 • Open
Retail Price: $50

2

VALUES: NM $142
▲ $125
I $110
⊷ $100
✝ $94
✦ $88

Variation

Be Not Weary And Well Doing

Be Not Weary In Well Doing
#E3111
Issued: 1980 • Retired: 1985
Retail Price: $14 – $19
Variation: "Be Not Weary And Well Doing" – $220

3

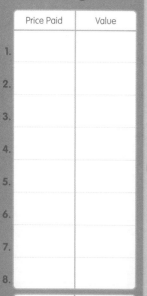

VALUES: NM $122
▲ $105
I $96
⊷ $88
✝ $85

Bear Ye One Another's Burdens
#E5200
Issued: 1981 • Susp.: 1984
Retail Price: $20 – $25

4

VALUES: ★ $50
⊙ $50

The Beauty Of God Blooms Forever
Four Seasons Series
#129143
Issued: 1999 • Open
Retail Price: $50

5

VALUES: 6∂ $36
★ $36
⊙ $35

Believe It Or Knot, I Luv You
#487910
Issued: 1999 • Open
Retail Price: $35

General Figurines

	Price Paid	Value
1.		
2.		
3.		
4.		
5.		
6.		
7.		
8.		

Totals

6

VALUES: ♠ $107
⚓ $88
⌖ $80
★ $76
🔔 $72

Believe The Impossible
#109487
Issued: 1988 • Susp.: 1991
Retail Price: $35 – $45

7

VALUES: ★ $50
⊙ $50

Beside The Still Waters
Four Seasons Series
#129127
Issued: 1999 • Open
Retail Price: $50

8

VALUES: ✝ $40
✦ $37
♪ $35
▲ $34
✣ $34
⌖ $32
★ $32
🔔 $30
& $30
⚪ $28
⌐ $28
⊿ $27
♡ $25
✝ $25
⚓ $25
★ $25
⊙ $25

Best Man
Bridal Party Series
#E2836
Issued: 1984 • Open
Retail Price: $13.50 – $25

KEY: NM *Pre-1981* ▲ 1981 I 1982 ⊷1983 ✝ 1984 ✦ 1985 ♪ 1986 ▲ 1987 ✣ 1988 ⌖ 1989 ★ 1990 🔔 1991 & 1992 ⚐ 1993 ⌐ 1994 ⊿ 1995 ♡ 1996 ✝ 1997 6∂ 1998 ★ 1999 ⊙ 2000 UM *Unmarked*

Value Guide — PRECIOUS MOMENTS®

1

VALUES: 🌒 $40
★ $40
🕐 $35

Birthday Figurine (personalized)
#163686
Issued: 1998 • Open
Retail Price: $35

2
New!

VALUES: ★ $50
🕐 $50

Bless Be The Tie That Binds
#520918
Issued: 2000 • Open
Retail Price: $50

3

VALUES: ✠ $260
◄ $230
✝ $222

Bless This House
#E7164
Issued: 1982 • Susp.: 1984
Retail Price: $45 – $50

4

VALUES: ⊓ $145
⊓ $130

Bless Those Who Serve Their Country
#526568
Issued: 1991 • Susp.: 1992
Retail Price: $32.50

5

VALUES: ⊓ $52
⊓ $48

Bless Those Who Serve Their Country
#526576
Issued: 1991 • Susp.: 1992
Retail Price: $32.50

6

VALUES: ⊓ $62
⊓ $57

Bless Those Who Serve Their Country
#526584
Issued: 1991 • Susp.: 1992
Retail Price: $32.50

7

VALUES: ⊓ $48
⊓ $48

Bless Those Who Serve Their Country
#527289
Issued: 1991 • Susp.: 1992
Retail Price: $32.50

8

VALUES: ⊓ $45
⊓ $45

Bless Those Who Serve Their Country
#527297
Issued: 1991 • Susp.: 1992
Retail Price: $32.50

9
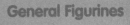
VALUES: ⊓ $70
⊓ $70

Bless Those Who Serve Their Country
#527521
Issued: 1991 • Susp.: 1992
Retail Price: $32.50

10
New!

VALUES: ★ $25
🕐 $25

Bless You
#679879
Issued: 2000 • Open
Retail Price: $25

General Figurines

	Price Paid	Value
1.		
2.		
3.		
4.		
5.		
6.		
7.		
8.		
9.		
10.		
Totals		

KEY: NM *Pre-1981* ▲ 1981 ✠ 1982 ◄ 1983 ✝ 1984 ❦ 1985 ♪ 1986 ♣ 1987 ✿ 1988 ⊕ 1989 ★ 1990
🌡 1991 ♬ 1992 ♈ 1993 ◄ 1994 ⚠ 1995 ♡ 1996 ↑ 1997 🌒 1998 ★ 1999 🕐 2000 UM *Unmarked*

Value Guide — PRECIOUS MOMENTS®

General Figurines (sidebar)

1 VALUES: $58 / $54 / $53 / $50 / $50 / $50 / $48 / $48 / $47 / $47 / $47 / $45 / $45 / $45 / $45 / $45 / $45

Bless You Two
#E9255
Issued: 1983 • Open
Retail Price: $21 – $45

2 VALUES: $44 / $35 / $28 / $27.50 / $27.50 / $27.50 / $27.50

Bless Your Soul
#531162
Issued: 1995 • Open
Retail Price: $25 – $27.50

3 VALUES: NM $130 / $115 / $97 / $86 / $81 / $75

Blessed Are The Peacemakers
#E3107
Issued: 1980 • Retired: 1985
Retail Price: $13 – $19

4 VALUES: NM $63 / $55 / $53 / $53 / $47 / $47 / $42 / $42 / $42 / $38 / $38 / $38

Blessed Are The Pure In Heart
#E3104
Issued: 1980 • Susp.: 1991
Retail Price: $9 – $19

5 VALUES: ★ $60

Blessed Are They With A Caring Heart
Century Circle Figurine
#163724
Issued: 1999 • Closed: 1999
Retail Price: $55

6 VALUES: $200 / ★ $200

Blessed Art Thou Amongst Women (LE-1999)
#261556
Issued: 1999 • Closed: 1999
Retail Price: $175

7 VALUES: ★ $114 / $104 / $98 / $92 / $86

Blessings From Above
#523747
Issued: 1990 • Retired: 1994
Retail Price: $45 – $50

8 VALUES: $90 / $83 / $80 / $77

Blessings From My House To Yours
#E0503
Issued: 1983 • Susp.: 1986
Retail Price: $27

9 VALUES: $48 / $44 / $38 / $38 / $37 / $37 / $37

Bless-Um You
#527335
Issued: 1993 • Retired: 1998
Retail Price: $35

10 VALUES: $148 / $136 / $126 / $120 / $112 / $112 / $110 / $110

Bon Voyage
#522201
Issued: 1989 • Susp.: 1996
Retail Price: $75 – $90

General Figurines

	Price Paid	Value
1.		
2.		
3.		
4.		
5.		
6.		
7.		
8.		
9.		
10.		
Totals		

KEY: NM *Pre*-1981 ▲1981 ♨1982 ◀1983 ✝1984 ✦1985 ♪1986 ▲1987 ✤1988 ⊕1989 ★1990 ♦1991 ♒1992 ♉1993 ◁1994 △1995 ♡1996 ✝1997 ↻1998 ★1999 ♕2000 UM *Unmarked*

1

VALUES: ♡ $40 / † $40 / 6⊃ $40 / ★ $40 / ⊙ $40

A Bouquet From God's Garden Of Love
Growing In God's Garden Of Love Series
#184268
Issued: 1997 • Open
Retail Price: $37.50 – $40

2

VALUES: ▲ $38 / ✤ $35 / ♋ $32 / ✦ $32 / ● $30 / ♂ $28 / ♋ $28 / ☷ $27.50 / △ $27.50 / ♡ $27.50 / † $27.50 / 6⊃ $27.50 / ★ $27.50 / ⊙ $27.50

Bride
Bridal Party Series
#E2846
Issued: 1987 • Open
Retail Price: $18 – $27.50

3

VALUES: † $42 / ✤ $35 / ♒ $34 / ▲ $33 / ✤ $31 / ✦ $31 / ♂ $29 / ● $29 / ♋ $27 / ♋ $27 / ☷ $25 / △ $25 / ♡ $25 / † $25 / 6⊃ $25 / ★ $25 / ⊙ $25

Bridesmaid
Bridal Party Series
#E2831
Issued: 1984 • Open
Retail Price: $13.50 – $25

4

VALUES: ● $115 / ♂ $105 / ✦ $98 / ☷ $95 / △ $92 / ♡ $90 / † $90 / 6⊃ $90 / ★ $90 / ⊙ $90

Bring The Little Ones To Jesus
Child Evangelism Fellowship Figurine
#527556
Issued: 1992 • Open
Retail Price: $90

5

VALUES: ♋ $92 / ▲ $85 / △ $80

Bringing You A Merry Christmas
#527599
Issued: 1993 • Retired: 1995
Retail Price: $45

6

VALUES: ♒ $108 / ▲ $97 / ✤ $90 / ♋ $86

Brotherly Love
#100544
Issued: 1986 • Susp.: 1989
Retail Price: $37 – $47.50

7

VALUES: Ⅱ $130 / ◄ $105 / † $92 / ✦ $90 / ♒ $85 / ▲ $85 / ✤ $85 / ✦ $82 / ♂ $82 / ♋ $80 / ♂ $80 / ♋ $78

Bundles Of Joy
#E2374
Issued: 1982 • Retired: 1993
Retail Price: $27.50 – $45

8

VALUES: NM $110 / Ⅰ $83 / Ⅱ $65 / ◄ $58 / † $55 / ✦ $50 / ♒ $48 / ▲ $48 / ✤ $44 / ♂ $42 / ♋ $42 / ♂ $42 / ♋ $42 / ☷ $40 / ♡ $40 / † $40 / 6⊃ $40 / ★ $40 / ⊙ $40

But Love Goes On Forever
#E3115
Issued: 1980 • Open
Retail Price: $16.50 – $40

9

VALUES: † $855 / UM $725

But Love Goes On Forever Retailer's Dome (Dealers' Only, Gift To Centers)
#E7350
Issued: 1984 • Closed: 1984
Retail Price: N/A

General Figurines

	Price Paid	Value
1.		
2.		
3.		
4.		
5.		
6.		
7.		
8.		
9.		
Totals		

KEY: NM *Pre-1981* ▲ 1981 Ⅱ 1982 ◄ 1983 † 1984 ✦ 1985 ♒ 1986 ▲ 1987 ✤ 1988 ♋ 1989 ★ 1990 ● 1991 ♂ 1992 ♋ 1993 ☷ 1994 △ 1995 ♡ 1996 † 1997 6⊃ 1998 ★ 1999 ⊙ 2000 UM *Unmarked*

81

1 VALUES: 6ð $30
★ $30
Ⓞ $30

**Caught Up In Sweet
Thoughts Of You**
#521973
Issued: 1999 • Open
Retail Price: $30

2 VALUES: 6ð $55

Charity Begins In The Heart
Victorian Girls Series
#307009
Issued: 1998 • Retired: 1998
Retail Price: $50

3 VALUES: ▲ $88
$80
Ⴛ $74
$70
$70
$ $67
$65
$65
△ $62
♡ $62

Cheers To The Leader
#104035
Issued: 1987 • Retired: 1997
Retail Price: $22.50 – $32.50

4 VALUES: ⬥ $64
$58
$ $56

Christmas Fireplace
Family Christmas Series
#524883
Issued: 1990 • Susp.: 1992
Retail Price: $37.50

5 VALUES: Ⅱ $90
$84
✝ $77
$73
$71

**Christmas Joy From
Head To Toe**
#E2361
Issued: 1982 • Susp.: 1986
Retail Price: $25 – $27.50

6 VALUES: ◀ $116
$104
$97
$92
▲ $88
⬥ $85
Ⴛ $80
$75

**Christmastime Is
For Sharing**
#E0504
Issued: 1983 • Retired: 1989
Retail Price: $37 – $50

General Figurines

	Price Paid	Value
1.		
2.		
3.		
4.		
5.		
6.		
7.		
8.		
9.		

Totals

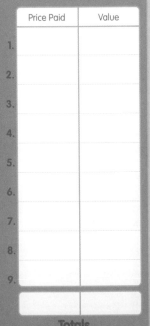

7 VALUES: ⬥ $188
$165
▲ $145
⬥ $140
Ⴛ $140
$140
$128
$ $128
♋ $128
⊟ $114
△ $114
♡ $114

Variation

Crowns

Clown Figurines (set/4)
#12238
Issued: 1985 • Susp.: 1996
Retail Price: $54 – $80
Variation: "Crowns" – $240

8 VALUES: ⬥ $40
$35
▲ $35
⬥ $35
Ⴛ $33
$33
$30
$ $30
♋ $30
⊟ $30
△ $30
♡ $30

**Clown Figurines –
Mini Boy Clown**
#12238A
Issued: 1985 • Susp.: 1996
Retail Price: $13.50 – $20

9 VALUES: ⬥ $42
$38
▲ $35
⬥ $35
Ⴛ $35
$33
$32
$ $32
♋ $30
⊟ $30
△ $30
♡ $30

**Clown Figurines –
Mini Boy Clown**
#12238C
Issued: 1985 • Susp.: 1996
Retail Price: $13.50 – $20

Value Guide — PRECIOUS MOMENTS®

1

VALUES:
🍃	$42
🦋	$38
♠	$36
✤	$36
➗	$36
✚	$34
↓	$34
§	$33
℗	$33
▱	$33
△	$33
♡	$33

**Clown Figurines –
Mini Girl Clown**
#12238B
Issued: 1985 • Susp.: 1996
Retail Price: $13.50 – $20

2

VALUES:
🍃	$43
🦋	$39
♠	$37
✤	$35
➗	$35
✚	$35
↓	$33
§	$33
℗	$33
▱	$32
△	$32
♡	$32

**Clown Figurines –
Mini Girl Clown**
#12238D
Issued: 1985 • Susp.: 1996
Retail Price: $13.50 – $20

3
New!

VALUES:
★	$25
⏱	$25

**Collection of Precious
Moments (LE-2000)**
#745510
Issued: 2000 • To Be Closed: 2000
Retail Price: $25

4

VALUES:
𝕀	$118
✚	$62
✝	$57
🍃	$54
🦋	$52
♠	$47

Collection Plaque
#E6901
Issued: 1982 • Susp.: 1986
Retail Price: $19 – $20

5

VALUES:
♡	$77
✝	$70
6↓	$55

**Color Your World
With Thanksgiving**
#183857
Issued: 1996 • Retired: 1998
Retail Price: $50

6

VALUES: NM $320

Come Let Us Adore Him
#E2011
Issued: 1979 • Retired: 1981
Retail Price: $10 – $14

7

VALUES:
6↓	$30
★	$30
⏱	$30

Confirmed In The Lord
#488178
Issued: 1999 • Open
Retail Price: $30

8
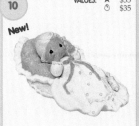
VALUES:
🦋	$65
♠	$45
✤	$42
➗	$40
✚	$38
↓	$38
§	$37
℗	$37
▱	$37
△	$35
♡	$35
✝	$35
6↓	$35
★	$35
⏱	$35

**Congratulations,
Princess**
#106208
Issued: 1987 • Open
Retail Price: $20 – $35

General Figurines

	Price Paid	Value
1.		
2.		
3.		
4.		
5.		
6.		
7.		
8.		
9.		
10.		

Totals

9

VALUES:
♠	$85
✤	$57
➗	$47
✚	$44
↓	$40
§	$40
℗	$37
▱	$37
△	$35
♡	$35
✝	$35
6↓	$35
★	$35
⏱	$35

December
Calendar Girl Series
#110116
Issued: 1988 • Open
Retail Price: $27.50 – $35

10
New!
VALUES:
★	$35
⏱	$35

Dedicated To God
#488232
Issued: 2000 • Open
Retail Price: $35

KEY: NM *Pre-1981* ▲ 1981 𝕀 1982 ◄1983 ✝ 1984 🍃 1985 🦋 1986 ♠ 1987 ✤ 1988 ➗ 1989 ★ 1990
§ 1991 § 1992 ℗ 1993 ◄ 1994 △ 1995 ♡ 1996 ✝ 1997 6↓ 1998 ★ 1999 ⏱ 2000 UM *Unmarked*

General Figurines

1

VALUES:
- ⊅ $110
- ⭐ $102
- 🌢 $95
- 🐚 $92
- ✿ $86

**Don't Let The Holidays
Get You Down**
#522112
Issued: 1989 • Retired: 1993
Retail Price: $42.50 – $45

2

VALUES:
- 🍥 $50
- △ $43
- ♡ $40
- † $40
- 6∂ $40
- ★ $40
- 🕐 $40

Dreams Really Do Come True
#128309
Issued: 1995 • Open
Retail Price: $37.50 – $40

3

VALUES:
- Ⅱ $89
- 🐚 $83
- † $79

Dropping In For Christmas
#E2350
Issued: 1982 • Susp.: 1984
Retail Price: $18

4

VALUES:
- 🍥 $53
- △ $48
- ♡ $48
- † $48
- 6∂ $48

**Dropping In For
The Holidays**
#531952
Issued: 1994 • Retired: 1998
Retail Price: $40 – $45

5

VALUES:
- Ⅱ $130
- 🍥 $105
- † $98
- 🐚 $93
- ℐ $90
- ♣ $90
- ⬧ $85
- ⊅ $81
- ⭐ $76
- 🌢 $76

**Dropping Over For
Christmas**
#E2375
Issued: 1982 • Retired: 1991
Retail Price: $30 – $45

6

VALUES:
- △ $82
- ♡ $74
- † $70
- 6∂ $70
- ★ $70
- 🕐 $70

**Each Hour Is Precious
With You**
#163791
Issued: 1996 • Open
Retail Price: $70

7

VALUES:
- ⊅ $84
- ⭐ $75
- 🌢 $72
- 🐚 $70
- 9∂ $68
- 🍥 $68
- △ $68
- ♡ $65
- † $65
- 6∂ $65
- ★ $65

Easter's On Its Way
#521892
Issued: 1990 • Retired: 1999
Retail Price: $60 – $65

8

VALUES:
- NM $135
- ▲ $115
- Ⅱ $100
- 🍥 $92

Eggs Over Easy
#E3118
Issued: 1980 • Retired: 1983
Retail Price: $12 – $15

9

VALUES:
- ⬧ $75
- ⊅ $70
- ⭐ $63
- 🌢 $58
- 🐚 $56
- 9∂ $54
- 🍥 $52
- △ $52
- † $50
- 6∂ $50
- ★ $50

Eggspecially For You
#520667
Issued: 1989 • Retired: 1999
Retail Price: $45 – $50

10

VALUES:
- Ⅱ $90
- 🐚 $79
- † $74
- 🍃 $68
- UM $140

The End Is In Sight
#E9253
Issued: 1983 • Susp.: 1985
Retail Price: $25

General Figurines

	Price Paid	Value
1.		
2.		
3.		
4.		
5.		
6.		
7.		
8.		
9.		
10.		
Totals		

KEY: NM *Pre-1981* ▲ 1981 Ⅱ 1982 ◀1983 † 1984 🍃 1985 ℐ 1986 ♣ 1987 ⬧ 1988 ⊅ 1989 ⭐ 1990 🌢 1991 🐚 1992 9∂ 1993 🍥 1994 △ 1995 ♡ 1996 † 1997 6∂ 1998 ★ 1999 🕐 2000 UM *Unmarked*

Value Guide — PRECIOUS MOMENTS®

1

VALUES: ⚜ $42
♡ $37
✝ $35
6∂ $35
★ $35
⏱ $35

Enter His Court With Thanksgiving
#521221
Issued: 1996 • Open
Retail Price: $35

2

VALUES: ✦ $44
✝ $40
✤ $40
♫ $36
♠ $34
⬥ $32
♂ $32
♀ $32
UM $52

Especially For Ewe
#E9282C
Issued: 1983 • Susp.: 1990
Retail Price: $8 – $13.50

3

VALUES: 6∂ $140

Even The Heavens Shall Praise Him (LE-15,000)
Century Circle Figurine
#150312
Issued: 1998 • Closed: 1998
Retail Price: $125

4

VALUES: ♪ $67
♀ $48

An Event For All Seasons (LE-1993)
Special Event Figurine
#530158
Issued: 1993 • Closed: 1993
Retail Price: $30

5

VALUES: ♠ $68
♪ $60

An Event Worth Wading For (LE-1992)
Special Event Figurine
#527319
Issued: 1992 • Closed: 1992
Retail Price: $32.50

6

VALUES: ♂ $176
★ $155
♠ $145
♪ $125
♀ $120

Faith Is A Victory
#521396
Issued: 1990 • Retired: 1993
Retail Price: $25 – $27.50

7

Variation

VALUES: ♠ $62
♂ $50
✤ $44
★ $42
♠ $40
♪ $40
♀ $38
⬫ $37
⚜ $37
♡ $37
✝ $37
6∂ $37

Faith Takes The Plunge
#111155
Issued: 1988 • Susp.: 1998
Retail Price: $27.50 – $35
Variation: Girl with smile – $60

8

VALUES: ♠ $60
✤ $49
♂ $45
★ $42
♠ $42
♪ $42
♀ $40
⬫ $40
⚜ $37.50
♡ $37.50
✝ $37.50
6∂ $37.50
★ $37.50
⏱ $37.50

February
Calendar Girl Series
#109991
Issued: 1988 • Open
Retail Price: $27.50 – $37.50

9

VALUES: ✝ $70

A Festival Of Precious Moments (LE-1997)
Regional Conference Figurine
#270741
Issued: 1997 • Closed: 1997
Retail Price: $30

General Figurines

	Price Paid	Value
1.		
2.		
3.		
4.		
5.		
6.		
7.		
8.		
9.		
Totals		

KEY: NM *Pre*-1981 ▲ 1981 ✇ 1982 ◀ 1983 ✝ 1984 ♡ 1985 ♫ 1986 ♠ 1987 ✤ 1988 ♂ 1989 ★ 1990
♪ 1991 ♪ 1992 ♀ 1993 ⬫ 1994 ⬥ 1995 ♡ 1996 ✝ 1997 6∂ 1998 ★ 1999 ⏱ 2000 UM *Unmarked*

1

VALUES: ⚜ $170
       💮 $138

**Fifteen Happy Years Together,
What A Tweet (LE-1993)**
*15th Anniversary
Commemorative Figurine*
#530786
Issued: 1993 • Closed: 1993
Retail Price: $100

2

VALUES: 👓 $80

Flight Into Egypt (LE-1998)
#455970
Issued: 1998 • Closed: 1998
Retail Price: $75

3

VALUES: ⚜ $37
       🌾 $32
       ▲ $30
       ⬥ $25
       ⬥ $25
       ☀ $22
       ♦ $22
       ⚜ $20
       💮 $20
       🛶 $18.50
       △ $18.50
       ♡ $18.50
       † $18.50
       👓 $18.50
       ★ $18.50
       🕐 $18.50

Flower Girl
Bridal Party Series
#E2835
Issued: 1985 • Open
Retail Price: $11 – $18.50

4

VALUES: 🛶 $58
       △ $48

Follow Your Heart (LE-1995)
Special Event Figurine
#528080
Issued: 1995 • Closed: 1995
Retail Price: $30

5

VALUES: † $34
       👓 $34
       ★ $34
       🕐 $32.50

**For The Sweetest
Tu-Lips In Town**
#306959
Issued: 1998 • Open
Retail Price: $30 – $32.50

6

VALUES: 🐟 $96
       † $88
       ⚜ $86
       🌾 $84
       ▲ $79
       ⬥ $74
       ⊕ $70

Forgiving Is Forgetting
#E9252
Issued: 1983 • Susp.: 1989
Retail Price: $37.50 – $47.50

General Figurines

	Price Paid	Value
1.		
2.		
3.		
4.		
5.		
6.		
7.		
8.		
9.		
Totals		

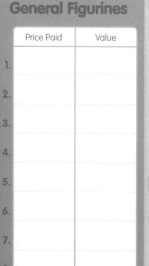

7

VALUES: ⬥ $95
       ⊕ $80
       ☀ $75
       ♦ $70
       ⚜ $68
       💮 $65
       🛶 $65
       △ $65

**A Friend Is Someone
Who Cares**
#520632
Issued: 1989 • Retired: 1995
Retail Price: $30 – $35

8

VALUES: 👓 $60
       ★ $60
       🕐 $60

**Friends Are Forever,
Sew Bee It**
#455903
Issued: 1998 • Open
Retail Price: $60

9

VALUES: ♡ $56
       † $55
       👓 $55
       ★ $55
       🕐 $55

**Friends From The
Very Beginning**
#261068
Issued: 1997 • Open
Retail Price: $50 – $55

KEY: NM *Pre-1981* ▲ 1981 ▆ 1982 ◀ 1983 ☀ 1984 ⚜ 1985 🌾 1986 ▲ 1987 ⬥ 1988 ⊕ 1989 ★ 1990 ♦ 1991 ⚜ 1992 💮 1993 🛶 1994 △ 1995 ♡ 1996 † 1997 👓 1998 ★ 1999 🕐 2000 UM *Unmarked*

Value Guide — PRECIOUS MOMENTS®

1

VALUES:
- 🦋 $92
- 🌲 $75
- ♠ $73
- ⚓ $70
- ☩ $65
- 🕯 $65
- 🌿 $65
- ♪ $65
- 🐚 $65
- ♡ $65
- † $65
- 👓 $65
- ★ $65
- ◯ $65

**Friends Never
Drift Apart**
#100250
Issued: 1986 • Open
Retail Price: $35 – $65

2

VALUES:
- ♥ $76
- 🐚 $72
- △ $70
- ♡ $66

Friends To The Very End
#526150
Issued: 1994 • Retired: 1997
Retail Price: $40 – $45

3

VALUES:
- 💧 $120
- ♪ $95
- ♥ $86
- 🐚 $82

**Friendship Grows When
You Plant A Seed**
#524271
Issued: 1992 • Retired: 1994
Retail Price: $40

4
Variation   *Variation*

PHOTO UNAVAILABLE

VALUES:
- ⚓ $95
- ♠ $83
- ♣ $80
- ♪ $77
- ♪ $77
- ♥ $74
- 🐚 $72
- △ $70
- ♡ $70
- † $70
- 👓 $70
- ★ $70
- ◯ $70

Friendship Hits The Spot
#520748
Issued: 1989 • Open
Retail Price: $55 – $70
Variations: "Freindship Hits The Spot" – $85, Missing Table – $280

5
New!

VALUES:
- ★ $35
- ◯ $35

Friendship's A Slice Of Life
#634964
Issued: 2000 • Open
Retail Price: $35

6

VALUES:
- 🐚 $40
- 🐚 $35
- △ $33
- ♡ $33
- † $32.50
- 👓 $32.50
- ★ $32.50

**The Fruit Of The Spirit
Is Love**
#521213
Issued: 1993 • Retired: 1999
Retail Price: $30 – $32.50

7

VALUES:
- † $56
- ♪ $44
- ♪ $42

**Get Into The Habit
Of Prayer**
#12203
Issued: 1985 • Susp.: 1986
Retail Price: $19

8

VALUES: ♪ $78

**God Bless America
(LE-1986)**
#102938
Issued: 1986 • Closed: 1986
Retail Price: $30

9

VALUES:
- ♠ $68
- ⚓ $63
- ♣ $60
- ♪ $57
- 🕯 $57
- ♪ $55
- ♥ $53
- 🐚 $52
- △ $50
- ♡ $50
- † $50
- 👓 $50
- ★ $50

God Bless Our Family
#100498
Issued: 1987 • Retired: 1999
Retail Price: $35 – $50

General Figurines

	Price Paid	Value
1.		
2.		
3.		
4.		
5.		
6.		
7.		
8.		
9.		

Totals

KEY: NM *Pre-1981* ▲1981 Ⅱ1982 ◀1983 †1984 🍃1985 ♪1986 ♠1987 ⚓1988 ♥1989 ★1990 🕯1991 ♪1992 ♥1993 🐚1994 △1995 ♡1996 †1997 👓1998 ★1999 ◯2000 UM *Unmarked*

87

VALUES:
- ▲ $68
- ✤ $63
- ⊕ $60
- ⚓ $58
- ✦ $58
- 𝄢 $56
- ♔ $54
- ♔ $54
- △ $52
- † $50
- ♡ $50
- ★ $50

God Bless Our Family
#100501
Issued: 1987 • Retired: 1999
Retail Price: $35 – $50

VALUES:
- 🍃 $87
- ✒ $81
- ▲ $77
- ✦ $77
- ⊕ $74
- ⚓ $72
- 𝄢 $72
- ♔ $69
- ♔ $69
- △ $66
- † $66
- 👓 $66

God Bless Our Home
#12319
Issued: 1985 • Retired: 1998
Retail Price: $40 – $65

VALUES:
- † $65
- ✒ $62
- ✦ $60
- ▲ $60
- ✦ $58
- ⊕ $57
- ⚓ $57
- ✦ $55
- 𝄢 $55
- 👓 $52
- ♔ $52
- △ $50
- ♡ $50
- † $50
- 👓 $50
- ★ $50
- ◔ $50

God Bless The Bride
#E2832
Issued: 1984 • Open
Retail Price: $35 – $50

VALUES:
- ✒ $126
- ▲ $120
- ✦ $115
- ⊕ $110
- ⚓ $105

God Bless The Day We Found You
#100145
Issued: 1986 • Susp.: 1990
Retail Price: $40 – $55

VALUES:
- 🍃 $70
- ♔ $65
- ♡ $60
- † $60
- 👓 $60
- ★ $60
- ◔ $60

God Bless The Day We Found You
#100145R
Issued: 1995 • Open
Retail Price: $60

VALUES:
- ✒ $120
- ▲ $112
- ✦ $105
- ⊕ $97
- ⚓ $94

God Bless The Day We Found You
#100153
Issued: 1986 • Susp.: 1990
Retail Price: $40 – $55

VALUES:
- 🍃 $67
- △ $62
- ♡ $60
- † $60
- 👓 $60
- ★ $60
- ◔ $60

God Bless The Day We Found You
#100153R
Issued: 1995 • Open
Retail Price: $60

VALUES:
- ⚓ $45
- 𝄢 $40

God Bless The U.S.A.
(LE-1992)
National Day Of Prayer Figurine
#527564
Issued: 1992 • Closed: 1992
Retail Price: $32.50

VALUES:
- ✒ $55
- ▲ $43
- ✦ $40
- ⊕ $40
- ⚓ $40
- ✦ $38
- 𝄢 $38
- ♔ $36
- ♔ $36
- △ $36
- † $36
- 👓 $36
- ★ $36
- ◔ $35

God Bless You Graduate
#106194
Issued: 1987 • Open
Retail Price: $20 – $35

General Figurines

	Price Paid	Value
1.		
2.		
3.		
4.		
5.		
6.		
7.		
8.		
9.		
Totals		

KEY: NM *Pre*-1981 ▲ 1981 ⊠ 1982 ◀ 1983 † 1984 🍃 1985 ✒ 1986 ▲ 1987 ✤ 1988 ⊕ 1989 ⚓ 1990 ✦ 1991 𝄢 1992 👓 1993 🍃 1994 △ 1995 ♡ 1996 † 1997 👓 1998 ★ 1999 ◔ 2000 ⅁M *Unmarked*

Value Guide — PRECIOUS MOMENTS®

1

Variation

VALUES:
✝ $69
🕊 $60
✣ $60
▲ $57
⚓ $57
🖂 $55
✦ $54
🔔 $54
🐚 $52
🌺 $52
🍤 $50
△ $50
♡ $50
† $50
🕶 $50
★ $50
🕐 $50

God Blessed Our Year Together With
So Much Love And Happiness
#E2854
Issued: 1984 • Open
Retail Price: $35 – $50
Variation: "God Blessed Our Years Together . . . " – $77

2

VALUES:
✝ $70
🕊 $63
✣ $62
▲ $62
⚓ $58
🖂 $56
✦ $54
🔔 $54
🐚 $52
🌺 $50
🍤 $50
△ $50
♡ $50
† $50
🕶 $50
★ $50
🕐 $50

God Blessed Our
Years Together With
So Much Love And
Happiness
#E2853
Issued: 1984 • Open
Retail Price: $35 – $50

3

VALUES: ✝ $76
🕊 $71
✣ $68
▲ $68
⚓ $68
🖂 $68
✦ $65
🔔 $65
🐚 $65
🌺 $65
🍤 $63
△ $63
♡ $63

God Blessed Our
Years Together With
So Much Love And
Happiness
#E2855
Issued: 1984 • Susp.: 1996
Retail Price: $35 – $50

4

VALUES: ✝ $78
🕊 $75
✣ $73
▲ $73
⚓ $73
🖂 $70
✦ $70
🔔 $68
🐚 $68
🌺 $66
🍤 $66
△ $66

God Blessed Our
Years Together With
So Much Love And
Happiness
#E2856
Issued: 1984 • Susp.: 1996
Retail Price: $35 – $50

5

VALUES: ✝ $67
🕊 $62
✣ $59
▲ $59
⚓ $56
🖂 $54
✦ $54
🔔 $52
🐚 $52
🌺 $50
🍤 $50
△ $50
♡ $50
† $50
★ $50
🕐 $50

God Blessed Our
Years Together With
So Much Love And
Happiness
#E2857
Issued: 1984 • Open
Retail Price: $35 – $50

6

VALUES: ✝ $80
🕊 $75
✣ $72
▲ $72
⚓ $72
🖂 $72
✦ $70
🔔 $70
🐚 $70
🌺 $68
🍤 $68
△ $68
♡ $68

God Blessed Our
Years Together With
So Much Love And
Happiness
#E2859
Issued: 1984 • Susp.: 1996
Retail Price: $35 – $50

7

VALUES: ✝ $80
🕊 $75
✣ $72
▲ $72
⚓ $72
🖂 $72
✦ $70
🔔 $70
🐚 $70
🌺 $68
🍤 $65
△ $60
† $55
🕶 $55
★ $50
🕐 $50

God Blessed Our
Years Together With
So Much Love And
Happiness
#E2860
Issued: 1984 • Open
Retail Price: $35 – $50

8

VALUES: 🍤 $90
△ $78
♡ $75

God Cared Enough To
Send His Best
#524476
Issued: 1994 • Retired: 1996
Retail Price: $50 – $55

9

VALUES: 🕊 $54
✣ $50
▲ $46
⚓ $42
🖂 $40
✦ $40
🔔 $36
🐚 $33

God Gave His Best
Family Christmas Series
#15806
Issued: 1985 • Susp.: 1992
Retail Price: $13 – $19

General Figurines

Price Paid	Value
1.	
2.	
3.	
4.	
5.	
6.	
7.	
8.	
9.	

Totals

KEY: NM *Pre-1981* ▲ 1981 ✣ 1982 🕊 1983 ✝ 1984 🕊 1985 ✣ 1986 ▲ 1987 ⚓ 1988 🖂 1989 ★ 1990
🔔 1991 🐚 1992 🌺 1993 🍤 1994 △ 1995 ♡ 1996 † 1997 🕶 1998 ★ 1999 🕐 2000 UM *Unmarked*

General Figurines (side tab)

1

VALUES: NM $130
▲ $94
✠ $85
✦ $80
✝ $72
✍ $70
⚓ $68
⚓ $65
⚓ $65
ⴲ $65

God Is Love
#E5213
Issued: 1981 • Susp.: 1989
Retail Price: $17 – $30

2

VALUES: ★ N/E

God Is Love
Special Event Figurine
#E5213R
Issued: 1999 • Closed: 1999
Retail Price: $17

3

VALUES: ▲ $60
✠ $45
✦ $40
✝ $35
✍ $35
✍ $32

God Is Love, Dear Valentine
#E7153
Issued: 1982 • Susp.: 1986
Retail Price: $16 – $17

4

VALUES: ▲ $60
✠ $50
✦ $40
✝ $40
✍ $35
✍ $35

God Is Love, Dear Valentine
#E7154
Issued: 1982 • Susp.: 1986
Retail Price: $16 – $17

5

VALUES: ⴲ $44
✚ $38
⚘ $37
⚘ $37
⚘ $34
⊟ $32
△ $30
♡ $30
✝ $30
ᏮᎧ $30
★ $30

God Is Love, Dear Valentine
#523518
Issued: 1990 • Retired: 1999
Retail Price: $27.50 – $30

6

VALUES: ✠ $115
✦ $104
✝ $93

God Is Watching Over You
#E7163
Issued: 1982 • Susp.: 1984
Retail Price: $27.50 – $30

General Figurines

	Price Paid	Value
1.		
2.		
3.		
4.		
5.		
6.		
7.		
8.		
9.		
10.		
Totals		

7

New!

VALUES: ★ $30
◔ $30

**God Knows Our Ups
And Downs**
#490318
Issued: 2000 • Open
Retail Price: $30

8

New!

VALUES: ★ $37.50
◔ $37.50

God Loves A Happy Camper
#587893
Issued: 2000 • Open
Retail Price: $37.50

9

VALUES: NM $1000

**God Loveth
A Cheerful Giver**
#E1378
Issued: 1979 • Retired: 1981
Retail Price: $9.50 – $15

10

VALUES: ᏮᎧ N/E

**God Loveth A
Cheerful Giver (LE-20)**
#456225
Issued: 1998 • Closed: 1998
Retail Price: N/A

KEY: NM Pre-1981 ▲ 1981 ✠ 1982 ✦ 1983 ✝ 1984 ✍ 1985 ✍ 1986 ⚓ 1987 ✦ 1988 ⴲ 1989 ★ 1990
✚ 1991 ⚘ 1992 ⚘ 1993 ⊟ 1994 △ 1995 ♡ 1996 ✝ 1997 ᏮᎧ 1998 ★ 1999 ◔ 2000 UM Unmarked

Value Guide — PRECIOUS MOMENTS®

1

VALUES: 🐟 $89
✝ $73
🌙 $67
🎋 $64
🔥 $62

God Sends The Gift Of His Love
#E6613
Issued: 1984 • Susp.: 1987
Retail Price: $22.50 – $25

2

VALUES: 🐟 $105
✝ $96
🌙 $92
🎋 $88
🔥 $80

God Sent His Son
#E0507
Issued: 1983 • Susp.: 1987
Retail Price: $32.50 – $37

3

VALUES: NM $148
▲ $112
Ⅰ $107
🐟 $97
✝ $94

God Understands
#E1379B
Issued: 1979 • Susp.: 1984
Retail Price: $8 – $19

4

VALUES: ♡ $240

God's Love Is Reflected In You (LE-15,000)
Century Circle Figurine
#175277
Issued: 1996 • Closed: 1996
Retail Price: $150

5

VALUES: Ⅰ $97
✝ $87
🎋 $80
🐟 $73
🌙 $71
🔥 $68

God's Promises Are Sure
#E9260
Issued: 1983 • Susp.: 1987
Retail Price: $30 – $33.50

6

VALUES: NM $125
▲ $97
Ⅰ $84
🐟 $68

God's Speed
#E3112
Issued: 1980 • Retired: 1983
Retail Price: $14 – $18

7

VALUES: 🔔 $77
🕊 $69
👒 $67
🍺 $64
△ $62
♡ $60
✝ $60
👓 $60
★ $60
🕐 $60

Going Home
#525979
Issued: 1992 • Open
Retail Price: $60

8
New!

VALUES: ★ $30
🕐 $30

Good Advice Has No Price
#679828
Issued: 2000 • Open
Retail Price: $30

General Figurines

	Price Paid	Value
1.		
2.		
3.		
4.		
5.		
6.		
7.		
8.		
9.		
Totals		

9
VALUES: 🔔 $45
🕊 $38
👒 $37
🍺 $35
△ $35
♡ $35
✝ $35
👓 $35
★ $35

Good Friends Are For Always
#524123
Issued: 1991 • Retired: 1999
Retail Price: $27.50 – $35

KEY: NM *Pre-1981* ▲ 1981 Ⅰ 1982 🐟 1983 ✝ 1984 🍀 1985 🌙 1986 ♣ 1987 🌸 1988 🕊 1989 ★ 1990 🔔 1991 🕊 1992 👒 1993 🍺 1994 △ 1995 ♡ 1996 ✝ 1997 👓 1998 ★ 1999 🕐 2000 UM *Unmarked*

91

1

VALUES: 1989 $74 · 1990 $65 · 1991 $62 · 1992 $60 · 1993 $57 · 1994 $57 · 1995 $55 · 1996 $55 · 1997 $55 · 1998 $55 · 1999 $55 · 2000 $55

Good Friends Are Forever
#521817
Issued: 1990 • Open
Retail Price: $50 – $55

2

VALUES: $760

Good Friends Are Forever
Special Event Figurine
#525049
Issued: 1990 • Closed: 1990
Retail Price: N/A

3

VALUES: 1989 $43 · 1990 $38 · 1991 $35 · 1992 $34 · 1993 $32 · 1994 $32 · 1995 $30 · 1996 $30 · 1997 $30 · 1998 $30 · 1999 $30 · 2000 $30

The Good Lord Always Delivers
#523453
Issued: 1990 • Open
Retail Price: $27.50 – $30

4

VALUES: 1987 $250 · 1988 $230

The Good Lord Has Blessed Us Tenfold (LE-1988)
10th Anniversary Commemorative Figurine
#114022
Issued: 1988 • Closed: 1988
Retail Price: $90

5

VALUES: 1997 $50 · 1998 $50 · 1999 $50 · 2000 $50

The Good Lord Will Always Uphold Us
#325325
Issued: 1998 • Open
Retail Price: $50

6

VALUES: 1991 $82 · 1992 $76 · 1993 $74 · 1994 $72 · 1995 $70 · 1996 $70 · 1997 $70 · 1998 $70 · 1999 $70

Good News Is So Uplifting
#523615
Issued: 1991 • Retired: 1999
Retail Price: $60 – $70

7

VALUES: 1987 $63 · 1988 $50 · 1989 $50 · 1990 $46 · 1991 $44 · 1992 $42 · 1993 $42 · 1994 $40 · 1995 $40 · 1996 $40 · 1997 $40 · 1998 $40 · 1999 $40

The Greatest Gift Is A Friend
#109231
Issued: 1987 • Retired: 1999
Retail Price: $30 – $40

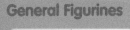

8

VALUES: 1989 $60 · 1990 $54 · 1991 $50

The Greatest Of These Is Love
#521868
Issued: 1989 • Susp.: 1991
Retail Price: $27.50 – $30

9

VALUES: 1986 $42 · 1987 $37 · 1988 $32 · 1989 $32 · 1990 $28 · 1991 $28 · 1992 $28 · 1993 $27.50 · 1994 $27.50 · 1995 $27.50 · 1996 $27.50 · 1997 $27.50 · 1998 $27.50 · 1999 $27.50 · 2000 $27.50

Groom
Bridal Party Series
#E2837
Issued: 1986 • Open
Retail Price: $15 – $27.50
Variation: Boy with no hands – $46

General Figurines

	Price Paid	Value
1.		
2.		
3.		
4.		
5.		
6.		
7.		
8.		
9.		
Totals		

KEY: NM *Pre*-1981 · 1981 · 1982 · 1983 · 1984 · 1985 · 1986 · 1987 · 1988 · 1989 · 1990 · 1991 · 1992 · 1993 · 1994 · 1995 · 1996 · 1997 · 1998 · 1999 · 2000 · UM *Unmarked*

Value Guide — PRECIOUS MOMENTS®

1

VALUES: 6ə $22.50
★ $22.50
🕐 $22.50

Growing In Wisdom
Exclusive To Japan
#481645
Issued: 1999 • Open
Retail Price: $22.50

2

VALUES: 6ə $22.50
★ $22.50
🕐 $22.50

Growing In Wisdom
Exclusive To Japan
#481653
Issued: 1999 • Open
Retail Price: $22.50

3

VALUES: ✥ $72
🕂 $65
$58
$55
$52
$50
$47
$45
♡ $45
† $45
6ə $45
★ $45
🕐 $45

Hallelujah Country
#105821
Issued: 1988 • Open
Retail Price: $35 – $45

4

VALUES: $39
△ $37
♡ $35
† $35
$35
6ə $35
★ $35

Hallelujah For The Cross
#532002
Issued: 1995 • Retired: 1999
Retail Price: $35

5

VALUES: △ $95
♡ $62

Hallelujah Hoedown
(LE-1996)
Special Event Figurine
#163864
Issued: 1996 • Closed: 1996
Retail Price: $32.50

6

VALUES: ✔ $225
🗲 $200
▲ $192
✥ $185

Halo, And Merry Christmas
#12351
Issued: 1985 • Susp.: 1988
Retail Price: $40 – $47.50

7

VALUES: NM $108
▲ $92
✗ $85
◄ $78
† $75

The Hand That Rocks
The Future
#E3108
Issued: 1980 • Susp.: 1984
Retail Price: $13 – $19

8

VALUES: ✥ $88
🕂 $80
★ $73
$67
🗲 $65

Happiness Divine
#109584
Issued: 1988 • Retired: 1992
Retail Price: $25 – $30

9

VALUES: 🗲 $97
🙢 $72

Happiness Is At Our
Fingertips (LE-1993)
Catalog Figurine
#529931
Issued: 1993 • Closed: 1993
Retail Price: $35

10

VALUES: ✔ $52
🗲 $50
▲ $45
✥ $45
🕂 $44
★ $42

Happiness Is The Lord
Rejoice In The Lord Band Series
#12378
Issued: 1985 • Susp.: 1990
Retail Price: $15 – $22.50

General Figurines

	Price Paid	Value
1.		
2.		
3.		
4.		
5.		
6.		
7.		
8.		
9.		
10.		
Totals		

KEY: NM *Pre-1981* ▲ 1981 ✗ 1982 ◄ 1983 † 1984 ✔ 1985 🗲 1986 ▲ 1987 ✥ 1988 🕂 1989 ★ 1990 ★ 1991 🗲 1992 🙢 1993 ◄ 1994 △ 1995 ♡ 1996 † 1997 6ə 1998 ★ 1999 🕐 2000 UM *Unmarked*

93

General Figurines

1 VALUES: ♡ $55

Happiness To The Core
(LE-1997)
Catalog Figurine
#261378
Issued: 1997 • Closed: 1997
Retail Price: $37.50

2 VALUES: † $37 / 6∂ $37 / ★ $37 / ◐ $35

Happy Birthday Jesus
#272523
Issued: 1997 • Open
Retail Price: $35

3 VALUES: ♣ $72 / ✿ $67 / ∂ $66 / ♨ $65 / ♨ $65 / ♒ $59 / ♒ $57

Happy Birthday Poppy
#106836
Issued: 1988 • Susp.: 1993
Retail Price: $27.50 – $35

4 VALUES: ★ $35 / ◐ $35

New!

Happy Birthday To Ewe
#531561
Issued: 2000 • Open
Retail Price: $35

5 VALUES: ♣ $85 / ✿ $78 / ∂ $75 / ♨ $70

Happy Days Are Here Again
#104396
Issued: 1987 • Susp.: 1990
Retail Price: $25 – $32.50

6 VALUES: △ $40 / ♡ $36 / † $34 / 6∂ $32.50 / ★ $32.50 / ◐ $32.50

Happy Hula Days
#128694
Issued: 1995 • Open
Retail Price: $30 – $32.50

General Figurines

	Price Paid	Value
1.		
2.		
3.		
4.		
5.		
6.		
7.		
8.		
9.		
10.		
Totals		

7 VALUES: ∂ $97 / ♨ $63 / ♨ $60 / ♒ $57 / ♒ $53 / ♒ $50

Happy Trip
#521280
Issued: 1990 • Susp.: 1994
Retail Price: $35

8 VALUES: ∂ $46 / ♨ $42 / ♨ $39 / ♒ $35

Have A Beary
Merry Christmas
Family Christmas Series
#522856
Issued: 1989 • Susp.: 1992
Retail Price: $15 – $16.50

9 VALUES: 6∂ $50 / ★ $50 / ◐ $50

Have A Cozy
Country Christmas
#455873
Issued: 1998 • Open
Retail Price: $50

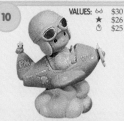

10 VALUES: 6∂ $30 / ★ $26 / ◐ $25

Have A Heavenly Journey
Care-A-Van Exclusive
#12416R
Issued: 1998 • Open
Retail Price: $25

KEY: NM *Pre-*1981 ▲1981 ∎1982 ◀1983 †1984 ✦1985 ♪1986 ♣1987 ✿1988 ∂1989 ★1990 ♨1991 ♒1992 ♘1993 ⊟1994 △1995 ♡1996 †1997 6∂1998 ★1999 ◐2000 UM *Unmarked*

Value Guide — PRECIOUS MOMENTS®

1
VALUES: ♡ $45

Have I Toad You Lately That I Love You? (LE-1996)
Catalog Figurine
#521329
Issued: 1996 • Closed: 1996
Retail Price: $30

2
VALUES: ♡ $42
        ☌ $35
        ★ $35
        ⏱ $35

Have You Any Room For Jesus
#261130
Issued: 1997 • Open
Retail Price: $35

3
VALUES: ★ $30
        ⏱ $30

He Came As The Gift Of God's Love (set/4)
Mini-Mini Nativity
#528128
Issued: 1999 • Open
Retail Price: $30

4
VALUES: 🍀 $66
   ⅋ $52
   ♠ $49
   ⚓ $47
   ⚓ $45
   ★ $45
   ♦ $42
   ⚜ $42
   ⊟ $40
   △ $40
   ♡ $40
   † $40
   ☌ $40
   ★ $40
   ⏱ $40

He Cleansed My Soul
#100277
Issued: 1986 • Open
Retail Price: $24 – $40

5
VALUES: ★ $50
        ⏱ $50

He Covers The Earth With His Glory
Four Seasons Series
#129135
Issued: 1999 • Open
Retail Price: $50

6
VALUES: ★ $50
        ⏱ $50

He Graces The Earth With Abundance
Four Seasons Series
#129119
Issued: 1999 • Open
Retail Price: $50

7
VALUES: 🍀 $50
   ⅋ $47
   ♠ $47
   ⚓ $42
   ♦ $42
   ★ $40

He Is My Song (set/2)
Rejoice In The Lord Band Series
#12394
Issued: 1985 • Susp.: 1990
Retail Price: $17.50 – $27.50

8
VALUES: † $80
        ☌ $80

He Is Our Shelter From The Storm
Boys & Girls Clubs Of America Commemorative Figurine
#523550
Issued: 1997 • Closed: 1997
Retail Price: $75

9
VALUES: ♦ $90
   ★ $85
   ♦ $80
   ♦ $80
   ♀ $76

He Is The Star Of Morning
#522252
Issued: 1989 • Susp.: 1993
Retail Price: $55 – $60

10
VALUES: ★ $58
        ♦ $48

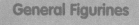

He Loves Me (LE-1991)
#524263
Issued: 1990 • Closed: 1991
Retail Price: $35

General Figurines

	Price Paid	Value
1.		
2.		
3.		
4.		
5.		
6.		
7.		
8.		
9.		
10.		

Totals

General Figurines

1 VALUES: ○ $160

New!

He Shall Lead The Children
Into The 21st Century (set/5)
Special Event Figurine
#127930
Issued: 2000 • Open
Retail Price: $160

2 VALUES: ⌒ $96
✝ $88
♣ $84

He Upholdeth Those
Who Fall
(all pieces inscribed with "He
Upholdeth Those Who Call")
#E0526
Issued: 1983 • Susp.: 1985
Retail Price: $28.50 – $35

3 VALUES: NM $98
♦ $90
Ⅰ $82
⌒ $75
✝ $67

He Watches Over Us All
#E3105
Issued: 1980 • Susp.: 1984
Retail Price: $11 – $17

4 VALUES: ♪ $68
▲ $64
♣ $62
Ð $60
★ $56
● $56
⅋ $52
♑ $52
⊟ $50
♡ $50
✝ $50
ᚼ $50
★ $50

He's The Healer Of
Broken Hearts
#100080
Issued: 1987 • Retired: 1999
Retail Price: $33 – $50

5 VALUES: Ð $126
★ $58
● $50
ℰ $45
⅋ $42
⊟ $37
⊟ $37
♡ $35
✝ $35
★ $35
★ $35

Heaven Bless You
#520934
Issued: 1990 • Open
Retail Price: $35

6 VALUES: ♪ $113
♣ $98
Ð $94
★ $92
● $92
ℰ $90
⊟ $90
♡ $90
✝ $90
ᚼ $90
★ $90

Heaven Bless
Your Togetherness
#106755
Issued: 1988 • Retired: 1999
Retail Price: $65 – $90

General Figurines

	Price Paid	Value
1.		
2.		
3.		
4.		
5.		
6.		
7.		
8.		
9.		
10.		
Totals		

7 VALUES: ✝ $65
ᚼ $65
★ $65
○ $65

Heaven Must Have
Sent You
#521388
Issued: 1998 • Open
Retail Price: $60 – $65

8 VALUES: ♪ $80
▲ $73
♣ $70
Ð $66

Help, Lord I'm In A Spot
#100269
Issued: 1986 • Retired: 1989
Retail Price: $18.50 – $25

9 VALUES: Ð $56
★ $52
● $49
ℰ $47
♑ $40

High Hopes
#521957
Issued: 1990 • Susp.: 1993
Retail Price: $30

10 VALUES: NM $165
▲ $145
Ⅰ $122
⌒ $105
✝ $95

His Burden Is Light
#E1380G
Issued: 1979 • Retired: 1984
Retail Price: $8 – $19

KEY: NM *Pre-1981* ▲1981 Ⅰ1982 ⌒1983 ✝1984 ♣1985 ♪1986 ▲1987 ♣1988 Ð1989 ★1990
● 1991 ℰ1992 ♑1993 ⊟1994 ⊟1995 ♡1996 ✝1997 ᚼ1998 ★1999 ○2000 UM *Unmarked*

1 VALUES: $138 / $124 / $115 / $105 / $97

His Eye Is On The Sparrow
#E0530
Issued: 1983 • Retired: 1987
Retail Price: $28.50 – $32.50

2 VALUES: $150 / $150 / $150

**His Love Will Uphold
The World**
Millennium Figurine
#539309
Issued: 1999 • Open
Retail Price: $150

3 VALUES: $144 / $130 / $123 / $118 / $112 / $107

Holy Smokes
#E2351
Issued: 1982 • Retired: 1987
Retail Price: $27 – $33.50

4 VALUES: $40 / $40

**Home Is Where
The Heart Is**
Catalog Figurine
#325481
Issued: 1998 • Closed: 1998
Retail Price: $37.50

5 VALUES: $77

**Hope Is Revealed Through
God's Word**
Victorian Girls Series
#488259
Issued: 1998 • Retired: 1998
Retail Price: $70

6 VALUES: $68 / $63 / $60 / $55 / $52

**Hope You're Up And On
The Trail Again**
#521205
Issued: 1990 • Susp.: 1993
Retail Price: $35

7 VALUES: $57 / $50 / $48 / $44 / $44 / $42 / $40 / $40 / $40 / $40

Hoppy Easter, Friend
#521906
Issued: 1991 • Retired: 1999
Retail Price: $40

8 VALUES: N/E

**How Can Three Work
Together Except
They Agree (LE-20)**
Care-A-Van Exclusive
N/A
Issued: 1998 • Closed: 1998
Retail Price: N/A

9 VALUES: $190 / $162 / $148 / $140

**How Can Two Walk
Together Except They Agree**
#E9263
Issued: 1983 • Susp.: 1985
Retail Price: $35

10 VALUES: $90 / $82 / $78 / $78 / $75 / $75

Hug One Another
#521299
Issued: 1991 • Retired: 1995
Retail Price: $45 – $50

General Figurines

	Price Paid	Value
1.		
2.		
3.		
4.		
5.		
6.		
7.		
8.		
9.		
10.		

Totals

KEY: NM *Pre-1981* ▲1981 ▮1982 ◄1983 †1984 ✿1985 ⌁1986 ♠1987 ✦1988 ꝺ1989 ★1990 ♦1991 ♗1992 ♒1993 ⊟1994 △1995 ♡1996 †1997 ꝺ1998 ★1999 ◷2000 UM *Unmarked*

97

General Figurines

1

VALUES: ♂ $110
† $100
✝ $92
⚓ $86

I Believe In Miracles
#E7156
Issued: 1982 • Susp.: 1985
Retail Price: $17 – $19

2

Variation

VALUES: ♠ $80
♧ $70
Ð $62
★ $60
♪ $56

I Believe In Miracles
#E7156R
Issued: 1987 • Retired: 1992
Retail Price: $22.50 – $27.50
Variation: Boy with small head/blue bird/no "Sam B." signature – $215

3

VALUES: ✎ $60
⚡ $52
♠ $46
♧ $43
Ð $43
★ $40
♪ $40
⚘ $37
♨ $37
△ $35
♡ $35
† $35
♫ $35
★ $35
♙ $35

I Believe In The Old Rugged Cross
#103632
Issued: 1986 • Open
Retail Price: $25 – $35

4

VALUES: ♧ $53
Ð $42
★ $35
♪ $32

I Belong To The Lord
#520853
Issued: 1989 • Susp.: 1991
Retail Price: $25 – $27.50

5

VALUES: ⬛ $62
△ $54
♡ $52
† $50
♨ $50
★ $50
♙ $50

I Can't Bear To Let You Go
#532037
Issued: 1995 • Retired: 1999
Retail Price: $50

6

VALUES: ★ $125
♧ $85
⚘ $73
♨ $73
★ $70

I Can't Spell Success Without You
#523763
Issued: 1991 • Susp.: 1994
Retail Price: $40 – $45

7

VALUES: ★ $60
♙ $60

I Couldn't Make It Without You
Boys & Girls Clubs Of America Commemorative Figurine
#635030
Issued: 1999 • Open
Retail Price: $60

8

VALUES: ✎ $88
⚡ $82
♠ $75
♧ $75
Ð $70
★ $67
♪ $67
⚘ $64
♨ $64
♫ $62
△ $62
♡ $62

I Get A Bang Out Of You
The Clown Series
#12262
Issued: 1985 • Retired: 1997
Retail Price: $30 – $45

9

VALUES: ⬛ $235
† $215
✎ $200
♫ $195

I Get A Kick Out Of You
#E2827
Issued: 1984 • Susp.: 1986
Retail Price: $50

General Figurines

	Price Paid	Value
1.		
2.		
3.		
4.		
5.		
6.		
7.		
8.		
9.		
Totals		

KEY: NM *Pre-1981* ▲1981 ♂1982 ◄1983 †1984 ✎1985 ♫1986 ♠1987 ♧1988 Ð1989 ★1990 ♪1991 ⚘1992 ♨1993 ⬛1994 △1995 ♡1996 †1997 ♙1998 ★1999 ♙2000 UM *Unmarked*

Value Guide — PRECIOUS MOMENTS®

1 VALUES: 🦢 $86 / △ $76 / ♡ $73 / † $70 / $70 / ★ $70 / ○ $70

I Give You My Love
Forever True
#129100
Issued: 1995 • Open
Retail Price: $70

2 VALUES: 6ð $30 / ★ $30 / ○ $30

I Now Pronounce You
Man And Wife
#455938
Issued: 1998 • Open
Retail Price: $30

3 VALUES: △ $59 / ♡ $55 / $55 / 6ð $55 / ★ $55

I Only Have Ice For You
#530956
Issued: 1995 • Retired: 1999
Retail Price: $55

4 VALUES: ⚘ $90 / ▲ $82

I Picked A Very Special
Mom (LE-1987)
#100536
Issued: 1987 • Closed: 1987
Retail Price: $40

5 VALUES: 6ð $65 / ★ $65 / ○ $65

I Saw Mommy Kissing
Santa Claus
#455822
Issued: 1998 • Open
Retail Price: $65

6 VALUES: ⚘ $50 / ⛢ $35 / △ $32 / ♡ $32 / † $30 / 6ð $30 / ★ $30 / ○ $30

I Still Do
#530999
Issued: 1994 • Open
Retail Price: $30

7 VALUES: ⚘ $50 / ⛢ $35 / △ $32 / ♡ $32 / † $30 / 6ð $30 / ★ $30 / ○ $30

I Still Do
#531006
Issued: 1994 • Open
Retail Price: $30

8 VALUES: † $42 / $40 / ★ $40 / ○ $40

I Think You're Just Divine
#272558
Issued: 1997 • Open
Retail Price: $40

9 VALUES: ⚘ $82 / ⛢ $75 / △ $68 / ♡ $63

I Will Always Be
Thinking Of You
#523631
Issued: 1994 • Retired: 1996
Retail Price: $45

10 VALUES: ♦ $42 / ⚶ $37 / ⚘ $33 / △ $32 / △ $30 / ♡ $30 / † $30 / 6ð $30 / ★ $30

I Would Be Lost
Without You
#526142
Issued: 1992 • Retired: 1999
Retail Price: $27.50 – $30

General Figurines

	Price Paid	Value
1.		
2.		
3.		
4.		
5.		
6.		
7.		
8.		
9.		
10.		

Totals

KEY: NM *Pre-1981* ▲ 1981 ⅠⅠ 1982 ◄1983 ✝ 1984 ✦ 1985 ✿ 1986 ▲ 1987 ✤ 1988 ⊕ 1989 ✦ 1990 ♦ 1991 ⚶ 1992 ⚘ 1993 ⛢ 1994 △ 1995 ♡ 1996 † 1997 6ð 1998 ★ 1999 ○ 2000 UM *Unmarked*

1 VALUES:
▲	$30
✣	$27
☩	$25
♣	$25
♨	$25
♨	$22
♋	$22
△	$20
♡	$20
†	$20
♆	$20
★	$20
⊙	$20

**I Would Be
Sunk Without You**
#102970
Issued: 1987 • Open
Retail Price: $15 – $20

2 VALUES:
△	$48
♡	$46
†	$46
6∂	$46

I'll Give Him My Heart
#150088
Issued: 1995 • Retired: 1998
Retail Price: $40 – $45

3 VALUES:
ꝑ	$90
♣	$78
♨	$76
♨	$76
♋	$75
☲	$75
△	$72
♡	$70

I'll Never Stop Loving You
#521418
Issued: 1990 • Retired: 1996
Retail Price: $37.50 – $40

4 VALUES:
⳾	$90
▲	$82
✣	$77
ꝑ	$75
♣	$72
♨	$72
♨	$68
♋	$68

I'm A Possibility
#100188
Issued: 1986 • Retired: 1993
Retail Price: $22 – $35

5 VALUES:
ꝑ	$53
♣	$50

**I'm A Precious Moments
Fan (LE-1990)**
Special Event Figurine
#523526
Issued: 1990 • Closed: 1990
Retail Price: $25

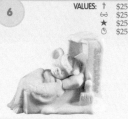

6 VALUES:
†	$25
6∂	$25
★	$25
⊙	$25

**I'm Dreaming Of A
White Christmas**
#272590
Issued: 1997 • Open
Retail Price: $25

	Price Paid	Value
1.		
2.		
3.		
4.		
5.		
6.		
7.		
8.		
9.		
10.		
Totals		

7 VALUES:
†	$87
♨	$75
⳾	$68
▲	$68
✣	$65
ꝑ	$65
♣	$65
♨	$65
♋	$65
☲	$65
△	$65
♡	$65
†	$65
6∂	$65
★	$65
⊙	$65

**I'm Sending You A
White Christmas**
#E2829
Issued: 1984 • Open
Retail Price: $37.50 – $65

8 VALUES:
♨	$120
♋	$92
☲	$85
△	$82

**I'm So Glad That God Has
Blessed Me With A Friend
Like You**
#523623
Issued: 1993 • Retired: 1995
Retail Price: $50 – $55

9 VALUES:
✣	$350
ꝑ	$300
♣	$285
♨	$265

**I'm So Glad You Fluttered
Into My Life**
#520640
Issued: 1989 • Retired: 1991
Retail Price: $40 – $45

10 VALUES:
★	$40
⊙	$40
	(Can.)

New!

Ice See In You A Champion
Exclusive To Canada
#649937
Issued: 2000 • Open
Retail Price: $40 (Canadian)

Value Guide — PRECIOUS MOMENTS®

1

VALUES: ◀ $108
✝ $90
$85

If God Be For Us, Who Can
Be Against Us
#E9285
Issued: 1983 • Susp.: 1985
Retail Price: $27.50

2

VALUES: ♡ $190
✝ $175

In God's Beautiful Garden
Of Love (LE-15,000)
Century Circle Figurine
#261629
Issued: 1997 • Closed: 1997
Retail Price: $150

3

VALUES: ★ $69
♠ $65
$ $60
⅌ $56
⌐ $56
△ $52
♡ $48

In The Spotlight Of
His Grace
#520543
Issued: 1991 • Susp.: 1996
Retail Price: $35 – $37.50

4

VALUES: ◀ $182
♪ $173
▲ $165

It Is Better To Give
Than To Receive
#12297
Issued: 1985 • Susp.: 1987
Retail Price: $19 – $21

5

VALUES: △ $45
♡ $37.50
✝ $37.50
⌐∂ $37.50
★ $37.50
○ $37.50

It May Be Greener, But It's
Just As Hard To Cut
#163899
Issued: 1996 • Open
Retail Price: $37.50

6

VALUES: ● $105
$ $98
⅌ $90
⌐ $86

It's No Yolk When I Say
I Love You
#522104
Issued: 1992 • Susp.: 1994
Retail Price: $60 – $65

7

VALUES: $ $57
⅌ $48
⌐ $47
△ $45
♡ $45
✝ $45
⌐∂ $45
★ $45

It's So Uplifting To Have
A Friend Like You
#524905
Issued: 1992 • Retired: 1999
Retail Price: $40 – $45

8

VALUES: NM $143
▲ $130
Ⅰ $124
◀ $115
✝ $105

It's What's Inside
That Counts
#E3119
Issued: 1980 • Susp.: 1984
Retail Price: $13 – $19

9

VALUES: ▲ $62
✛ $57
Ð $53
⚡ $50
● $50
$ $47
⅌ $47
△ $45
♡ $45
✝ $45
⌐∂ $45
★ $45
○ $45

January
Calendar Girl Series
#109983
Issued: 1988 • Open
Retail Price: $37.50 – $45

10

VALUES: ◀ $60
♪ $50

Jesus Is Coming Soon
#12343
Issued: 1985 • Susp.: 1986
Retail Price: $19 – $22.50

General Figurines

	Price Paid	Value
1.		
2.		
3.		
4.		
5.		
6.		
7.		
8.		
9.		
10.		
Totals		

KEY: NM *Pre-1981* ▲1981 Ⅰ1982 ◀1983 ✝1984 ◀1985 ♪1986 ▲1987 ✛1988 Ð1989 ★1990
● 1991 $ 1992 ⅌1993 ⌐1994 △1995 ♡1996 ✝1997 ⌐∂1998 ★1999 ○2000 UM *Unmarked*

VALUES: ★ $75
☾ $75

Jesus Is My Lighthouse
(lighted)
#487945
Issued: 1999 • Open
Retail Price: $75

VALUES: NM $195
▲ $177
I $155
◀ $145
✝ $135

Jesus Is The Answer
#E1381
Issued: 1979 • Susp.: 1984
Retail Price: $11.50 – $22.50

VALUES: ♣ $90
↭ $82
⬩ $75
△ $72
♡ $68

Jesus Is The Answer
St. Jude Children's Research
Hospital Figurine
#E1381R
Issued: 1992 • Retired: 1996
Retail Price: $55

VALUES: NM $133
▲ $82
I $74
◀ $69
✝ $66
⫯ $58
✳ $55
▲ $50
⚓ $45

Jesus Is The Light
#E1373G
Issued: 1979 • Retired: 1988
Retail Price: $7 – $21

VALUES: ✝ $78
⬩ $72
✦ $65
℣ $56

Jesus Is The Light
That Shines
#E0502
Issued: 1983 • Susp.: 1986
Retail Price: $22.50 – $23

VALUES: ✣ $82
ϸ $73
★ $70
⬩ $70
⚘ $65
⚲ $65

Jesus Is The Only Way
#520756
Issued: 1989 • Susp.: 1993
Retail Price: $40 – $45

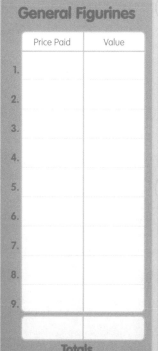

VALUES: NM $130
▲ $75
I $55
◀ $45
✝ $42
✦ $42
✳ $37
▲ $37
⚓ $33
ϸ $33
★ $33
⬩ $33
⚘ $33
△ $32
♡ $32
✝ $32
6d $32

Jesus Loves Me
#E1372B
Issued: 1979 • Retired: 1998
Retail Price: $7 – 27.50

VALUES: NM $132
▲ $85
I $60
◀ $48
✝ $44
✦ $42
✳ $40
▲ $35
ϸ $33
★ $33
⬩ $32
⚘ $30
⚑ $30
△ $27.50
♡ $27.50
✝ $27.50
6d $27.50
★ $27.50
☾ $27.50

Jesus Loves Me
#E1372G
Issued: 1979 • Open
Retail Price: $7 – $27.50

VALUES: I $45
◀ $35
✝ $28
✦ $25
✳ $23
▲ $23
⚓ $23
ϸ $23
★ $23
⬩ $23
⚘ $23
△ $20
♡ $20
✝ $20
6d $20

Jesus Loves Me
#E9278
Issued: 1983 • Retired: 1998
Retail Price: $9 – $17.50

General Figurines

	Price Paid	Value
1.		
2.		
3.		
4.		
5.		
6.		
7.		
8.		
9.		
Totals		

KEY: NM *Pre-1981* ▲ 1981 I 1982 ◀ 1983 ✝ 1984 ✦ 1985 ✳ 1986 ▲ 1987 ⚓ 1988 ϸ 1989 ★ 1990 ⬩ 1991 ⚘ 1992 ⚲ 1993 ⚑ 1994 △ 1995 ♡ 1996 ✝ 1997 6d 1998 ★ 1999 ☾ 2000 UM *Unmarked*

1

VALUES: $43, $33, $32, $32, $30, $30, $26, $24, $22, $22, $20, $20, $18.50, $18.50, $18.50, $18.50, $18.50, $18.50

Jesus Loves Me
#E9279
Issued: 1983 • Open
Retail Price: $9 – $18.50

2

VALUES: $120, $84, $67, $62, $58, $57, $57, $55, $55, $55, $55, $55, $55, $55, $55

The Joy Of The Lord Is My Strength
#100137
Issued: 1986 • Open
Retail Price: $35 – $55

3

VALUES: $74, $68, $60, $58, $57, $55, $55, $55, $55, $55, $55

Joy On Arrival
#523178
Issued: 1991 • Open
Retail Price: $50 – $55

4

VALUES: $62, $52, $50, $48, $48, $47, $47, $45, $45, $45, $45, $45, $45

July
Calendar Girl Series
#110051
Issued: 1988 • Open
Retail Price: $35 – $45

5

VALUES: $145, $68, $65, $60, $58, $57, $55, $55, $55, $55, $55, $55, $55

June
Calendar Girl Series
#110043
Issued: 1988 • Open
Retail Price: $40 – $55

6

VALUES: $35, $32, $29, $27, $27, $25, $25, $24, $24, $22.50, $22.50, $22.50, $22.50, $22.50, $22.50

Junior Bridesmaid
Bridal Party Series
#E2845
Issued: 1986 • Open
Retail Price: $12.50 – $22.50

7

VALUES: $62, $54, $50, $50, $50, $50

Just A Line To Say You're Special
#522864
Issued: 1995 • Retired: 1999
Retail Price: $45 – $50

8

VALUES: $116, $108, $102, $96, $94, $90, $90, $90, $90

Just A Line To Wish You A Happy Day
#520721
Issued: 1989 • Susp.: 1996
Retail Price: $65 – $75

9

VALUES: $55, $48, $45, $45, $45, $45, $45

Just Poppin' In To Say Halo!
#523755
Issued: 1994 • Retired: 1999
Retail Price: $45

10

VALUES: $44, $39

Lead Me To Calvary
(Dated 1997)
The Dated Cross Series
#260916
Issued: 1997 • Closed: 1997
Retail Price: $37.50

General Figurines

	Price Paid	Value
1.		
2.		
3.		
4.		
5.		
6.		
7.		
8.		
9.		
10.		

Totals

KEY: NM *Pre-1981* ▲ 1981 Ⅱ 1982 ◀ 1983 ✝ 1984 ✔ 1985 ♪ 1986 ♠ 1987 ✤ 1988 ⊅ 1989 ★ 1990 ♦ 1991 ♒ 1992 ♋ 1993 ⊟ 1994 △ 1995 ♡ 1996 ✝ 1997 ⌒ 1998 ★ 1999 ○ 2000 UM *Unmarked*

Value Guide — PRECIOUS MOMENTS®

1

VALUES: [Century Circle] $45

Let Freedom Ring (special year mark available)
#681059
Issued: 1999 • Open
Retail Price: $45

2

VALUES: [Hourglass] $120 · [Fish] $88 · [Cross] $88 · [Dove] $85 · [Olive Branch] $79 · [Cedar Tree] $74

Let Love Reign
#E9273
Issued: 1983 • Retired: 1987
Retail Price: $22.50 – $30

3

VALUES: NM $215 · [Triangle] $178 · [Hourglass] $165 · [Fish] $150 · [Cross] $145

Let Not The Sun Go Down Upon Your Wrath
#E5203
Issued: 1981 • Susp.: 1984
Retail Price: $22.50 – $30

4

VALUES: [Hourglass] $146 · [Fish] $137 · [Cross] $126 · [Dove] $120 · [Olive Branch] $115 · [Cedar Tree] $110

Let The Whole World Know
#E7165
Issued: 1982 • Susp.: 1987
Retail Price: $45 – $55

5

VALUES: [Star] $37.50 · [Century Circle] $37.50 (Can.)

Let's Keep Our Eyes On The Goal
Exclusive To Canada
#549975
Issued: 1999 • Open
Retail Price: $37.50 (Canadian)

6

VALUES: [Sword] $63 · [Eyeglasses] $60 · [Star] $60 · [Century Circle] $60

Let's Put The Pieces Together
#525928
Issued: 1998 • Open
Retail Price: $60

General Figurines

	Price Paid	Value
1.		
2.		
3.		
4.		
5.		
6.		
7.		
8.		
9.		
10.		
Totals		

7

VALUES: [Heart] $25 · [Sword] $17.50 · [Eyeglasses] $17.50 · [Star] $17.50

Lettuce Pray
#261122
Issued: 1997 • Retired: 1999
Retail Price: $17.50

8

VALUES: [Eyeglasses] $40

Life Can Be A Jungle
Special Event Figurine
#325457
Issued: 1998 • Closed: 1998
Retail Price: $37.50

9

VALUES: NM $97 · [Triangle] $85 · [Hourglass] $73 · [Fish] $64 · [Cross] $60 · [Dove] $57 · [Olive Branch] $55 · [Cedar Tree] $53 · [Flower] $53 · [Bow & Arrow] $52 · [Flame] $50 · [Vessel] $50 · [G-Clef] $50 · [Butterfly] $50 · [Trumpet] $50 · [Ship] $50 · [Heart] $50 · [Sword] $50 · [Eyeglasses] $50 · [Star] $50 · [Century Circle] $50

The Lord Bless You And Keep You
#E3114
Issued: 1980 • Open
Retail Price: $16 – $50

10

VALUES: NM $55 · [Triangle] $47 · [Hourglass] $44 · [Fish] $44 · [Cross] $42 · [Dove] $40 · [Olive Branch] $40 · [Cedar Tree] $38

The Lord Bless You And Keep You
#E4720
Issued: 1981 • Susp.: 1987
Retail Price: $14 – $22.50

KEY: NM *Pre*-1981 · [Triangle] 1981 · [Hourglass] 1982 · [Fish] 1983 · [Cross] 1984 · [Dove] 1985 · [Olive Branch] 1986 · [Cedar Tree] 1987 · [Flower] 1988 · [Bow & Arrow] 1989 · [Flame] 1990 · [Vessel] 1991 · [G-Clef] 1992 · [Butterfly] 1993 · [Trumpet] 1994 · [Ship] 1995 · [Heart] 1996 · [Sword] 1997 · [Eyeglasses] 1998 · [Star] 1999 · [Century Circle] 2000 · UM *Unmarked*

1

VALUES: NM $82
$59
$52
$48
$46
$44
$44
$40
$40
$38
$38
$37
$35
$35
$35
$35
$35
$35
$35
$35

The Lord Bless You
And Keep You
#E4721
Issued: 1981 • Open
Retail Price: $14 – $35

2

VALUES: $56
$54
$52
$50
$50
$50
$50
$50

The Lord Bless You
And Keep You
#532118
Issued: 1994 • Open
Retail Price: $40 – $50

3

VALUES: $42
$37
$35
$35
$35
$35
$35
$35
$35

The Lord Bless You
And Keep You
#532126
Issued: 1994 • Open
Retail Price: $30 – $35

4

VALUES: $40
$37
$35
$35
$35
$35
$35
$35

The Lord Bless You
And Keep You
#532134
Issued: 1994 • Open
Retail Price: $30 – $35

5

New!

VALUES: ★ $37
$37

The Lord Bless You
And Keep You
#E4721B
Issued: 2000 • Open
Retail Price: $37

6

New!

VALUES: ★ $37
$37

The Lord Bless You
And Keep You
#E4721DB
Issued: 2000 • Open
Retail Price: $37

7

VALUES: $60
$53
$53
$48
$46
$44
$42

Lord, Give Me A Song
Rejoice In The Lord Band Series
#12386
Issued: 1985 • Susp.: 1990
Retail Price: $15 – $22.50

8

VALUES: I $68
$62
$60
$54

Lord, Give Me Patience
#E7159
Issued: 1982 • Susp.: 1985
Retail Price: $25 – $27.50

9

VALUES: $90
$85
$80
$77
$77
$75
$75
$73
$73

The Lord Giveth, And The
Lord Taketh Away
#100226
Issued: 1987 • Retired: 1995
Retail Price: $33.50 – $40

10

VALUES: $64
$60
$57
$55

Lord, Help Me Make
The Grade
#106216
Issued: 1987 • Susp.: 1990
Retail Price: $25 – $32.50

General Figurines

	Price Paid	Value
1.		
2.		
3.		
4.		
5.		
6.		
7.		
8.		
9.		
10.		
Totals		

KEY: NM *Pre-1981* ▲ 1981 I 1982 ◄ 1983 ✝ 1984 ✿ 1985 ♪ 1986 ▲ 1987 ✤ 1988 ✈ 1989 ⬇ 1990
♦ 1991 ✦ 1992 ✿ 1993 ⬅ 1994 △ 1995 ♡ 1996 ✝ 1997 ♋ 1998 ★ 1999 ♌ 2000 �llM *Unmarked*

105

General Figurines

1

VALUES: ⌇ $78
♦ $73
♪ $67
⚘ $65
⚘ $65
⚺ $62
△ $59
♡ $59

**Lord, Help Me Stick
To My Job**
#521450
Issued: 1990 • Retired: 1997
Retail Price: $30 – $35

2

VALUES: △ $42
♡ $40
⚺ $35
66 $35
★ $35
⚹ $35

**Lord Help Me To Stay
On Course**
#532096
Issued: 1995 • Open
Retail Price: $35

3

VALUES: ⌇ $140
♣ $125
♦ $118
♦ $118
★ $110
♪ $110

**Lord, Help Us Keep Our
Act Together**
#101850
Issued: 1987 • Retired: 1992
Retail Price: $35 – $50

4

VALUES: ⚘ $96
⚹ $60
♣ $53
♦ $46
♦ $46
♪ $43
⚘ $43
⚘ $43
⚺ $40
⚱ $38
♡ $37
⚹ $35
† $35
★ $35
⚹ $35

**Lord, I'm Coming
Home**
#100110
Issued: 1986 • Open
Retail Price: $22.50 – $35

5

New!

VALUES: ★ $50
⚹ $50

Lord, I'm In It Again
#525944
Issued: 2000 • Open
Retail Price: $50

6

VALUES: ⚹ $43
△ $38
♡ $35
† $35
66 $35
★ $35
⚹ $35

**The Lord Is Counting
On You**
#531707
Issued: 1994 • Open
Retail Price: $32.50 – $35

General Figurines

	Price Paid	Value
1.		
2.		
3.		
4.		
5.		
6.		
7.		
8.		
9.		
10.		

Totals

7

VALUES: ♡ $46
† $40
66 $40
★ $40
⚹ $40

**The Lord Is The Hope
Of Our Future**
#261564
Issued: 1997 • Open
Retail Price: $40

8

New!

VALUES: ★ $42
⚹ $42

**The Lord Is The Hope Of
Our Future**
#261564B
Issued: 2000 • Open
Retail Price: $42

9

New!

VALUES: ★ $42
⚹ $42

**The Lord Is The Hope Of
Our Future**
#261564G
Issued: 2000 • Open
Retail Price: $42

10

VALUES: △ $35
♡ $30
† $27.50
66 $27.50
★ $27.50

The Lord Is With You
#526835
Issued: 1996 • Retired: 1999
Retail Price: $27.50

KEY: NM *Pre-1981* ▲1981 ℐ1982 ⌇1983 †1984 ⚘1985 ⌇1986 ♣1987 ⚹1988 ♦1989 ★1990
⚹1991 ⚹1992 ♀1993 ⚺1994 △1995 ♡1996 †1997 66 1998 ★1999 ⚹2000 UM *Unmarked*

Value Guide — PRECIOUS MOMENTS®

1

VALUES:
- ❖ $77
- ⊕ $73
- ✦ $70
- 🍖 $70
- ⚜ $67
- ❀ $67
- 🍤 $67
- △ $67
- † $65
- ∞ $65
- ★ $65
- ⊙ $65

The Lord Is Your Light To Happiness
#520837
Issued: 1989 • Open
Retail Price: $50 – $65

2

VALUES:
- 🍃 $118
- ⅊ $97
- ♠ $88
- ⚓ $85

Lord, Keep Me On My Toes
#100129
Issued: 1986 • Retired: 1988
Retail Price: $22.50 – $27

3

VALUES:
- ⅊ $72
- ♠ $62
- ⚓ $59
- ⊕ $59
- ✦ $56
- 🍖 $56
- ⚜ $54
- ❀ $50
- 🍤 $48
- △ $48
- ♡ $48
- † $48
- ∞ $48

Lord, Keep Me On The Ball
The Clown Series
#12270
Issued: 1986 • Susp.: 1998
Retail Price: $30 – $45

4

VALUES:
- ★ $45
- ⊙ $45

Lord, Police Protect Us
#539953
Issued: 1999 • Open
Retail Price: $45

5

VALUES:
- ♡ $40
- † $40
- ∞ $40
- ★ $40
- ⊙ $40

Lord, Spare Me
#521191
Issued: 1997 • Open
Retail Price: $37.50 – $40

6

VALUES:
- ∞ $50
- ★ $45
- ⊙ $45

Lord Speak To Me
#531987
Issued: 1999 • Open
Retail Price: $45

7

VALUES: 🍤 $47

Lord Teach Us To Pray
(LE-1994)
National Day Of Prayer Figurine
#524158
Issued: 1994 • Closed: 1994
Retail Price: $35

8

VALUES:
- ⊕ $70
- ✦ $64
- 🍖 $60
- ⚜ $60
- ❀ $56
- 🍤 $56
- △ $52
- ♡ $50

Lord, Turn My Life Around
#520551
Issued: 1990 • Susp.: 1996
Retail Price: $35 – $37.50

9

VALUES:
- ⚜ $60
- ❀ $58
- 🍤 $55
- △ $53
- ♡ $52

The Lord Turned My Life Around
#520535
Issued: 1992 • Susp.: 1996
Retail Price: $35.50 – $37.50

10

VALUES:
- 🍃 $95
- ⅊ $92
- ♠ $86
- ⚓ $82

The Lord Will Carry You Through
The Clown Series
#12467
Issued: 1986 • Retired: 1988
Retail Price: $30 – $35

General Figurines

	Price Paid	Value
1.		
2.		
3.		
4.		
5.		
6.		
7.		
8.		
9.		
10.		

Totals

KEY: NM *Pre-1981* ▲1981 Ⅱ1982 ◀1983 †1984 🍃1985 ⅊1986 ♠1987 ⚓1988 ⊕1989 ✦1990 🍖1991 ⚜1992 ❀1993 🍤1994 △1995 ♡1996 †1997 ∞1998 ★1999 ⊙2000 UM *Unmarked*

107

General Figurines

1

VALUES: ♣ $70
❀ $60

**The Lord Will Provide
(LE-1993)**
#523593
Issued: 1993 • Closed: 1993
Retail Price: $40

2
VALUES: ⚓ $76
✠ $56
✝ $56
♫ $55
♪ $52
▲ $50
♦ $50
⟊ $48
♠ $48
♦ $47
♨ $47
❀ $45
⚖ $45
♡ $45
† $45
ᏻᏻ $45
★ $45
⏾ $45

**Love Beareth
All Things**
#E7158
Issued: 1982 • Open
Retail Price: $25 – $45

3
VALUES: ⛨ $46
⚖ $40

**Love Blooms Eternal
(Dated 1995)**
The Dated Cross Series
#127019
Issued: 1995 • Closed: 1995
Retail Price: $35

4
VALUES: NM $160
▲ $145
⚓ $128
♦ $120
† $115
🍂 $105

**Love Cannot Break A
True Friendship**
#E4722
Issued: 1981 • Susp.: 1985
Retail Price: $22.50 – $27.50

5
VALUES: † $87
✠ $82
♪ $80
⟊ $75
⚓ $75
⟊ $72
♦ $70
♦ $65

Love Covers All
#12009
Issued: 1985 • Susp.: 1991
Retail Price: $27.50 – $37.50

6
VALUES: ᏻᏻ $65
★ $65

Love Is Color Blind
*Boys & Girls Clubs Of America
Commemorative Figurine*
#524204
Issued: 1998 • Closed: 1998
Retail Price: $60

7
VALUES: ⟊ $80
★ $75
♦ $70
♣ $70
❀ $68
⚱ $68
⚖ $66
♡ $60

Love Is From Above
#521841
Issued: 1990 • Susp.: 1996
Retail Price: $45 – $50

8
VALUES: NM $145
▲ $120
⚓ $105
◀ $100
† $97

Love Is Kind
#E1379A
Issued: 1979 • Susp.: 1984
Retail Price: $8 – $19

9
VALUES: ᏻᏻ $40

Love Is Kind
Special Event Figurine
#E1379R
Issued: 1998 • Closed: 1998
Retail Price: $8

General Figurines

	Price Paid	Value
1.		
2.		
3.		
4.		
5.		
6.		
7.		
8.		
9.		
Totals		

KEY: NM *Pre-1981* ▲ 1981 ⚓ 1982 ◀ 1983 † 1984 🍂 1985 ♪ 1986 ▲ 1987 ⟊ 1988 ⟊ 1989 ★ 1990
♦ 1991 ♣ 1992 ❀ 1993 ⚱ 1994 ⚖ 1995 ♡ 1996 † 1997 ᏻᏻ 1998 ★ 1999 ⏾ 2000 UM *Unmarked*

Value Guide — PRECIOUS MOMENTS®

1
VALUES: ✝ $105
🐚 $95
♫ $89
🔔 $84

Love Is Kind
#E5377
Issued: 1984 • Retired: 1987
Retail Price: $27.50 – $30

2
VALUES: 🐟 $98
✝ $88
⚓ $80

Love Is Patient
#E9251
Issued: 1983 • Susp.: 1985
Retail Price: $35

3
VALUES: ▮ $187
✝ $172
✝ $165

Love Is Sharing
#E7162
Issued: 1982 • Susp.: 1984
Retail Price: $25 – $27.50

4
VALUES: 🔔 $82
❖ $74
Ð $67
⚓ $65

**Love Is The Glue
That Mends**
#104027
Issued: 1987 • Susp.: 1990
Retail Price: $33.50 – $40

5
VALUES: 6∂ $33

Love Is The Key
*Century Circle/
Avon Figurine*
#482242 / #033-949
Issued: 1998 • Closed: 1998
Retail Price: $29.99

6
VALUES: ♡ $42
† $36
6∂ $35
★ $35
🕐 $35

Love Letters In The Sand
#129488
Issued: 1997 • Open
Retail Price: $35

7
VALUES: NM $178
▲ $115
▮ $100
🐚 $94
✝ $86
🐚 $83
♫ $80
🔔 $78
❖ $75
Ð $75
⚓ $73
⚓ $73
♦ $68
♀ $68

Love Lifted Me
#E1375A
Issued: 1979 • Retired: 1993
Retail Price: $11 – $37.50

8
VALUES: NM $130
▲ $110
▮ $95
🐚 $90
✝ $85

Love Lifted Me
#E5201
Issued: 1981 • Susp.: 1984
Retail Price: $25 – $33

9 New!
VALUES: ★ $45
🕐 $45

A Love Like No Other
#681075
Issued: 2000 • Open
Retail Price: $45

10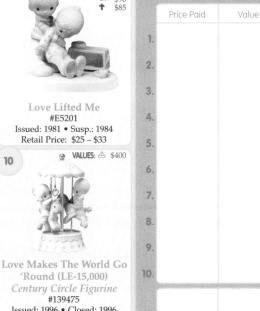
VALUES: △ $400

**Love Makes The World Go
'Round (LE-15,000)**
Century Circle Figurine
#139475
Issued: 1996 • Closed: 1996
Retail Price: $200

General Figurines

	Price Paid	Value
1.		
2.		
3.		
4.		
5.		
6.		
7.		
8.		
9.		
10.		

Totals

KEY: NM *Pre-1981* ▲ 1981 ▮ 1982 🐚 1983 ✝ 1984 🐚 1985 ♫ 1986 🔔 1987 ❖ 1988 Ð 1989 ★ 1990
♦ 1991 ♦ 1992 ♀ 1993 🐚 1994 △ 1995 ♡ 1996 † 1997 6∂ 1998 ★ 1999 🕐 2000 UM *Unmarked*

109

1

VALUES:
	$68
	$55
	$52
	$48
	$48
	$45
	$45
	$45
	$42
	$42
	$40
	$40
	$40
	$40
	$40

Love Never Fails
#12300
Issued: 1985 • Open
Retail Price: $25 – $40

2

VALUES:
	$49
	$43
	$40
	$40
	$40
	$40

Love Never Leaves A Mother's Arms
#523941
Issued: 1996 • Open
Retail Price: $40

3

VALUES: NM $138
	$92
	$72
	$60
	$57
	$52
	$50
	$50
	$48
	$46
	$45
	$45
	$43
	$43
	$42
	$40
	$40
	$40
	$40

Love One Another
#E1376
Issued: 1979 • Open
Retail Price: $10 – $40

4

VALUES:
	$59
	$52
	$47
	$44
	$40
	$40
	$40
	$40
	$37.50
	$37.50
	$37.50
	$37.50

Love Rescued Me
#102393
Issued: 1986 • Retired: 1999
Retail Price: $22.50 – $37.50

5

VALUES:
	$77
	$72
	$70
	$70
	$70
	$70

Love Vows To Always Bloom
#129097
Issued: 1996 • Open
Retail Price: $70

6

VALUES: NM $146
	$118
	$105
	$88
	$85
	$83
	$80
	$80
	$80
	$75
	$75
	$72
	$72

Loving Is Sharing
#E3110B
Issued: 1980 • Retired: 1993
Retail Price: $13 – $30

General Figurines

	Price Paid	Value
1.		
2.		
3.		
4.		
5.		
6.		
7.		
8.		
9.		
Totals		

7
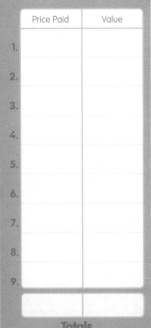

VALUES: NM $112
	$80
	$68
	$50
	$45
	$42
	$40
	$40
	$38
	$38
	$35
	$35
	$35
	$35
	$35
	$35
	$35
	$35

Loving Is Sharing
#E3110G
Issued: 1980 • Open
Retail Price: $13 – $35

8

VALUES:
	$35
	$35

New!

lovingcaringsharing.com
#679860
Issued: 2000 • Open
Retail Price: $35

9

VALUES:
	$39
	$39
	$39
	$37.50
	$37.50
	$37.50

Luke 2:10-11
#532916
Issued: 1994 • Retired: 1999
Retail Price: $35 – $37.50

KEY: NM *Pre-1981* ▲1981 Ⅱ1982 ➾1983 ✝1984 ✣1985 ♪1986 ▲1987 ✤1988 ♱1989 ★1990 ♒1991 ✦1992 ♨1993 ➾1994 △1995 ♡1996 ✝1997 ➿1998 ★1999 ☉2000 UM *Unmarked*

Value Guide — PRECIOUS MOMENTS®

1

VALUES: NM $135
▲ $87
I $56
◄ $44
✝ $42
🍂 $40
♫ $40
♣ $37
✤ $37
Ð $37
⚓ $35
🔔 $35
§ $35
☰ $33
△ $33
♡ $32.50
✝ $32.50
6∂ $32.50
△ $32.50
★ $32.50
◐ $32.50

Make A Joyful Noise
#E1374G
Issued: 1979 • Open
Retail Price: $8 – $32.50

2

VALUES: ♫ $140
▲ $98
✤ $92
Ð $85
⚓ $79

Make Me A Blessing
#100102
Issued: 1987 • Retired: 1990
Retail Price: $35 – $50

3

VALUES: 6∂ $60
★ $60
◐ $60

Make Me Strong (set/4)
Exclusive To Japan
#481688
Issued: 1999 • Open
Retail Price: $60

4

VALUES: ◄ $44
♡ $43
✝ $41
6∂ $41

Making Spirits Bright
#150118
Issued: 1995 • Retired: 1998
Retail Price: $37.50

5

VALUES: ✤ $360
Ð $330
⚓ $320

**Many Moons In Same
Canoe, Blessum You**
#520772
Issued: 1989 • Retired: 1990
Retail Price: $50 – $55

6

VALUES: 6∂ $65

**Many Years Of Blessing You
(LE-1998)**
#384887
Issued: 1998 • Closed: 1998
Retail Price: $60

7

VALUES: ▲ $64
✤ $48
Ð $47
⚓ $43
🔔 $42
§ $40
♣ $40
☰ $40
△ $40
♡ $40
✝ $40
6∂ $40
★ $40
◐ $40

March
Calendar Girl Series
#110019
Issued: 1988 • Open
Retail Price: $27.50 – $40

8

VALUES: △ $44
♡ $38
✝ $35
6∂ $35
★ $35
◐ $35

**Marching To The Beat Of
Freedom's Drum**
#521981
Issued: 1996 • Open
Retail Price: $35

9

VALUES: 6∂ $57

Marvelous Grace (LE-1998)
Century Circle Figurine
#325503
Issued: 1998 • Closed: 1998
Retail Price: $50

10

VALUES: ▲ $125
✤ $50
Ð $44
⚓ $42
🔔 $40
§ $40
♣ $37
☰ $37
△ $35
♡ $35
✝ $35
6∂ $35
★ $35
◐ $35

May
Calendar Girl Series
#110035
Issued: 1988 • Open
Retail Price: $25 – $35

General Figurines

	Price Paid	Value
1.		
2.		
3.		
4.		
5.		
6.		
7.		
8.		
9.		
10.		

Totals

KEY: NM *Pre-1981* ▲ 1981 I 1982 ◄ 1983 ✝ 1984 🍂 1985 ♫ 1986 ▲ 1987 ✤ 1988 Ð 1989 ★ 1990 🔔 1991 § 1992 ♣ 1993 ☰ 1994 △ 1995 ♡ 1996 ✝ 1997 6∂ 1998 ★ 1999 ◐ 2000 ⊞M *Unmarked*

111

Value Guide — PRECIOUS MOMENTS®

General Figurines

1

VALUES:	
☀	$70
⬥	$53
⬧	$47
⬨	$44
⬱	$40
♡	$40
†	$40
∞	$40

May Only Good Things Come Your Way
#524425
Issued: 1991 • Retired: 1998
Retail Price: $30 – $37.50

2

VALUES:	
♡	$70

May The Sun Always Shine On You (LE-1996)
Century Circle Figurine
#184217
Issued: 1996 • Closed: 1996
Retail Price: $37.50

3

VALUES:	
⬥	$55
⬦	$50
▲	$47
⬥	$47
⬧	$45
☀	$42
⬨	$42
⬧	$40

May You Have The Sweetest Christmas
Family Christmas Series
#15776
Issued: 1985 • Susp.: 1992
Retail Price: $17 – $25

4

VALUES:	
⬱	$130
†	$105
⬥	$100
⬧	$95

May Your Birthday Be A Blessing
#E2826
Issued: 1984 • Susp.: 1986
Retail Price: $37.50

5

VALUES:	
☀	$58
⬥	$48
⬧	$43
⬨	$40
⬱	$38
⬧	$37
♡	$35
†	$35
∞	$35
★	$35
⬤	$35

May Your Birthday Be A Blessing
#524301
Issued: 1991 • Open
Retail Price: $30 – $35

6

VALUES:	
†	$85
⬧	$76
⬧	$72

May Your Christmas Be Blessed
#E5376
Issued: 1984 • Susp.: 1986
Retail Price: $37.50

7

VALUES:	
▥	$94
⬥	$83
†	$78

May Your Christmas Be Cozy
#E2345
Issued: 1982 • Susp.: 1984
Retail Price: $23 – $25

8

VALUES:	
⬥	$69
⬥	$64
▲	$62
⬥	$60
⬧	$60
⬧	$58
⬥	$58
⬧	$56
⬨	$54
⬱	$52

May Your Christmas Be Delightful
#15482
Issued: 1985 • Susp.: 1994
Retail Price: $25 – $35

9

VALUES:	
†	$48
∞	$40
★	$40
⬤	$40

May Your Christmas Be Delightful
#604135
Issued: 1997 • Open
Retail Price: $40

10

VALUES:	
▥	$150
⬥	$135
†	$127
⬧	$127
⬧	$122
▲	$117
⬥	$114

May Your Christmas Be Warm
#E2348
Issued: 1982 • Susp.: 1988
Retail Price: $30 – $38.50

General Figurines

	Price Paid	Value
1.		
2.		
3.		
4.		
5.		
6.		
7.		
8.		
9.		
10.		
Totals		

112

KEY: NM *Pre*-1981 ▲1981 ▥1982 ⬱1983 †1984 ⬥1985 ⬧1986 ▲1987 ⬥1988 ⬧1989 ☀1990 ⬥1991 ⬧1992 ⬨1993 ⬱1994 ⬧1995 ♡1996 †1997 ∞1998 ★1999 ⬤2000 UM *Unmarked*

Value Guide — PRECIOUS MOMENTS®

1 VALUES: 🐚 $68
🐞 $63
🍴 $58
△ $55
♡ $53
† $50
★ $50
⭐ $50
🕐 $50

May Your Every Wish
Come True
#524298
Issued: 1993 • Open
Retail Price: $50

2 VALUES: 🐚 $47
🐞 $45
🍴 $42
△ $42
♡ $40
† $40
★ $40
🕐 $40

May Your Future Be Blessed
#525316
Issued: 1993 • Open
Retail Price: $35 – $40

3 VALUES: ♱ $68
★ $62
🍴 $58
🐞 $56
🐚 $52
🍴 $52
△ $52
♡ $52
† $52
⭐ $52

May Your Life Be Blessed
With Touchdowns
#522023
Issued: 1989 • Retired: 1998
Retail Price: $45 – $50

4 VALUES: ★ $37.50
🕐 $37.50

May Your Seasons Be Jelly
And Bright
#587885
Issued: 1999 • Open
Retail Price: $37.50

5 VALUES: 🐚 $88
🐞 $82
🍴 $78
🍴 $74
△ $70
♡ $70

May Your World Be
Trimmed With Joy
#522082
Issued: 1991 • Susp.: 1996
Retail Price: $55

6 VALUES: 🐞 $52
🍴 $46

Memories Are Made
Of This (LE-1994)
Special Event Figurine
#529982
Issued: 1994 • Closed: 1994
Retail Price: $30

7 VALUES: ♱ $56
🍴 $46
★ $43
🍴 $40
🐚 $38
🐞 $38
🍴 $37
△ $37
♡ $35
† $35
⭐ $35
★ $35
🕐 $35

Meowie Christmas
#109800
Issued: 1998 • Open
Retail Price: $30 – $35

8 VALUES: ♱ $108
★ $98
🍴 $95
🐚 $93
🍴 $93
🍴 $90
△ $90
♡ $87

Merry Christmas Deer
#522317
Issued: 1989 • Retired: 1997
Retail Price: $50 – $60

9 VALUES: † $50
⭐ $45
★ $45
🕐 $45

Missum You
#306991
Issued: 1998 • Open
Retail Price: $45

10 VALUES: ⭐ $40

Mom, You Always Make Our
House A Home (LE-1998)
Catalog Figurine
#325465
Issued: 1998 • Closed: 1998
Retail Price: $37.50

General Figurines

	Price Paid	Value
1.		
2.		
3.		
4.		
5.		
6.		
7.		
8.		
9.		
10.		
Totals		

KEY: NM *Pre-1981* ▲1981 ✕1982 ◀1983 †1984 🍴1985 ✗1986 ♠1987 ♣1988 ♱1989 ★1990
🐚1991 🐞1992 🐞1993 🍴1994 △1995 ♡1996 †1997 ⭐1998 ★1999 🕐2000 UM *Unmarked*

1 VALUES: ★ $33

Mom, You're A Royal Gem
Avon Figurine
#588083
Issued: 1999 • Closed: 1999
Retail Price: $30

2 VALUES: ᴦᴦ $40
★ $40

**Mom, You're My
Special-tea (LE-1999)**
#325473
Issued: 1999 • Closed: 1999
Retail Price: $25 – $30

3 VALUES: ᴦᴦ $37
★ $35
◔ $35

**Mom, You've Given
Me So Much**
#488046
Issued: 1999 • Open
Retail Price: $35

4 VALUES: ♠ $46
⬩ $42
Ɒ $40
⚓ $37
✦ $35
§ $32
♣ $32
⌇ $30
♡ $30
† $30
⟋ $30
★ $30
◔ $30

Mommy, I Love You
#109975
Issued: 1988 • Open
Retail Price: $22.50 – $30

5 VALUES: ♠ $50
⬩ $44
Ɒ $40
⚓ $38
✦ $35
§ $33
♣ $32
⌇ $30
♡ $30
† $30
⟋ $30
★ $30
◔ $30

Mommy, I Love You
#112143
Issued: 1988 • Open
Retail Price: $22.50 – $30

6 VALUES: ♠ $85
△ $78
♡ $74

**Money's Not The Only
Green Thing Worth Saving**
#531073
Issued: 1995 • Retired: 1996
Retail Price: $50

7 VALUES: ♡ $45
★ $45
◔ $45

Mornin' Pumpkin
#455687
Issued: 1998 • Retired: 1999
Retail Price: $45

8 VALUES: ♡ $47
† $44

The Most Precious Gift Of All
Catalog Figurine
#183814
Issued: 1997 • Closed: 1997
Retail Price: $37.50 – $40

9 VALUES: NM $92
▲ $74
Ɪ $53
◄ $48
† $44
♫ $44
♫ $42
♠ $40
⬩ $38
Ɒ $38
⚓ $36
✦ $36
§ $36
♣ $36
⌇ $36
♡ $35
† $35
⟋ $35
★ $35
◔ $35

Mother Sew Dear
#E3106
Issued: 1980 • Open
Retail Price: $13 – $35

KEY: NM *Pre-1981* ▲ 1981 Ɪ 1982 ◄ 1983 † 1984 ✦ 1985 ♫ 1986 ♠ 1987 ⬩ 1988 Ɒ 1989 ⚓ 1990 ♣ 1991 § 1992 ♞ 1993 ⌇ 1994 △ 1995 ♡ 1996 † 1997 ᴦᴦ 1998 ★ 1999 ◔ 2000 UM *Unmarked*

Value Guide — PRECIOUS MOMENTS®

General Figurines

1

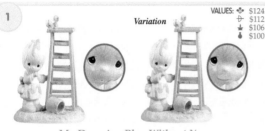

Variation

VALUES: $124 / $112 / $106 / $100

My Days Are Blue Without You
#520802
Issued: 1989 • Susp.: 1991
Retail Price: $65 – $70
Variation: Girl smiling – $130

2

VALUES: $78 / $70 / $68 / $67 / $64 / $62 / $62 / $60 / $60 / $60 / $60 / $60

My Heart Is Exposed With Love
#520624
Issued: 1989 • Retired: 1999
Retail Price: $45 – $60

3

VALUES: $37.50 / $37.50

My Life Is A Vacuum Without You
#587907
Issued: 1999 • Open
Retail Price: $37.50

4

VALUES: $58 / $53 / $50 / $50 / $50 / $50

My Love Blooms For You
#521728
Issued: 1996 • Open
Retail Price: $50

5

VALUES: $40 / $40 / $40 / $40

My Love Will Keep You Warm
Catalog Figurine
#272957
Issued: 1998 • Closed: 1998
Retail Price: $37.50

6

VALUES: $63 / $57 / $50 / $47 / $44 / $44 / $42 / $40 / $40 / $40 / $40 / $40 / $40 / $40

My Love Will Never Let You Go
#103497
Issued: 1987 • Open
Retail Price: $25 – $40

7

VALUES: $43 / $40 / $40 / $40 / $40

My True Love Gave To Me
#529273
Issued: 1996 • Open
Retail Price: $40

8

VALUES: $48 / $48

My Universe Is You
#487902
Issued: 1999 • Retired: 1999
Retail Price: $45

9

VALUES: $110 / $105 / $100 / $96 / $94 / $94

My Warmest Thoughts Are You
#524085
Issued: 1992 • Retired: 1996
Retail Price: $55 – $60

General Figurines

	Price Paid	Value
1.		
2.		
3.		
4.		
5.		
6.		
7.		
8.		
9.		

Totals

KEY: NM *Pre-1981* ▲ 1981 ▮ 1982 ◄ 1983 ✝ 1984 ✔ 1985 ✎ 1986 ♠ 1987 ✿ 1988 ✞ 1989 ★ 1990 ♨ 1991 ♣ 1992 ✿ 1993 ✈ 1994 △ 1995 ♡ 1996 ✝ 1997 ∞ 1998 ★ 1999 ○ 2000 UM *Unmarked*

General Figurines

1 VALUES:
- ▲ $104
- ✣ $85
- ⚜ $80
- ⚓ $78
- ❦ $76
- ⚘ $76
- ஐ $74
- ▦ $72
- △ $70
- ♡ $70
- † $70
- ◠ $70
- ★ $70
- ◷ $70

No Tears Past The Gate
#101826
Issued: 1987 • Open
Retail Price: $40 – $70

2 VALUES:
- ▮ $93
- ✝ $85
- ✣ $82
- ஐ $79
- ▦ $77
- ▲ $73
- ✣ $70
- ✣ $68
- ⚓ $65

Variation

Nobody's Perfect
#E9268
Issued: 1983 • Retired: 1990
Retail Price: $21 – $30
Variation: Boy smiling – $557

3 VALUES:
- ஐ $45
- ▦ $38
- △ $35
- ♡ $35
- † $35
- ◠ $35
- ★ $35
- ◷ $35

Nothing Can Dampen The Spirit Of Caring
The Good Samaritan Series
#603864
Issued: 1994 • Open
Retail Price: $35

4 VALUES:
- ✣ $58
- ✣ $48
- ★ $45
- ⚓ $43
- ❦ $42
- ⚘ $42
- ஐ $40
- ▦ $37.50
- △ $37.50
- ♡ $37.50
- † $37.50
- ◠ $37.50
- ★ $37.50
- ◷ $37.50

November
Calendar Girl Series
#110108
Issued: 1988 • Open
Retail Price: $32.50 – $37.50

5 VALUES:
- ▦ $59
- △ $50
- ♡ $47

Now I Lay Me Down To Sleep
#522058
Issued: 1994 • Retired: 1997
Retail Price: $30 – $35

General Figurines

	Price Paid	Value
1.		
2.		
3.		
4.		
5.		
6.		
7.		
8.		
9.		
Totals		

6 VALUES:
- ▮ $110
- ▲ $94
- † $88
- ⚘ $82
- ⚓ $78

O Come All Ye Faithful
#E2353
Issued: 1982 • Retired: 1986
Retail Price: $27.50 – $30

7 VALUES:
- NM $157
- ▲ $137
- ▮ $114
- ◀ $102
- † $95

O, How I Love Jesus
#E1380B
Issued: 1979 • Retired: 1984
Retail Price: $8 – $19

8 VALUES:
- ⚘ $58
- ⚘ $52
- ▲ $48
- ✣ $45
- ✣ $44
- ⚓ $42
- ❦ $42
- ⚘ $40
- ஐ $40
- ▦ $40
- △ $40
- ♡ $40
- † $40
- ◠ $40
- ★ $40
- ◷ $40

O Worship The Lord
#100064
Issued: 1986 • Open
Retail Price: $24 – $40

9 VALUES:
- ⚘ $55
- ⚘ $48
- ▲ $45
- ✣ $44
- ✣ $44
- ⚓ $42
- ❦ $42
- ⚘ $40
- ஐ $40
- ▦ $40
- △ $40
- ♡ $40
- † $40
- ◠ $40
- ★ $40
- ◷ $40

O Worship The Lord
#102229
Issued: 1986 • Open
Retail Price: $24 – $40

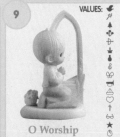

KEY: NM *Pre-1981* ▲ 1981 ▮ 1982 ◀ 1983 † 1984 ⚘ 1985 ஐ 1986 ▲ 1987 ✣ 1988 ✣ 1989 ⚓ 1990 ❦ 1991 ⚘ 1992 ஐ 1993 ◀ 1994 △ 1995 ♡ 1996 † 1997 ◠ 1998 ★ 1999 ◷ 2000 ⅃M *Unmarked*

Value Guide — PRECIOUS MOMENTS®

1

VALUES:
✿	$62
♧	$57
✦	$50
✠	$48
◈	$47
☙	$45
△	$45
♡	$45
†	$45
★	$45
◐	$45

October
Calendar Girl Series
#110094
Issued: 1988 • Open
Retail Price: $35 – $45

2

VALUES:
♠	$135
✿	$124
♧	$120
✦	$118
☙	$114
◈	$112
♥	$112
△	$112
♡	$112
†	$112
◐	$112

Oh What Fun It Is To Ride
#109819
Issued: 1987 • Retired: 1998
Retail Price: $85 – $110

3

VALUES:
♡	$50
†	$45
👁	$45
★	$45
◐	$45

On My Way To A Perfect Day
#522872
Issued: 1997 • Open
Retail Price: $45

4

VALUES:
👁	$17.50
★	$17.50
◐	$17.50

On Our Way To A Special Day
Exclusive To Japan
#481602
Issued: 1999 • Open
Retail Price: $17.50

5
VALUES:
👁	$17.50
★	$17.50
◐	$17.50

On Our Way To A Special Day
Exclusive To Japan
#481610
Issued: 1999 • Open
Retail Price: $17.50

6

VALUES:
†	$37
👁	$35
★	$35
◐	$35

Only One Life To Offer
#325309
Issued: 1998 • Open
Retail Price: $35

7
VALUES:
⬷	$68
†	$52
≫	$50
♠	$47
✿	$45
♧	$43
✦	$43
☙	$43
◈	$40
♥	$40
△	$40
♡	$40
†	$40
👁	$40
★	$40
◐	$40
UM	$150

Onward Christian Soldiers
#E0523
Issued: 1983 • Open
Retail Price: $24 – $40

8

VALUES:
✠	$108
⬷	$97
†	$90
⬷	$82

Our First Christmas Together
#E2377
Issued: 1982 • Susp.: 1985
Retail Price: $35 – $37.50

General Figurines

	Price Paid	Value
1.		
2.		
3.		
4.		
5.		
6.		
7.		
8.		
9.		
10.		

Totals

9

VALUES:
✿	$90
♧	$79
✦	$77
☙	$75

Our First Christmas Together
#115290
Issued: 1988 • Susp.: 1991
Retail Price: $50 – $60

10

VALUES:
☙	$82
♥	$75
◈	$73
△	$70
♡	$70
†	$70
👁	$70
★	$70

Our Friendship Is Soda-licious
#524336
Issued: 1993 • Retired: 1999
Retail Price: $65 – $70

KEY: NM *Pre-1981* ▲1981 ✠1982 ⬷1983 †1984 ⬷1985 ≫1986 ♠1987 ✿1988 ♧1989 ✦1990 ☙1991 ◈1992 ♥1993 ⬷1994 △1995 ♡1996 †1997 👁1998 ★1999 ◐2000 UM *Unmarked*

117

General Figurines

1

VALUES: 6∂ N/E

**Our Future Is Looking
Much Brighter**
*PRECIOUS MOMENTS
Collection 20th Anniversary
Cruise Figurine*
#325511
Issued: 1998 • Closed: 1998
Retail Price: N/A

2

VALUES: ⚓ $95
⚜ $89
♫ $85
✠ $83
✿ $78
Ð $73

**Part Of Me Wants
To Be Good**
#12149
Issued: 1985 • Susp.: 1989
Retail Price: $19 – $25

3

VALUES: NM $112
▲ $93
Ⅱ $87
⬛ $85
✝ $80

Peace Amid The Storm
#E4723
Issued: 1981 • Susp.: 1984
Retail Price: $22.50 – $27.50

4

VALUES: ⏱ $125

New!

PHOTO
UNAVAILABLE

**Peace In The Valley
(LE-12,500)**
#649929
Issued: 2000 • Open
Retail Price: $125

5

VALUES: NM $158
▲ $152
Ⅱ $140
⬛ $140
✝ $136

Peace On Earth
#E2804
Issued: 1980 • Susp.: 1984
Retail Price: $20 – $27.50

6

VALUES: ⏱ $55

PHOTO
UNAVAILABLE

Peace On Earth (LE-1999)
#E2804R
Issued: 1999 • Closed: 1999
Retail Price: $50

General Figurines

	Price Paid	Value
1.		
2.		
3.		
4.		
5.		
6.		
7.		
8.		
9.		
10.		
Totals		

7

VALUES: NM $112
▲ $88
Ⅱ $80
⬛ $75
✝ $73

Peace On Earth
#E4725
Issued: 1981 • Susp.: 1984
Retail Price: $25 – $30

8

VALUES: ◄ $200
✝ $190
✎ $182
♫ $175

Peace On Earth
#E9287
Issued: 1983 • Susp.: 1986
Retail Price: $37.50

9

VALUES: ✝ $75

**The Pearl Of Great Price
(LE-1997)**
Century Circle Figurine
#526061
Issued: 1997 • Closed: 1997
Retail Price: $50

10

VALUES: 6∂ $35
★ $35
⏱ $35

Peas On Earth
#455768
Issued: 1998 • Open
Retail Price: $35

KEY: NM *Pre-1981* ▲ 1981 Ⅱ 1982 ◄ 1983 ✝ 1984 ✎ 1985 ♫ 1986 ▲ 1987 ✤ 1988 Ð 1989 ✦ 1990 ♦ 1991 ⚜ 1992 ♋ 1993 ⬛ 1994 △ 1995 ♡ 1996 ✝ 1997 6∂ 1998 ★ 1999 ⏱ 2000 UM *Unmarked*

Value Guide — PRECIOUS MOMENTS®

1

VALUES: 𝐈 $85 / ✝ $80 / 🐟 $72 / 🍂 $66 / ♫ $60

The Perfect Grandpa
#E7160
Issued: 1982 • Susp.: 1986
Retail Price: $25 – $27.50

2

VALUES: 🐚 $62 / △ $58 / ♡ $55 / ✝ $55 / 6⊃ $55 / ★ $55

Perfect Harmony
#521914
Issued: 1994 • Retired: 1999
Retail Price: $55

3

VALUES: ✝ $56 / 6⊃ $56 / ★ $56 / ⏾ $55

Pizza On Earth
#521884
Issued: 1997 • Open
Retail Price: $55

4

VALUES: 🐚 $45 / △ $39 / ♡ $37 / ✝ $37 / 6⊃ $37

A Poppy For You
#604208
Issued: 1995 • Susp.: 1998
Retail Price: $35

5

VALUES: ♡ $32 / ✝ $25 / 6⊃ $25 / ★ $25 / ⏾ $25

Potty Time
#531022
Issued: 1997 • Open
Retail Price: $25

6

VALUES: 6⊃ $40 / ★ $40 / ⏾ $40

Praise God From Whom All Blessings Flow
#455695
Issued: 1998 • Open
Retail Price: $40

7

VALUES: 6⊃ $50 / ★ $50 / ⏾ $50

Praise The Lord And Dosie-Do
#455733
Issued: 1998 • Open
Retail Price: $50

8

VALUES: NM $110 / ▲ $92 / 𝐈 $75

Praise The Lord Anyhow
#E1374B
Issued: 1979 • Retired: 1982
Retail Price: $8 – $17

9

VALUES: 𝐈 $126 / ✝ $98 / 🐟 $95 / 🍂 $90 / ♫ $90 / ▲ $85 / △ $85 / ♇ $83 / ♣ $82 / ♯ $80 / ♊ $72 / 🐚 $70 / 🐚 $65

Praise The Lord Anyhow
#E9254
Issued: 1983 • Retired: 1994
Retail Price: $35 – $55

10

VALUES: NM $240 / ▲ $175 / 𝐈 $163 / 🐚 $155 / ✝ $150

Prayer Changes Things
#E1375B
Issued: 1979 • Susp.: 1984
Retail Price: $11 – $22.50

General Figurines

	Price Paid	Value
1.		
2.		
3.		
4.		
5.		
6.		
7.		
8.		
9.		
10.		
Totals		

KEY: NM Pre-1981 / ▲ 1981 / 𝐈 1982 / 🐚 1983 / ✝ 1984 / 🍂 1985 / ♫ 1986 / ▲ 1987 / 🐚 1988 / ♇ 1989 / ★ 1990 / ♣ 1991 / ♯ 1992 / ♊ 1993 / 🐚 1994 / △ 1995 / ♡ 1996 / ✝ 1997 / 6⊃ 1998 / ★ 1999 / ⏾ 2000 / UM Unmarked

Value Guide — PRECIOUS MOMENTS®

1

Variation

VALUES:	
NM	$180
Triangle	$160
Hourglass	$125
Fish	$110
Cross	$105
Dove	$102

Prayer Changes Things
#E5214
Issued: 1981 • Susp.: 1984
Retail Price: $35 – $37.50
Variation: "Holy Bible" on back cover – NM – *$184* ▲ – *$160*

2

VALUES:	
Fish	$137
Cross	$85
Dove	$80
Olive Branch	$80
Cedar Tree	$77
Flower	$75
Bow & Arrow	$75
Flame	$73
Vessel	$70
G-Clef	$70
Butterfly	$68
Trumpet	$68
Ship	$65
Heart	$65
Torch	$65
Eyeglasses	$65
Star	$65

Precious Memories
#E2828
Issued: 1984 • Retired: 1999
Retail Price: $45 – $65

3

VALUES:	
Cedar Tree	$79
Flower	$64
Bow & Arrow	$60
Flame	$57
Vessel	$55
G-Clef	$55
Butterfly	$55
Trumpet	$55
Ship	$55
Heart	$55
Torch	$55
Eyeglasses	$55
Star	$55
Clock	$55

Precious Memories
#106763
Issued: 1988 • Open
Retail Price: $37.50 – $55

4

VALUES:	
Ship	$78
Heart	$73
Torch	$70
Eyeglasses	$70
Star	$70
Clock	$70

Precious Moments To Remember
#163848
Issued: 1996 • Open
Retail Price: $70

5

VALUES:	
Star	$40

Precious Moments Will Last Forever
Special Event Figurine
#681008
Issued: 1999 • Closed: 1999
Retail Price: $35

General Figurines

	Price Paid	Value
1.		
2.		
3.		
4.		
5.		
6.		
7.		
8.		
9.		
Totals		

6

VALUES:	
Hourglass	$110
Fish	$87
Cross	$82
Dove	$78
Olive Branch	$75
Cedar Tree	$73
Flower	$73
Bow & Arrow	$69
Flame	$67
Vessel	$67
G-Clef	$67
Butterfly	$65
Trumpet	$65
Ship	$65
Heart	$65
Torch	$65
Eyeglasses	$65
Star	$65

Press On
#E9265
Issued: 1983 • Retired: 1999
Retail Price: $40 – $65

7

VALUES:	
Ship	$44
Heart	$38
Torch	$35
Eyeglasses	$35
Star	$35
Clock	$35

Pretty As A Princess
#526053
Issued: 1996 • Open
Retail Price: $35

8

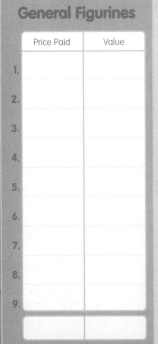

VALUES:	
Ship	$44
Heart	$38
Torch	$35
Eyeglasses	$35
Star	$35
Clock	$35

A Prince Of A Guy
#526037
Issued: 1996 • Open
Retail Price: $35

9

VALUES:	
Flower	$30
Bow & Arrow	$25
Flame	$23
Vessel	$23
G-Clef	$20
Butterfly	$20
Trumpet	$20
Ship	$20
Heart	$17.50
Torch	$17.50
Eyeglasses	$17.50
Star	$17.50

Puppy Love
#520764
Issued: 1989 • Retired: 1999
Retail Price: $12.50 – $17.50

KEY: NM *Pre*-1981 • ▲ (Triangle) 1981 • Hourglass 1982 • Fish 1983 • Cross 1984 • Dove 1985 • Olive Branch 1986 • Cedar Tree 1987 • Flower 1988 • Bow & Arrow 1989 • Flame 1990 • Vessel 1991 • G-Clef 1992 • Butterfly 1993 • Trumpet 1994 • Ship 1995 • Heart 1996 • Torch 1997 • Eyeglasses 1998 • ★ (Star) 1999 • Clock 2000 • UM *Unmarked*

1

VALUES: ▲ $100
⚜ $94
🕀 $90
★ $88
🔔 $86
♧ $86
❀ $83
🍶 $80
🛆 $80

Puppy Love Is From Above
#106798
Issued: 1988 • Retired: 1995
Retail Price: $45 – $55

2

VALUES: ★ $29

Purr-fect Friends
Catalog Figurine
#488364
Issued: 1999 • Closed: 1999
Retail Price: $25

3

VALUES: NM $83
$73
I $48
$45
✝ $42
✦ $40
♪ $38
▲ $35
⚜ $35
🕀 $35
❀ $35
🍶 $35
♧ $35
❀ $35
🛆 $35
♡ $35
✝ $35
6◠ $35
★ $35
🕚 $35

The Purr-fect Grandma
#E3109
Issued: 1980 • Open
Retail Price: $13 – $35

4

VALUES: 🍶 $70
♧ $65
♧ $60
❀ $56
🛆 $54
🛆 $52
♡ $52
✝ $50
6◠ $50
★ $50

A Reflection Of His Love
#522279
Issued: 1991 • Retired: 1999
Retail Price: $50

5

VALUES: NM $110
▲ $82
I $75
◄ $72
✝ $68
♪ $65
♪ $65
▲ $62
⚓ $60
🕀 $57
🍶 $57
♧ $57
❀ $57
❀ $55
🛆 $55
♡ $55
✝ $55
6◠ $55
★ $55
🕚 $55

Rejoicing With You
#E4724
Issued: 1981 • Open
Retail Price: $25 – $55

6

VALUES: ✝ $37
🕚 $32
♪ $29
▲ $27
⚜ $25
🕀 $23
🍶 $23
♧ $22
❀ $22
❀ $20
🍴 $18.50
🛆 $18.50
♡ $18.50
✝ $18.50
★ $18.50
🕚 $18.50

Ring Bearer
Bridal Party Series
#E2833
Issued: 1985 • Open
Retail Price: $11 – $18.50

7

VALUES: ♧ $170
❀ $152
🍴 $148
🛆 $134
♡ $128

Ring Those Christmas Bells
#525898
Issued: 1992 • Retired: 1996
Retail Price: $95 – $100

8

VALUES: ★ $45
🕚 $45

RV Haven' Fun Or What
#587915
Issued: 1999 • Open
Retail Price: $45

9

VALUES: ♧ $40
❀ $36
🍴 $34
🛆 $32.50
♡ $32.50
✝ $32.50
6◠ $32.50
★ $32.50
🕚 $32.50

Safe In The Arms Of Jesus
*Child Evangelism
Fellowship Figurine*
#521922
Issued: 1993 • Open
Retail Price: $30 – $32.50

10

VALUES: 🍴 $550

Sailabration Cruise (LE-1995)
*PRECIOUS MOMENTS
Collectors' Club 15th
Anniversary Cruise Figurine*
#150061
Issued: 1995 • Closed: 1995
Retail Price: N/A

General Figurines

	Price Paid	Value
1.		
2.		
3.		
4.		
5.		
6.		
7.		
8.		
9.		
10.		

Totals

KEY: NM *Pre-1981* ▲ 1981 I 1982 ◄ 1983 ✝ 1984 ✦ 1985 ♪ 1986 ▲ 1987 ⚜ 1988 🕀 1989 ★ 1990 🍶 1991 ♧ 1992 ❀ 1993 🍴 1994 🛆 1995 ♡ 1996 ✝ 1997 6◠ 1998 ★ 1999 🕚 2000 ⅡM *Unmarked*

General Figurines (side)

1
VALUES: ♡ $60
† $60
6◊ $60
★ $60
◔ $60

Say I Do
#261149
Issued: 1997 • Open
Retail Price: $55 – $60

2
VALUES: ♫ $85
▲ $80
✧ $75
Ð $66
✚ $60
♠ $58

Scent From Above
#100528
Issued: 1987 • Retired: 1991
Retail Price: $19 – $27.50

3
VALUES: ★ $25
◔ $25

**Scootin' Your Way To A
Perfect Day**
Care-A-Van Exclusive
#634999
Issued: 1999 • Open
Retail Price: $25

4
VALUES: ♠ $92
♀ $88
$84
△ $80
♡ $75

Sealed With A Kiss
#524441
Issued: 1993 • Retired: 1996
Retail Price: $50 – $60

5
VALUES: ✦ $52
† $48
♣ $46
✿ $42

Seek Ye The Lord
#E9261
Issued: 1983 • Susp.: 1986
Retail Price: $21

6
VALUES: † $77
♣ $68
♫ $65
♠ $58

Seek Ye The Lord
#E9262
Issued: 1983 • Susp.: 1986
Retail Price: $21

General Figurines

	Price Paid	Value
1.		
2.		
3.		
4.		
5.		
6.		
7.		
8.		
9.		
10.		
Totals		

7
VALUES: ♣ $77
♫ $70
▲ $68
✧ $65
Ð $65
★ $63
♠ $62

Sending My Love
#100056
Issued: 1986 • Susp.: 1991
Retail Price: $22.50 – $32.50

8
VALUES: ☐ $62
△ $56

Sending My Love Your Way
(LE-1995)
Catalog Figurine
#528609
Issued: 1995 • Closed: 1995
Retail Price: $40

9
VALUES: ◀ $114
† $100
Ð $97
♫ $92

Sending You A Rainbow
#E9288
Issued: 1983 • Susp.: 1986
Retail Price: $22.50

10
VALUES: ▲ $72
✧ $58
Ð $55
★ $52
♠ $50
♀ $48
♀ $45
△ $45
♡ $45
† $45
6◊ $45
★ $45
◔ $45

Sending You My Love
#109967
Issued: 1988 • Open
Retail Price: $35 – $45

KEY: NM *Pre*-1981 ▲ 1981 ✕ 1982 ◀ 1983 ✚ 1984 ♣ 1985 ♫ 1986 ▲ 1987 ✧ 1988 Ð 1989 ★ 1990 ♠ 1991 ♀ 1992 ♀ 1993 ☐ 1994 △ 1995 ♡ 1996 † 1997 6◊ 1998 ★ 1999 ◔ 2000 UM *Unmarked*

Value Guide — PRECIOUS MOMENTS®

1

VALUES:
$65
$48
$45

Sending You Oceans
Of Love
#532010
Issued: 1995 • Retired: 1996
Retail Price: $35 – $37.50

2

VALUES:
$92
$82
$75
$72
$68

Sending You Showers
Of Blessings
#520683
Issued: 1989 • Retired: 1992
Retail Price: $32.50 – $35

3

VALUES:
$55
$48
$43
$42
$40
$40
$37.50
$37.50
$37.50
$37.50
$37.50
$37.50
$37.50

September
Calendar Girl Series
#110086
Issued: 1988 • Open
Retail Price: $27.50 – $37.50

4

VALUES:
$43
$40
$39
$37.50
$37.50
$37.50
$37.50
$37.50

Serenity Prayer Boy
#530700
Issued: 1994 • Open
Retail Price: $35 – $37.50

5

VALUES:
$45
$40
$40
$37.50
$37.50
$37.50
$37.50
$37.50

Serenity Prayer Girl
#530697
Issued: 1994 • Open
Retail Price: $35 – $37.50

6

VALUES:
$82
$75
$70
$65
$65
$60

Serving The Lord
#100161
Issued: 1986 • Susp.: 1990
Retail Price: $19 – $27.50

7

VALUES:
$65
$58
$52
$48
$45
$42

Serving The Lord
#100293
Issued: 1986 • Susp.: 1990
Retail Price: $19 – $27.50

8

VALUES:
$97
$92
$89
$86
$86
$84
$82
$80
$78
$74

Sew In Love
#106844
Issued: 1988 • Retired: 1997
Retail Price: $45 – $55

9

VALUES:
$82
$50

Sharing Begins In The
Heart (LE-1989)
Special Event Figurine
#520861
Issued: 1989 • Closed: 1989
Retail Price: $25

10

VALUES:
$95
$88
$82

Sharing Our Christmas
Together
#102490
Issued: 1986 • Susp.: 1988
Retail Price: $37 – $45

General Figurines

	Price Paid	Value
1.		
2.		
3.		
4.		
5.		
6.		
7.		
8.		
9.		
10.		

Totals

KEY: NM *Pre-1981* ▲ 1981 Ⅱ 1982 ◄1983 ✝1984 ✿1985 ℐ 1986 ♠ 1987 ✤ 1988 ᚦ 1989 ✦ 1990
🕯 1991 ⚜ 1992 ⁕ 1993 ⌐ 1994 ⚏ 1995 ♡ 1996 ✝ 1997 ୫୬ 1998 ★ 1999 ◔ 2000 UM *Unmarked*

123

General Figurines

1 VALUES: ✝ $35   6ᴈ $35   ★ $35   🕐 $35

Sharing Our Christmas Together
#531944
Issued: 1997 • Open
Retail Price: $35

2 VALUES: ℳ $70   ⚓ $65   ⚓ $63   ⊅ $57 $55 $52

Sharing Our Joy Together
#E2834
Issued: 1986 • Susp.: 1991
Retail Price: $31 – $40

3 VALUES: ➳ $170   ✝ $155   🍃 $148   ℳ $140

Sharing Our Season Together
#E0501
Issued: 1983 • Susp.: 1986
Retail Price: $50

4 VALUES: ★ $119

Sharing Our Time Is So Precious (LE-15,000)
Century Circle Figurine
#456349
Issued: 1999 • Closed: 1999
Retail Price: $110

5 VALUES: ★ $78

Sharing Our Winter Wonderland (LE-1999)
#539988
Issued: 1999 • Closed: 1999
Retail Price: $75

6 VALUES: ꙮ $55   🍽 $48   ⌂ $45   ♡ $45   ✝ $45   6ᴈ $45   ★ $45

Sharing Sweet Moments Together
#526487
Issued: 1994 • Retired: 1999
Retail Price: $45

General Figurines

	Price Paid	Value
1.		
2.		
3.		
4.		
5.		
6.		
7.		
8.		
9.		
10.		
Totals		

7 VALUES: ⌂ $80   ♡ $74   ✝ $70   6ᴈ $70   ★ $70   🕐 $70

Sharing The Gift Of 40 Precious Years
#163821
Issued: 1996 • Open
Retail Price: $70

8 VALUES: ✝ $35   6ᴈ $35   ★ $35   🕐 $35

Sharing The Light Of Love
#272531
Issued: 1997 • Open
Retail Price: $35

9 VALUES: 6ᴈ $20   ★ $20   🕐 $20

Shiny New And Ready For School
Exclusive To Japan
#481637
Issued: 1999 • Open
Retail Price: $20

10 VALUES: 6ᴈ $20   ★ $20   🕐 $20

Shiny New And Ready For School
Exclusive To Japan
#481629
Issued: 1999 • Open
Retail Price: $20

KEY: NM *Pre-1981* ▲ 1981 ▮ 1982 ◄ 1983 ✝ 1984 ✦ 1985 ℳ 1986 ♠ 1987 ✤ 1988 ♄ 1989 ✧ 1990 ♦ 1991 ✦ 1992 ꙮ 1993 ⊷ 1994 ⌂ 1995 ♡ 1996 ✝ 1997 6ᴈ 1998 ★ 1999 🕐 2000 UM *Unmarked*

Value Guide — PRECIOUS MOMENTS®

General Figurines

1

VALUES: ♡ $67 / $67

Shoot For The Stars You'll Never Strike Out
Boys & Girls Clubs Of America Commemorative Figurine
#521701
Issued: 1996 • Closed: 1996
Retail Price: $60

2

VALUES: ⌂ $78 / ♡ $74 / $70 / 6⊃ $70 / ★ $70 / ☾ $70

A Silver Celebration To Share
#163813
Issued: 1996 • Open
Retail Price: $70

3

VALUES: ♠ $70 / ⟡ $62 / Ð $58 / ⚓ $55 / ⚱ $50

Sitting Pretty
#104825
Issued: 1987 • Susp.: 1990
Retail Price: $22.50 – $30

4

VALUES: ℘ $205 / ♠ $190 / ⟡ $170 / Ð $158 / ★ $145 / ⚱ $140

Smile Along The Way
#101842
Issued: 1987 • Retired: 1991
Retail Price: $30 – $45

5

VALUES: NM $114 / ▲ $88 / ✗ $75 / ↩ $72 / † $57

Smile, God Loves You
#E1373B
Issued: 1979 • Retired: 1984
Retail Price: $7 – $17

6

VALUES: ★ $55 / ☾ $55

Snow Man Like My Man
#587877
Issued: 1999 • Open
Retail Price: $55

7

VALUES: ♡ $22 / † $18.50 / 6⊃ $18.50 / ★ $18.50 / ☾ $18.50

Snowbunny Loves You Like I Do
#183792
Issued: 1996 • Open
Retail Price: $18.50

8

VALUES: ✿ $58 / ⛻ $50

So Glad I Picked You As A Friend (LE-1994)
Catalog Figurine
#524379
Issued: 1994 • Closed: 1994
Retail Price: $40

9

VALUES: ♡ $40 / † $40 / 6⊃ $40 / ★ $40 / ☾ $40

Some Plant, Some Water, But God Giveth The Increase
Growing In God's Garden Of Love Series
#176958
Issued: 1996 • Open
Retail Price: $37.50 – $40

10

VALUES: ⟡ $86 / Ð $80 / ⚓ $80 / ⚱ $77 / ⸸ $70

Someday My Love
#520799
Issued: 1989 • Retired: 1992
Retail Price: $40 – $45

General Figurines

	Price Paid	Value
1.		
2.		
3.		
4.		
5.		
6.		
7.		
8.		
9.		
10.		
Totals		

KEY: NM *Pre-1981* ▲ 1981 ✗ 1982 ◄ 1983 † 1984 ✦ 1985 ℘ 1986 ♠ 1987 ⟡ 1988 Ð 1989 ⚓ 1990 ⚱ 1991 ⛻ 1992 ✿ 1993 ⌐ 1994 ⌂ 1995 ♡ 1996 † 1997 6⊃ 1998 ★ 1999 ☾ 2000 UM *Unmarked*

1

VALUES: ♡ $55
† $55
6ð $55
★ $55
ⓞ $55

**Something Precious
From Above**
#524360
Issued: 1997 • Open
Retail Price: $50 – $55

2

VALUES: ✣ $85
Ð $80
♨ $75
⬧ $70

**Something's Missing When
You're Not Around**
#105643
Issued: 1988 • Susp.: 1991
Retail Price: $32.50 – $37.50

3

VALUES: ♡ $55
† $50
6ð $50
★ $50
ⓞ $50

**Sometimes You're Next
To Impossible**
#530964
Issued: 1997 • Open
Retail Price: $50

4

VALUES: △ $42
♡ $38
† $35
6ð $35
★ $35

**Soot Yourself To A
Merry Christmas**
#150096
Issued: 1995 • Retired: 1999
Retail Price: $35

5

VALUES: △ $45
♡ $40
† $37.50
6ð $37.50
★ $37.50
ⓞ $37.50

Sowing Seeds Of Kindness
*Growing In God's
Garden Of Love Series*
#163856
Issued: 1996 • Open
Retail Price: $37.50

6

VALUES: ♀ $56
✣ $52
△ $48
♡ $48

A Special Chime For Jesus
#524468
Issued: 1993 • Retired: 1997
Retail Price: $32.50 – $35

General Figurines

	Price Paid	Value
1.		
2.		
3.		
4.		
5.		
6.		
7.		
8.		
9.		
10.		
Totals		

7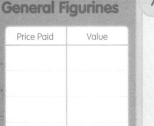

VALUES: ♦ $42
♠ $40
♀ $35
⬒ $33
△ $33
♡ $32.50
† $32.50
6ð $32.50
★ $32.50
ⓞ $32.50

A Special Delivery
#521493
Issued: 1991 • Open
Retail Price: $30 – $32.50

8

VALUES: ▲ $90
✣ $85
Ð $80
♨ $75
⬧ $70

**The Spirit Is Willing, But
The Flesh Is Weak**
#100196
Issued: 1987 • Retired: 1991
Retail Price: $19 – $30

9

VALUES: △ $47
♡ $40

**Standing In The Presence
Of The Lord (Dated 1996)**
The Dated Cross Series
#163732
Issued: 1996 • Closed: 1996
Retail Price: $37.50

10

VALUES: ✦ $65
♫ $56
▲ $53
✣ $53
Ð $52
♨ $52
♀ $47
♠ $47

The Story Of God's Love
Family Christmas Series
#15784
Issued: 1985 • Susp.: 1992
Retail Price: $22.50 – $35

KEY: NM *Pre-1981* ▲1981 ✖1982 ◀1983 † 1984 ⬧1985 ♫ 1986 ▲ 1987 ✣ 1988 Ð 1989 ♨ 1990 ♦ 1991 ♠ 1992 ♀ 1993 ⬒ 1994 △ 1995 ♡ 1996 † 1997 6ð 1998 ★ 1999 ⓞ 2000 UM *Unmarked*

Value Guide — PRECIOUS MOMENTS®

1

VALUES: ✝ $115
🐦 $100

Summer's Joy (LE-1985)
*The Four Seasons
Figurine Series*
#12076
Issued: 1985 • Closed: 1985
Retail Price: $30

2

VALUES: △ $42
♡ $40
✝ $37.50
∞ $37.50
★ $37.50

The Sun Is Always
Shining Somewhere
#163775
Issued: 1996 • Retired: 1999
Retail Price: $37.50

3

VALUES: ➤ $92
✝ $88
🐦 $85
♫ $83
♠ $78
✦ $78
Ꝺ $75

Surrounded With Joy
#E0506
Issued: 1983 • Retired: 1989
Retail Price: $21 – $27.50

4

VALUES: Ꝺ $139
★ $88
♦ $78
♀ $65
♀ $60
🍴 $60
△ $55
♡ $55

Sweep All Your
Worries Away
#521779
Issued: 1990 • Retired: 1996
Retail Price: $40

5

VALUES: ♡ $68
✝ $63
∞ $63

Sweeter As The Years
Go By
#522333
Issued: 1996 • Retired: 1998
Retail Price: $60

6

VALUES: ♦ $82
♦ $77
♀ $73
🍴 $67

Take Heed When You Stand
#521272
Issued: 1991 • Susp.: 1994
Retail Price: $55

7

VALUES: △ $38
♡ $33
✝ $30
∞ $30
★ $30
🕐 $30

Take It To The Lord
In Prayer
#163767
Issued: 1996 • Open
Retail Price: $30

8

VALUES: ★ $41

Take Time To Smell The
Roses (LE-1999)
Carlton Cards Exclusive
#634980C
Issued: 1999 • Closed: 1999
Retail Price: $35

9

VALUES: ➤ $83
✝ $77
🐦 $73
♫ $70

Taste And See That The
Lord Is Good
#E9274
Issued: 1983 • Retired: 1986
Retail Price: $22.50

10

VALUES: Ꝺ $63
♦ $50
★ $47
♀ $43
♀ $42
🍴 $40
△ $40
♡ $40
✝ $40
∞ $40
★ $40
🕐 $40

Tell It To Jesus
#521477
Issued: 1989 • Open
Retail Price: $35 – $40

General Figurines

	Price Paid	Value
1.		
2.		
3.		
4.		
5.		
6.		
7.		
8.		
9.		
10.		

Totals

KEY: NM *Pre*-1981 ▲1981 ✠1982 ◀1983 ✝1984 🐦1985 ♫1986 ♠1987 ✦1988 Ꝺ1989 ★1990 ♦1991 ♀1992 ♀1993 🍴1994 △1995 ♡1996 ✝1997 ∞1998 ★1999 🕐2000 UM *Unmarked*

127

Value Guide — PRECIOUS MOMENTS®

General Figurines

1
VALUES: 🐛 $42
🎋 $35
⚜ $35
⚓ $32
🔱 $30
⚖ $30
🔔 $27
🕯 $25

Tell Me A Story
Family Christmas Series
#15792
Issued: 1985 • Susp.: 1992
Retail Price: $10 – $15

2
VALUES: Ⅱ $130
✝ $112
✝ $107
🐛 $100

Tell Me The Story Of Jesus
#E2349
Issued: 1983 • Susp.: 1985
Retail Price: $30 – $33

3
VALUES: △ $79
♡ $73
✝ $70
👓 $70
★ $70
🕐 $70

Ten Years Heart To Heart
#163805
Issued: 1996 • Open
Retail Price: $70

4
VALUES: NM $170
▲ $145
Ⅱ $130
◀ $122
✝ $115

**Thank You For Coming
To My Ade**
#E5202
Issued: 1981 • Susp.: 1984
Retail Price: $22.50 – $30

5
VALUES: ⅁ $100
🔱 $90
⚖ $87
🕯 $84
🎣 $84

**Thank You, Lord,
For Everything**
#522031
Issued: 1989 • Susp.: 1993
Retail Price: $60

6
VALUES: ★ $25
🕐 $25

Thank You Sew Much
#587923
Issued: 1999 • Open
Retail Price: $25

General Figurines

	Price Paid	Value
1.		
2.		
3.		
4.		
5.		
6.		
7.		
8.		
9.		
10.		
Totals		

7
VALUES: Ⅱ $65
🔱 $52
✝ $48

Thanking Him For You
#E7155
Issued: 1982 • Susp.: 1984
Retail Price: $16 – $17

8
VALUES: 🔱 $63
⚖ $56
🕯 $54
🎣 $52
🍞 $50
△ $50
♡ $50
✝ $50
👓 $50
★ $50
🕐 $50

That's What Friends Are For
#521183
Issued: 1990 • Open
Retail Price: $45 – $50

9
VALUES: NM $164
▲ $110
Ⅱ $90
◀ $85
✝ $82
🐛 $82
🎋 $78
⚜ $78
⚓ $75
⅁ $73
🔱 $73
⚖ $70
🕯 $70
🎣 $68
🍞 $68

Thee I Love
#E3116
Issued: 1980 • Retired: 1994
Retail Price: $16.50 – $40

10
VALUES: ✝ $18
👓 $15
★ $15
🕐 $15

**There Are Two Sides
To Every Story**
#325368
Issued: 1998 • Open
Retail Price: $15

KEY: NM *Pre*-1981 ▲ 1981 Ⅱ 1982 ◀ 1983 ✝ 1984 🐛 1985 🎋 1986 ⚜ 1987 ⚓ 1988 ⅁ 1989 🔱 1990 ⚖ 1991 🕯 1992 🎣 1993 🍞 1994 △ 1995 ♡ 1996 ✝ 1997 👓 1998 ★ 1999 🕐 2000 UM *Unmarked*

Value Guide — PRECIOUS MOMENTS®

1

VALUES:
- ✠ $76
- † $63
- ✝ $60
- ✿ $56
- ✢ $54

There Is Joy In Serving Jesus
#E7157
Issued: 1982 • Retired: 1986
Retail Price: $17 – $19

2

VALUES:
- ✿ $44
- ✾ $37
- ✠ $33
- ⟁ $32
- † $32
- ✝ $32
- ∽ $32

There Is No Greater Treasure Than To Have A Friend Like You
#521000
Issued: 1993 • Retired: 1998
Retail Price: $30

3

VALUES:
- ⊕ $88
- ✦ $82
- ✜ $78
- ✿ $78
- ✎ $75
- ✎ $72
- ✝ $72
- ♡ $70
- † $70
- ∽ $70
- ★ $70

There Shall Be Showers Of Blessings
#522090
Issued: 1990 • Retired: 1999
Retail Price: $60 – $70

4

VALUES:
- ✦ $90
- ✜ $85
- ✿ $82
- ✾ $80
- ⟁ $77
- ♡ $75
- ♡ $72

There's A Light At The End Of The Tunnel
#521485
Issued: 1991 • Susp.: 1996
Retail Price: $55 – $60

5

VALUES:
- ✿ $60
- ✎ $55
- ✦ $53
- ✜ $53
- ⊕ $50
- ✦ $50

There's A Song In My Heart
Rejoice In The Lord Band Series
#12173
Issued: 1985 • Susp.: 1990
Retail Price: $11 – $16.50

6

VALUES:
- ⊕ $65
- ✦ $54
- ✜ $50
- ✿ $48
- ✾ $44
- ✎ $44
- ⟁ $42
- ♡ $42

Thinking Of You Is What I Really Like To Do
#522287
Issued: 1990 • Susp.: 1996
Retail Price: $30 – $32.50

7

VALUES:
- ⊕ $49
- ✦ $42
- ✜ $38
- ✿ $37
- ✾ $37
- ⟁ $35
- ⟁ $35
- † $35
- ∽ $35
- ★ $35
- ✦ $35

This Day Has Been Made In Heaven
#523496
Issued: 1990 • Open
Retail Price: $30 – $35

8

VALUES:
- ★ $30
- ○ $30

New!

This Day Has Been Made In Heaven
#679852
Issued: 2000 • Open
Retail Price: $30

9

VALUES:
- ✎ $105
- ✦ $76
- ✜ $74
- ⊕ $70
- ✦ $64

This Is The Day Which The Lord Has Made
#12157
Issued: 1987 • Susp.: 1990
Retail Price: $20 – $30

General Figurines

	Price Paid	Value
1.		
2.		
3.		
4.		
5.		
6.		
7.		
8.		
9.		
Totals		

KEY: NM *Pre-1981* ▲ *1981* ✠ *1982* ◄ *1983* † *1984* ✿ *1985* ✎ *1986* ✦ *1987* ✜ *1988* ⊕ *1989* ✦ *1990* ✦ *1991* ✾ *1992* ✾ *1993* ✎ *1994* ⟁ *1995* ♡ *1996* † *1997* ∽ *1998* ★ *1999* ○ *2000* UM *Unmarked*

Value Guide — PRECIOUS MOMENTS®

1 VALUES: ♠ $227

This Is The Day Which The Lord Hath Made (LE-1987)
Bridal Party Series
#E2838
Issued: 1987 • Closed: 1987
Retail Price: $185

2 VALUES: ✝ $113 / ✿ $105 / ✈ $97 / ♠ $95 / ⚓ $90

This Is Your Day To Shine
#E2822
Issued: 1984 • Retired: 1988
Retail Price: $37.50 – $40

3 VALUES: ♪ $43

This Land Is Our Land (LE-1992)
#527777
Issued: 1992 • Closed: 1992
Retail Price: $35

4 VALUES: ♠ $47 / ⚘ $42 / ★ $40 / ♥ $37 / ♪ $35 / ♫ $33 / ⊟ $32 / ⚑ $32 / △ $30 / ✝ $30 / ೲ $30 / ★ $30

This Too Shall Pass
#114014
Issued: 1988 • Retired: 1999
Retail Price: $23 – $30

5 VALUES: NM $98 / ⚔ $74 / ✕ $62 / ☜ $57 / ✝ $55 / ✿ $51 / ✈ $50 / ♠ $47 / ♦ $47 / ★ $45 / ♥ $43 / ♪ $43 / ♫ $42 / ⚑ $42 / ⊟ $40 / ♡ $40 / ✝ $40 / ೲ $40 / ★ $40 / ☉ $40

Thou Art Mine
#E3113
Issued: 1980 • Open
Retail Price: $16 – $40

6 VALUES: ♪ $90 / ♫ $80 / ♪ $77 / ೲ $73 / △ $70 / ♡ $70

Thumb-body Loves You
#521698
Issued: 1991 • Susp.: 1996
Retail Price: $55 – $60

7 VALUES: ೲ $66 / △ $57 / ⚑ $55 / ♡ $53

Tied Up For The Holidays
#527580
Issued: 1993 • Susp.: 1996
Retail Price: $40 – $45

8 VALUES: ೲ $35 / ★ $35 / ☉ $35

Time For A Holy Holiday
#455849
Issued: 1998 • Open
Retail Price: $35

9 VALUES: ♦ $52 / ♪ $45 / ♫ $42 / ೲ $42 / ⚑ $40 / △ $40 / ♡ $40 / ✝ $40 / ೲ $40 / ★ $40 / ☉ $40

Time Heals
#523739
Issued: 1990 • Open
Retail Price: $37.50 – $40

10 VALUES: ♦ $66 / ⚘ $62 / ★ $57 / ♪ $54 / ♫ $50 / ೲ $47 / ⚑ $47 / △ $45 / ♡ $45

'Tis The Season
#111163
Issued: 1988 • Susp.: 1996
Retail Price: $27.50 – $35

General Figurines

	Price Paid	Value
1.		
2.		
3.		
4.		
5.		
6.		
7.		
8.		
9.		
10.		
Totals		

KEY: NM *Pre-1981* ▲1981 ✕1982 ◄1983 ✝1984 ✿1985 ♪1986 ♠1987 ♦1988 ⚘1989 ★1990 ♦1991 ♪1992 ೲ1993 ☜1994 △1995 ♡1996 ✝1997 ೲ1998 ★1999 ☉2000 UM *Unmarked*

Value Guide — PRECIOUS MOMENTS®

1

VALUES: NM $75
$62
$52
$47
$45
$43
$42
$42
$42
$40
$39
$37
$37
$37
$37
$37
$37
$37

To A Special Dad
#E5212
Issued: 1981 • Susp.: 1998
Retail Price: $20 – $35

2

VALUES: $52
$45
$40
$40
$36
$35
$35
$35
$35
$35

To A Special Mum
#521965
Issued: 1991 • Retired: 1999
Retail Price: $30 – $35

3
VALUES: $62
$57
$52
$50
$48
$47
$47
$43
$42
$42
$40
$40
$40
$40
$40
$40

**To A Very
Special Mom**
#E2824
Issued: 1984 • Open
Retail Price: $27.50 – $40

4
VALUES: $57
$53
$50

**To A Very Special
Mom And Dad**
#521434
Issued: 1991 • Susp.: 1993
Retail Price: $35

5

VALUES: $82
$66
$62
$60
$60
$60
$58
$55
$55
$52
$52
$50
$50
$50
$50
$50

**To A Very
Special Sister**
#E2825
Issued: 1984 • Open
Retail Price: $37.50 – $50

6

VALUES: $70
$65
$65
$65
$65
$65
$65

To A Very Special Sister
#528633
Issued: 1994 • Open
Retail Price: $60 – $65

7
VALUES: $135
$100
$94
$90
$85

To God Be The Glory
#E2823
Issued: 1984 • Susp.: 1987
Retail Price: $40 – $45

8
VALUES: $105
$74
$65
$62
$56
$54
$52
$52
$50
$50
$50
$50
$50
$50

To My Deer Friend
#100048
Issued: 1987 • Open
Retail Price: $33 – $50

9

VALUES: $90
$75
$70
$65

To My Favorite Paw
#100021
Issued: 1986 • Susp.: 1988
Retail Price: $22.50 – $27

10
VALUES: $120
$75
$68
$62
$60
$58
$58
$57
$55
$55
$55
$55
$55
$55
$55
$55

To My Forever Friend
#100072
Issued: 1986 • Open
Retail Price: $33 – $55

General Figurines

	Price Paid	Value
1.		
2.		
3.		
4.		
5.		
6.		
7.		
8.		
9.		
10.		

Totals

KEY: NM *Pre-1981* ▲ 1981 ▮ 1982 ◀ 1983 † 1984 ✿ 1985 ♪ 1986 ♣ 1987 ✧ 1988 ♏ 1989 ★ 1990 ♦ 1991 ✦ 1992 ✪ 1993 ⊐ 1994 △ 1995 ♡ 1996 † 1997 ◔ 1998 ★ 1999 ◐ 2000 UM *Unmarked*

131

General Figurines

1
VALUES: ✕ $47
⸸ $43
✝ $43
⚓ $40
⚓ $37
⚓ $37
⚓ $33
⚓ $33
⚓ $32
ᵁᴹ $45

To Some Bunny Special
#E9282A
Issued: 1983 • Susp.: 1990
Retail Price: $8 – $13.50

2
VALUES: ⚓ $245
⚓ $237
⚓ $225
⚓ $218

**To Tell The Tooth,
You're Special**
#105813
Issued: 1987 • Susp.: 1990
Retail Price: $38.50 – $50

3
VALUES: ⚓ $42
⚓ $38
⚓ $37
♡ $35
⚓ $35
⚓ $35
★ $35

To The Apple Of God's Eye
#522015
Issued: 1993 • Retired: 1999
Retail Price: $32.50 – $35

4
VALUES: NM $97
⚓ $83
✕ $74
✝ $72
⚓ $72
⚓ $62
⚓ $62

To Thee With Love
#E3120
Issued: 1980 • Susp.: 1986
Retail Price: $13 – $19

5
VALUES: ✝ $88
⚓ $82
⚓ $77
⚓ $72
⚓ $67

Trust In The Lord
#E9289
Issued: 1983 • Susp.: 1987
Retail Price: $20 – $23

6
VALUES: ⚓ $44
⚓ $42
⚓ $40
⚓ $38
⚓ $36
⚓ $35
⚓ $34
⚓ $34
⚓ $34
♡ $34
✝ $34
★ $34

A Tub Full Of Love
#104817
Issued: 1987 • Susp.: 1998
Retail Price: $22.50 – $32.50

General Figurines

	Price Paid	Value
1.		
2.		
3.		
4.		
5.		
6.		
7.		
8.		
9.		
10.		

Totals

7
VALUES: ⚓ $46
⚓ $42
⚓ $40
⚓ $38
⚓ $36
⚓ $35
⚓ $34
⚓ $32.50
⚓ $32.50
♡ $32.50
✝ $32.50
⚓ $32.50
★ $32.50
⚓ $32.50

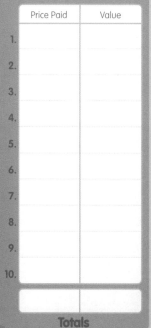

A Tub Full Of Love
#112313
Issued: 1987 • Open
Retail Price: $22.50 – $32.50

8
VALUES: ✝ $65
⚓ $65

**Twenty Years And The
Vision's Still The Same
(LE-1998)**
*20th Anniversary
Commemorative Figurine*
#306843
Issued: 1998 • Closed: 1998
Retail Price: $55

9
VALUES: ⚓ $47

**Under His Wings I Am
Safely Abiding (Dated 1998)**
The Dated Cross Series
#306835
Issued: 1998 • Closed: 1998
Retail Price: $40

10
VALUES: NM $140
⚓ $110
✕ $110
⚓ $105
✝ $100

Unto Us A Child Is Born
#E2013
Issued: 1979 • Susp.: 1984
Retail Price: $12 – $25

KEY: NM *Pre-1981* ▲ *1981* ✕ *1982* ⚓*1983* ✝ *1984* ⚓ *1985* ⚓ *1986* ⚓ *1987* ⚓ *1988* ⚓ *1989* ⚓ *1990* ⚓ *1991* ⚓ *1992* ⚓ *1993* ⚓ *1994* ⚓ *1995* ♡ *1996* ✝ *1997* ⚓ *1998* ★ *1999* ⚓ *2000* ᵁᴹ *Unmarked*

Value Guide — PRECIOUS MOMENTS®

1

VALUES: 🐦 $42 / 🔺 $37 / ♡ $35 / ✝ $35 / 👓 $35 / ★ $35 / 🕐 $35

Vaya Con Dios
#531146
Issued: 1995 • Open
Retail Price: $32.50 – $35

2

VALUES: 👓 $70 / ★ $70 / 🕐 $70

A Very Special Bond
#488240
Issued: 1999 • Open
Retail Price: $70

3

VALUES: ✝ $300 / 🐦 $280

The Voice Of Spring
(LE-1985)
The Four Seasons
Figurine Series
#12068
Issued: 1985 • Closed: 1985
Retail Price: $30

4

VALUES: ✝ $113 / $106 / 🎵 $102 / 🔺 $99 / ✤ $93 / 🔔 $90

Waddle I Do Without You
The Clown Series
#12459
Issued: 1985 • Retired: 1989
Retail Price: $30 – $40

5

VALUES: 🔺 $42 / ♡ $35 / ✝ $35 / 👓 $35 / ★ $35 / 🕐 $35

Walk In The Sonshine
#524212
Issued: 1995 • Open
Retail Price: $35

6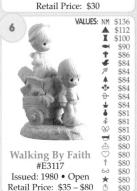

VALUES: NM $136 / $112 / 🕮 $100 / ✦ $90 / ✝ $86 / 🎵 $84 / 🔺 $84 / ✤ $84 / 🔔 $84 / ♦ $84 / 🔔 $81 / ♦ $81 / ✿ $81 / 🐦 $80 / ♡ $80 / ✝ $80 / 👓 $80 / ★ $80 / 🕐 $80

Walking By Faith
#E3117
Issued: 1980 • Open
Retail Price: $35 – $80

7

VALUES: ★ $50 / 🕐 $50

Warmest Wishes For The Holidays
#455830
Issued: 1999 • Open
Retail Price: $50

8

VALUES: ✝ $40 / 👓 $35 / ★ $35 / 🕐 $35

Water-Melancholy Day Without You
#521515
Issued: 1998 • Open
Retail Price: $35

9

VALUES: ♡ $38 / ✝ $35 / 👓 $35 / ★ $35 / 🕐 $35

We All Have Our Bad Hair Days
#261157
Issued: 1997 • Open
Retail Price: $35

10

VALUES: 🔺 $80

We Are All Precious In His Sight (LE-1987)
#102903
Issued: 1987 • Closed: 1987
Retail Price: $30

General Figurines

	Price Paid	Value
1.		
2.		
3.		
4.		
5.		
6.		
7.		
8.		
9.		
10.		

Totals

General Figurines

KEY: NM *Pre-1981* ▲ 1981 🕮 1982 ◄ 1983 ✝ 1984 ✦ 1985 🎵 1986 🔺 1987 ✤ 1988 🔔 1989 ★ 1990 🔔 1991 ♦ 1992 ✿ 1993 ◄ 1994 🔺 1995 ♡ 1996 ✝ 1997 👓 1998 ★ 1999 🕐 2000 UM *Unmarked*

133

General Figurines

1

VALUES:
- ✕ $63
- ◄ $46
- ✝ $44
- ♫ $42
- ✦ $42
- ⚓ $40
- ✤ $40
- ⊕ $37
- ↓ $37
- ♣ $37
- ⊗ $35
- ♡ $35
- ⊞ $35
- ♡ $35
- ✝ $35
- 🎀 $35
- ★ $35
- ◔ $35

We Are God's Workmanship
#E9258
Issued: 1983 • Open
Retail Price: $19 – 35

2

VALUES: ♦ $240

We Belong To The Lord
Damien-Dutton Figurine
#103004
Issued: 1986 • Closed: 1986
Retail Price: $50

3

VALUES:
- ▲ $340
- ✤ $290
- ⊕ $280
- ↓ $270
- ♣ $265
- ✦ $265
- ♀ $260
- ♀ $260
- △ $255

We Gather Together To Ask The Lord's Blessing (set/6)
#109762
Issued: 1987 • Retired: 1995
Retail Price: $130 – 150

4

New!

VALUES:
- ★ $40
- ◔ $40

We Knead You Grandma
#679844
Issued: 2000 • Open
Retail Price: $40

5

VALUES:
- ✤ $65
- ⊕ $60
- ↓ $58
- ↓ $55

We Need A Good Friend Through The Ruff Times
#520810
Issued: 1989 • Susp.: 1991
Retail Price: $35 – 37.50

6

VALUES:
- ↓ $74
- ↓ $67
- ♣ $62
- ♀ $60
- ⊟ $60
- △ $60
- ♡ $60
- ✝ $60
- 🎀 $60
- ★ $60
- ◔ $60

We're Going To Miss You
#524913
Issued: 1990 • Open
Retail Price: $50 – 60

General Figurines

	Price Paid	Value
1.		
2.		
3.		
4.		
5.		
6.		
7.		
8.		
9.		
10.		
Totals		

7

VALUES:
- ✕ $98
- ◄ $89
- ✝ $85
- ♫ $80
- ♫ $78
- ▲ $76
- ✦ $70
- ⊕ $70
- ↓ $66

We're In It Together
#E9259
Issued: 1983 • Susp.: 1990
Retail Price: $24 – 35

8

VALUES:
- ▲ $85
- ✤ $78
- ⊕ $74
- ↓ $69
- ↓ $67

We're Pulling For You
#106151
Issued: 1987 • Susp.: 1991
Retail Price: $40 – 55

9

VALUES: ♡ $45

We're So Hoppy You're Here (LE-1997)
Special Event Figurine
#261351
Issued: 1997 • Closed: 1997
Retail Price: $32.50

10

VALUES:
- ♫ $62
- ✦ $58
- ✤ $53
- ⊕ $50
- ↓ $48
- ↓ $46
- ♣ $40

Wedding Arch
Bridal Party Series
#102369
Issued: 1987 • Susp.: 1992
Retail Price: $22.50 – 30

KEY: NM *Pre-1981* ▲ 1981 ✕ 1982 ◄ 1983 ✝ 1984 ♫ 1985 ♫ 1986 ▲ 1987 ✤ 1988 ⊕ 1989 ↓ 1990 ↓ 1991 ♣ 1992 ♀ 1993 ⊟ 1994 △ 1995 ♡ 1996 ✝ 1997 🎀 1998 ★ 1999 ◔ 2000 UM *Unmarked*

Value Guide — PRECIOUS MOMENTS®

1 VALUES: † $55 6ᴥ $50 ★ $50 ◔ $50

Well, Blow Me Down It's Yer Birthday
#325538
Issued: 1998 • Open
Retail Price: $50

2 VALUES: ◮ $58 ♡ $53 † $50 6ᴥ $50 ★ $50 ◔ $50

What A Difference You've Made In My Life
#531138
Issued: 1996 • Open
Retail Price: $50

3 VALUES: 6ᴥ $30 ★ $30 ◔ $30

What Better To Give Than Yourself
#487988
Issued: 1999 • Open
Retail Price: $30

4 VALUES: ◮ $55 ◔ $50 ♡ $48 † $45 ᴥ $45 ★ $45

What The World Needs Is Love
#531065
Issued: 1995 • Retired: 1999
Retail Price: $45

5 VALUES: ♦ $85 ᴥ $80 ☙ $76 ◮ $73 ◮ $72 ♡ $72

What The World Needs Now
#524352
Issued: 1992 • Retired: 1997
Retail Price: $50

6 VALUES: ♡ $55 † $47 6ᴥ $40 ★ $40 ◔ $40

Who's Gonna Fill Your Shoes
Catalog Early Release
#531634
Issued: 1997 • Open
Retail Price: $37.50 – $40

7 VALUES: † $40 6ᴥ $40 ★ $40 ◔ $40

Who's Gonna Fill Your Shoes
Catalog Early Release
#532061
Issued: 1998 • Open
Retail Price: $37.50 – $40

8 VALUES: ✔ $142 ✔ $128

Winter's Song (LE-1986)
The Four Seasons Figurine Series
#12092
Issued: 1986 • Closed: 1986
Retail Price: $30

9 VALUES: ★ $41

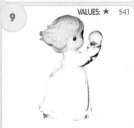

Wishes For The World
Special Event Figurine
#530018
Issued: 1999 • Closed: 1999
Retail Price: $35

General Figurines

	Price Paid	Value
1.		
2.		
3.		
4.		
5.		
6.		
7.		
8.		
9.		
Totals		

KEY: NM *Pre-1981* ▲ 1981 Ⅱ 1982 ◀ 1983 † 1984 ✔ 1985 ✎ 1986 ▲ 1987 ✿ 1988 ✢ 1989 ★ 1990 ♦ 1991 ♣ 1992 ✿ 1993 ✐ 1994 ◮ 1995 ♡ 1996 † 1997 6ᴥ 1998 ★ 1999 ◔ 2000 UM *Unmarked*

135

General Figurines

1

VALUES: ♠ $50
♣ $44
♊ $40
♦ $40
♨ $38
♒ $35
♇ $35
♎ $35
♡ $35
† $35
♋ $35
★ $35

Wishing You A Basket Full Of Blessings
#109924
Issued: 1988 • Retired: 1999
Retail Price: $23 – $35

2

VALUES: ★ $30
♧ $30

New!

PHOTO UNAVAILABLE

Wishing You A Blow Out Birthday (personalized)
#680184
Issued: 2000 • Open
Retail Price: $30

3

VALUES: ♊ $70
♌ $67
♦ $63
♒ $63
♋ $60

Wishing You A Cozy Season
#521949
Issued: 1989 • Susp.: 1993
Retail Price: $42.50 – $50

4

VALUES: ♠ $50
♣ $43
♊ $38
♌ $35
♦ $35
♒ $35
♇ $35
♎ $35
♡ $35
† $35
♋ $35
★ $35

Wishing You A Happy Easter
#109886
Issued: 1988 • Retired: 1999
Retail Price: $23 – $35

5

VALUES: ♒ $52
♇ $48
♎ $47
♨ $45
♡ $45
† $45
♋ $45
★ $45
♧ $45

Wishing You A Ho, Ho, Ho
#527629
Issued: 1992 • Open
Retail Price: $40 – $45

6

VALUES: ♣ $85
♊ $75
♌ $70
♦ $70
♒ $70
♇ $70
♎ $70
♡ $70
† $70
♋ $70
★ $70
♧ $70

Wishing You A Perfect Choice
#520845
Issued: 1989 • Open
Retail Price: $55 – $70

General Figurines	
Price Paid	Value
1.	
2.	
3.	
4.	
5.	
6.	
7.	
8.	
9.	
Totals	

7

VALUES: NM $125
▲ $117
Ⅱ $102
♦ $92
† $89
♥ $84

Wishing You A Season Filled With Joy
#E2805
Issued: 1980 • Retired: 1985
Retail Price: $20 – $27.50

8

VALUES: ♊ $85
♌ $79
♦ $77
♒ $75
♇ $72
♎ $70
♎ $70
♡ $70
† $70
♋ $70
★ $70

Wishing You A Very Successful Season
#522120
Issued: 1989 • Retired: 1999
Retail Price: $60 – $70

9

VALUES: ♠ $72
♣ $68
♊ $64
♌ $60
♦ $58
♒ $56
♇ $54
♎ $54

Wishing You A Yummy Christmas
#109754
Issued: 1987 • Susp.: 1994
Retail Price: $35 – $50

136

Value Guide — PRECIOUS MOMENTS®

1 VALUES: 6ᴅ $30 / ★ $30 / ☾ $30

Wishing You A Yummy Christmas
#455814
Issued: 1998 • Open
Retail Price: $30

2 VALUES: ★ $182

Wishing You An Old Fashioned Christmas
(set/6, LE-1999, with lighted tree)
#534778
Issued: 1999 • Closed: 1999
Retail Price: $175

3 VALUES: ❖ $95 / ❖ $88 / ♣ $86 / ♣ $80 / ● $80 / ✿ $77 / ⌒ $77 / △ $75 / ♡ $75 / † $75 / 6ᴅ $75 / ★ $75 / ☾ $75

Wishing You Roads Of Happiness
#520780
Issued: 1989 • Open
Retail Price: $60 – $75

4 VALUES: ★ $25 / ☾ $25

Witch Way Do You Spell Love?
#587869
Issued: 1999 • Open
Retail Price: $25

5 VALUES: ▲ $83 / ❖ $76 / Ꝺ $73 / ♣ $72 / ● $70 / ✿ $68 / ✦ $67 / ⌒ $65 / △ $65 / ♡ $65 / † $65 / 6ᴅ $65 / ★ $65 / ☾ $65

With This Ring I . . .
#104019
Issued: 1987 • Open
Retail Price: $40 – $65

6 VALUES: △ $80 / ♡ $72 / † $70 / 6ᴅ $70 / ★ $70 / ☾ $70

A Year Of Blessings
#163783
Issued: 1996 • Open
Retail Price: $70

7 VALUES: ★ $60 / ☾ $60

New!

PHOTO UNAVAILABLE

Yes Dear, You Are Always Right
Century Circle Exclusive
#523186
Issued: 2000 • Open
Retail Price: $60

8 VALUES: Ꝺ $58 / ♣ $55 / ● $49 / ✦ $47 / ✿ $47

Yield Not To Temptation
#521310
Issued: 1990 • Susp.: 1993
Retail Price: $27.50 – $30

9 VALUES: 6ᴅ $50 / ★ $50 / ☾ $50

You Always Stand Behind Me
#492140
Issued: 1999 • Open
Retail Price: $50

General Figurines

	Price Paid	Value
1.		
2.		
3.		
4.		
5.		
6.		
7.		
8.		
9.		

Totals

KEY: NM *Pre-1981* ▲ 1981 ❙ 1982 ◄ 1983 † 1984 ✔ 1985 ♪ 1986 ▲ 1987 ❖ 1988 Ꝺ 1989 ✦ 1990 ● 1991 ✿ 1992 ✇ 1993 ⌒ 1994 △ 1995 ♡ 1996 † 1997 6ᴅ 1998 ★ 1999 ☾ 2000 UM *Unmarked*

137

1

VALUES: † $40 · 👓 $40 · ★ $40 · ⏲ $40

You Are Always On My Mind
#306967
Issued: 1998 • Open
Retail Price: $37.50 – $40

2

VALUES: ♡ $55 · † $50 · 👓 $50 · ★ $50 · ⏲ $50

You Are Always There For Me
#163597
Issued: 1997 • Open
Retail Price: $50

3

VALUES: △ $58 · ♡ $55 · † $55 · 👓 $55 · ★ $55 · ⏲ $55

You Are Always There For Me
#163600
Issued: 1996 • Open
Retail Price: $50 – $55

4

VALUES: ♡ $55 · † $55 · 👓 $55 · ★ $55 · ⏲ $55

You Are Always There For Me
#163619
Issued: 1997 • Open
Retail Price: $50 – $55

5

VALUES: △ $59 · ♡ $53 · † $50 · 👓 $50 · ★ $50 · ⏲ $50

You Are Always There For Me
#163627
Issued: 1996 • Open
Retail Price: $50

6

VALUES: ♡ $55 · † $50 · 👓 $50 · ★ $50 · ⏲ $50

You Are Always There For Me
#163635
Issued: 1996 • Open
Retail Price: $50

General Figurines

	Price Paid	Value
1.		
2.		
3.		
4.		
5.		
6.		
7.		
8.		
9.		
Totals		

7

VALUES: (1992) $102 · (1993) $96 · (1994) $92 · △ $87 · ♡ $82

You Are My Favorite Star
#527378
Issued: 1992 • Retired: 1997
Retail Price: $60

8

VALUES: (1991) $76 · (1992) $68

You Are My Happiness (LE-1992)
#526185
Issued: 1992 • Closed: 1992
Retail Price: $37.50

9

VALUES: (1987) $62 · (1988) $57

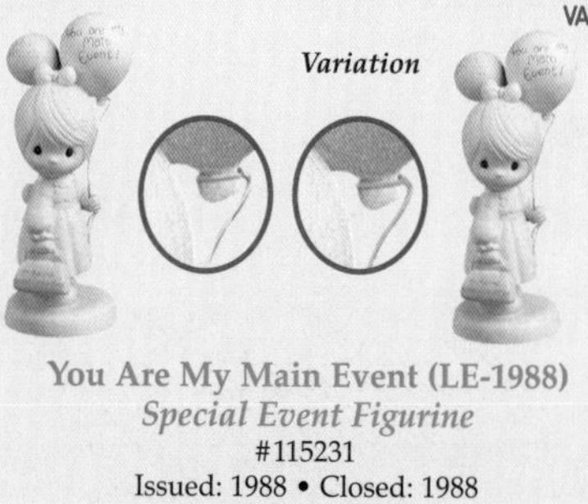

You Are My Main Event (LE-1988)
Special Event Figurine
#115231
Issued: 1988 • Closed: 1988
Retail Price: $30
Variation: Pink strings – $82

KEY: NM *Pre*-1981 · ▲ 1981 · 1982 · 1983 · ✝ 1984 · 1985 · 1986 · 1987 · 1988 · 1989 · 1990 · 1991 · 1992 · 1993 · 1994 · △ 1995 · ♡ 1996 · † 1997 · 👓 1998 · ★ 1999 · ⏲ 2000 · UM *Unmarked*

1

VALUES:
- ❖ $50
- ✦ $43
- ☆ $40
- 🛒 $38
- 🔔 $36
- ⚘ $36
- 🍶 $36
- ♡ $36
- ✝ $36
- 👓 $36

You Are My Number One
#520829
Issued: 1989 • Susp.: 1998
Retail Price: $25 – $35

2

VALUES:
- ✝ $45
- 👓 $45
- ★ $45
- ☉ $45

You Are My Once In A Lifetime
#531030
Issued: 1998 • Open
Retail Price: $45

3

VALUES:
- ⚘ $50
- ⚘ $42
- 🛒 $38
- ⚘ $37
- ♡ $35
- ✝ $35
- ⚘ $35
- ★ $35
- ☉ $35

You Are Such A Purr-fect Friend
#524395
Issued: 1993 • Open
Retail Price: $35

4

VALUES:
- 🔔 $60
- ⚘ $52
- ⚘ $48
- 🛒 $45
- ♡ $45
- ✝ $45
- ⚘ $45
- ⚘ $45
- ★ $45
- ☉ $45

You Are The Type I Love
#523542
Issued: 1992 • Open
Retail Price: $40 – $45

5

VALUES:
- ⚓ $58
- 🔔 $48

You Can Always Bring A Friend (LE-1991)
Special Event Figurine
#527122
Issued: 1991 • Closed: 1991
Retail Price: $27.50

6

VALUES:
- 👓 $35
- ★ $35
- ☉ $35

You Can Always Count On Me
#487953
Issued: 1999 • Open
Retail Price: $35

7

VALUES:
- ✦ $35
- ★ $35
- ☉ $35

You Can Always Fudge A Little During The Season
#455792
Issued: 1998 • Open
Retail Price: $35

8

VALUES:
- ♫ $75
- ★ $68
- ⚓ $64

You Can Fly
#12335
Issued: 1986 • Susp.: 1988
Retail Price: $25 – $30

General Figurines

	Price Paid	Value
1.		
2.		
3.		
4.		
5.		
6.		
7.		
8.		
9.		
Totals		

9

VALUES:
- ✕ $174
- ◀ $115
- ✝ $102
- ✦ $93
- ♫ $92
- ▲ $90
- ❖ $88
- ⊕ $85

You Can't Run Away From God
#E0525
Issued: 1983 • Retired: 1989
Retail Price: $28.50 – $38.50

General Figurines

1

VALUES: 👓 $25
★ $25
🕐 $25

You Can't Take It With You
#488321
Issued: 1999 • Open
Retail Price: $25

2

VALUES: ★ $30

You Color Our World With Loving Caring And Sharing
10th Anniversary Chapel Commemorative Figurine
#644463
Issued: 1999 • Closed: 1999
Retail Price: $19 – $30

3

VALUES: ★ $37.50
🕐 $37.50

New!

You Complete My Heart
#681067
Issued: 2000 • Open
Retail Price: $37.50

4

VALUES: 👓 $25
★ $25
🕐 $25

You Count
#488372
Issued: 1999 • Open
Retail Price: $25

5

VALUES: △ $65
♡ $58
† $58
👓 $58

You Deserve A Halo – Thank You
#531693
Issued: 1996 • Retired: 1998
Retail Price: $55

6

VALUES: 🐚 $47
🐟 $44
🍴 $42
△ $37.50
♡ $37.50
† $37.50
👓 $37.50
★ $37.50
🕐 $37.50

You Deserve An Ovation
#520578
Issued: 1992 • Open
Retail Price: $35 – $37.50

7

VALUES: 👓 $42

You Have Mastered The Art Of Caring
Catalog Early Release
#456276
Issued: 1998 • Closed: 1998
Retail Price: $40

8

VALUES: ★ $25
🕐 $25

New!

You Have The Sweetest Heart
#689548
Issued: 2000 • Open
Retail Price: $25

9

VALUES: 🐟 $83
† $73
🦋 $66
🐟 $63
▲ $60
⚜ $60
🔱 $56
★ $56
🍾 $54
⚓ $54
🍴 $52
△ $50
♡ $50
♡ $47

You Have Touched So Many Hearts
#E2821
Issued: 1984 • Susp.: 1996
Retail Price: $25 – $37.50

General Figurines

	Price Paid	Value
1.		
2.		
3.		
4.		
5.		
6.		
7.		
8.		
9.		

Totals

KEY: NM *Pre-1981* ▲ 1981 ✕ 1982 ◀ 1983 † 1984 🍃 1985 ♪ 1986 ♠ 1987 ⚜ 1988 ⊕ 1989 ★ 1990
🍷 1991 ⚜ 1992 ♀ 1993 🐟 1994 △ 1995 ♡ 1996 † 1997 👓 1998 ★ 1999 🕐 2000 UM *Unmarked*

Value Guide — PRECIOUS MOMENTS®

1

VALUES: ♡ $40
　　　　 † $40
　　　　 6∂ $40
　　　　 ★ $40
　　　　 ◷ $40

You Have Touched So Many Hearts
#261084
Issued: 1997 • Open
Retail Price: $37.50 – $40

2

VALUES: ♦ $42
　　　　 ⚘ $40
　　　　 ⚘ $40
　　　　 ⊟ $39
　　　　 ⚖ $39
　　　　 ♡ $39

You Have Touched So Many Hearts (personalized)
#527661
Issued: 1992 • Susp.: 1996
Retail Price: $35 – $37.50

3

VALUES: 6∂ $35
　　　　 ★ $35
　　　　 ◷ $35

You Just Can't Replace A Good Friendship
#488054
Issued: 1999 • Open
Retail Price: $35

4

VALUES: 6∂ $35

You Make Such A Lovely Pair
Catalog Figurine
#531588
Issued: 1998 • Closed: 1998
Retail Price: $32.50

5

VALUES: ★ $38

You Oughta Be In Pictures
Special Event Figurine
#490327
Issued: 1999 • Closed: 1999
Retail Price: $32.50

6

VALUES: ⊟ $40
　　　　 ◇ $38
　　　　 ♡ $35
　　　　 † $35
　　　　 6∂ $35
　　　　 ★ $35

You Suit Me To A Tee
#526193
Issued: 1994 • Retired: 1999
Retail Price: $35

7

VALUES: ⚖ $50

You Will Always Be Our Hero (LE-1995)
WWII Commemorative Figurine
#136271
Issued: 1995 • Closed: 1995
Retail Price: $40

8

VALUES: ◇ $38
　　　　 † $35
　　　　 6∂ $35
　　　　 ★ $35
　　　　 ◷ $35

You're A Life Saver To Me
#204854
Issued: 1997 • Open
Retail Price: $35

9

VALUES: † $60
　　　　 6∂ $55
　　　　 ★ $55
　　　　 ◷ $55

You're Just Too Sweet To Be Scary
#183849
Issued: 1997 • Open
Retail Price: $55

General Figurines

	Price Paid	Value
1.		
2.		
3.		
4.		
5.		
6.		
7.		
8.		
9.		
Totals		

KEY: NM *Pre-1981* ▲1981 ∐ 1982 ◄1983 †1984 ⚘1985 ⚘1986 ⚘1987 ⚘1988 ⚘1989 ★1990 ♦1991 ⚘1992 ⚘1993 ⊟1994 ⚖1995 ♡1996 †1997 6∂1998 ★1999 ◷2000 UM *Unmarked*

141

General Figurines

1 VALUES: 6ᕍ $20
★ $20
◐ $20

You're My Honey Bee
#487929
Issued: 1999 • Open
Retail Price: $20

2 VALUES: ❚ $43
✝ $40
✝ $38
✿ $36
✤ $36
♣ $35
♣ $35
♪ $33
♪ $33
UM $50

You're Worth Your Weight In Gold
#E9282B
Issued: 1983 • Susp.: 1990
Retail Price: $8 – $13.50

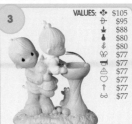

3 VALUES: ✤ $105
♪ $95
★ $88
♣ $80
♣ $80
♡ $77
△ $77
♡ $77
✝ $77
6ᕍ $77

Your Love Is So Uplifting
#520675
Issued: 1989 • Retired: 1998
Retail Price: $60 – $75

4 VALUES: ♡ $110

Your Precious Spirit Comes Shining Through (LE-1996)
Regional Conference Figurine
#212563
Issued: 1996 • Closed: 1996
Retail Price: $30

General Figurines

	Price Paid	Value
1.		
2.		
3.		
4.		
Totals		

KEY: NM *Pre-1981* ▲ 1981 ❚ 1982 ◀ 1983 ✝ 1984 ✦ 1985 ♪ 1986 ♣ 1987 ✤ 1988 ♪ 1989 ★ 1990 ♦ 1991 ♧ 1992 ♀ 1993 ◀ 1994 △ 1995 ♡ 1996 ✝ 1997 6ᕍ 1998 ★ 1999 ◐ 2000 UM *Unmarked*

COUNTRY LANE

The COUNTRY LANE collection made its debut in 1998 and is based on PRECIOUS MOMENTS artist Sam Butcher's fond memories of his Grandma Ethel's farm. Originally consisting of six figurines and one musical piece, the collection now boasts 14 pieces, including "Hay Good Lookin'," the only debut to date for the year 2000.

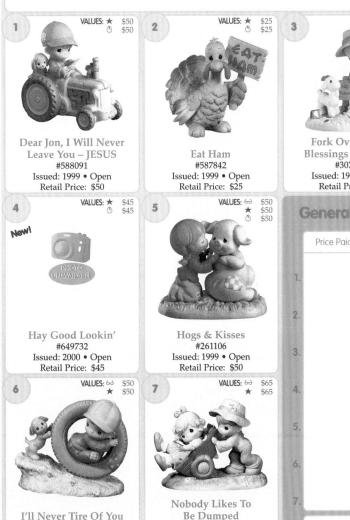

1

VALUES: ★ $50
🕐 $50

Dear Jon, I Will Never Leave You – JESUS
#588091
Issued: 1999 • Open
Retail Price: $50

2

VALUES: ★ $25
🕐 $25

Eat Ham
#587842
Issued: 1999 • Open
Retail Price: $25

3

VALUES: 🔶 $50
★ $50
🕐 $45

Fork Over Those Blessings To Others
#307033
Issued: 1998 • Open
Retail Price: $45

4

VALUES: ★ $45
🕐 $45

New!

Hay Good Lookin'
#649732
Issued: 2000 • Open
Retail Price: $45

5

VALUES: 🔶 $50
★ $50
🕐 $50

Hogs & Kisses
#261106
Issued: 1999 • Open
Retail Price: $50

6

VALUES: 🔶 $50
★ $50

I'll Never Tire Of You
#307068
Issued: 1998 • Retired: 1999
Retail Price: $50

7

VALUES: 🔶 $65
★ $65

Nobody Likes To Be Dumped
#307041
Issued: 1998 • Retired: 1999
Retail Price: $65

General Figurines

Price Paid	Value
1.	
2.	
3.	
4.	
5.	
6.	
7.	

Totals

KEY: NM *Pre-1981* ▲1981 ✕1982 ◄1983 ✝1984 🍂1985 ✒1986 ♦1987 ✤1988 🐝1989 ✚1990 🔥1991 ✤1992 ❀1993 ✂1994 △1995 ♡1996 ✝1997 🔶1998 ★1999 🕐2000 UM *Unmarked*

1 VALUES: 6ᵭ $55
★ $55
Ⓞ $55

Oh Taste And See That The Lord Is Good
#307025
Issued: 1998 • Open
Retail Price: $55

2 VALUES: 6ᵭ $42
★ $42
Ⓞ $35

Peas Pass The Carrots
#307076
Issued: 1998 • Open
Retail Price: $35

3 VALUES: ★ $40
Ⓞ $40

Shear Happiness And Hare Cuts
#539910
Issued: 1999 • Open
Retail Price: $40

4 VALUES: ★ $60
Ⓞ $60

Wishing You A Moo-ie Christmas
#455865
Issued: 1999 • Open
Retail Price: $60

5 VALUES: ★ $55
Ⓞ $55

You Brighten My Field Of Dreams
#587850
Issued: 1999 • Open
Retail Price: $55

6 VALUES: 6ᵭ $45
★ $45
Ⓞ $45

You're Just As Sweet As Pie
#307017
Issued: 1998 • Open
Retail Price: $45

General Figurines

	Price Paid	Value
1.		
2.		
3.		
4.		
5.		
6.		

Musicals

7.		

Totals

7 VALUES: 6ᵭ $270

Bringing In The Sheaves (LE-12,000)
♪ *"Bringing In The Sheaves"*
#307084
Issued: 1998 • Closed: 1998
Retail Price: $90

KEY: NM *Pre-1981* ▲ 1981 Ⅱ 1982 ◄1983 ✝1984 🍃1985 ♫1986 ▲1987 ✿1988 ϑ·1989 ★1990 ♨1991 ⚘1992 ⁹⁹1993 ☜1994 ⚠1995 ♡1996 ⚑1997 6ᵭ1998 ★1999 Ⓞ2000 UM *Unmarked*

LITTLE MOMENTS

Since their debut in 1996, LITTLE MOMENTS, a collection of smaller-sized PRECIOUS MOMENTS figurines, has grown to include 63 pieces. While many of the pieces are from the general line, several belong to the five series in the collection. So far, for the year 2000, there have been three new introductions, all of which belong to the *Bible Stories* series which was initially released in 1999.

1 VALUES: UM $25 New!

Baby Moses
#649953
Issued: 2000 • Open
Retail Price: $25

2 VALUES: UM $25

Daniel And The Lion's Den
#488291
Issued: 1999 • Open
Retail Price: $25

3 VALUES: UM $25 New!

The Good Samaritan
#649988
Issued: 2000 • Open
Retail Price: $25

4 VALUES: UM $20 New!

The Great Pearl
#649996
Issued: 2000 • Open
Retail Price: $20

5 VALUES: UM $25

Jonah And The Whale
#488283
Issued: 1999 • Open
Retail Price: $25

6 VALUES: UM $25

Joseph's Special Coat
#488305
Issued: 1999 • Open
Retail Price: $25

Bible Stories

	Price Paid	Value
1.		
2.		
3.		
4.		
5.		
6.		
Totals		

KEY: NM Pre-1981 ▲1981 Ⅱ1982 ◄1983 ✝1984 ◄1985 ✗1986 ▲1987 ❖1988 ⊕1989 ★1990 ♦1991 ✿1992 ♋1993 ✇1994 △1995 ♡1996 ✝1997 ⬷1998 ★1999 ◐2000 UM Unmarked

145

LITTLE MOMENTS

VALUES: UM $20

1

January
#261203
Issued: 1997 • Open
Retail Price: $20

VALUES: UM $20

2

February
#261246
Issued: 1997 • Open
Retail Price: $20

VALUES: UM $20

3

March
#261270
Issued: 1997 • Open
Retail Price: $20

VALUES: UM $20

4

April
#261300
Issued: 1997 • Open
Retail Price: $20

VALUES: UM $20

5

May
#261211
Issued: 1997 • Open
Retail Price: $20

VALUES: UM $20

6

June
#261254
Issued: 1997 • Open
Retail Price: $20

Birthstone Collection

	Price Paid	Value
1.		
2.		
3.		
4.		
5.		
6.		
7.		
8.		
9.		
10.		
Totals		

VALUES: UM $20

7

July
#261289
Issued: 1997 • Open
Retail Price: $20

VALUES: UM $20

8

August
#261319
Issued: 1997 • Open
Retail Price: $20

VALUES: UM $20

9

September
#261238
Issued: 1997 • Open
Retail Price: $20

VALUES: UM $20

10

October
#261262
Issued: 1997 • Open
Retail Price: $20

KEY: NM *Pre-1981* ▲1981 ▣1982 ◀1983 ✿1984 ✦1985 ✺1986 ♣1987 ✦1988 ✝1989 ✦1990 ♦1991 ✦1992 ✷1993 ✾1994 △1995 ♡1996 ✝1997 ∞1998 ★1999 ○2000 UM *Unmarked*

Value Guide — PRECIOUS MOMENTS®

LITTLE MOMENTS

1 VALUES: UM $20

November
#261297
Issued: 1997 • Open
Retail Price: $20

2 VALUES: UM $20

December
#261327
Issued: 1997 • Open
Retail Price: $20

3 VALUES: UM $20

Cross Walk
#649511
Issued: 1999 • Open
Retail Price: $20

4 VALUES: UM $20

Go For It
#649538
Issued: 1999 • Open
Retail Price: $20

5 VALUES: UM $20

God's Children At Play
#649481
Issued: 1999 • Open
Retail Price: $20

6 VALUES: UM $20

Highway To Happiness
#649457
Issued: 1999 • Open
Retail Price: $20

7 VALUES: UM $20

I'll Never Stop Loving You
#649465
Issued: 1999 • Open
Retail Price: $20

8 VALUES: UM $20

There's No Wrong Way With You
#649473
Issued: 1999 • Open
Retail Price: $20

9 VALUES: UM $20
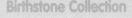
Afri-can Be There For You, I Will Be (Kenya)
#456462
Issued: 1998 • Open
Retail Price: $20

10 VALUES: UM $20

Don't Rome Too Far From Home (Italy)
#456403
Issued: 1998 • Open
Retail Price: $20

Birthstone Collection
	Price Paid	Value
1.		
2.		

Highway To Happiness
3.		
4.		
5.		
6.		
7.		
8.		

International Collection
9.		
10.		

Totals

KEY: NM Pre-1981 ▲1981 ▣1982 ◄1983 ✝1984 ✦1985 ✦1986 ▲1987 ✦1988 ✦1989 ★1990 ●1991 ✦1992 ✿1993 ✦1994 △1995 ♡1996 ✝1997 ✦1998 ★1999 ✪2000 UM Unmarked

147

LITTLE MOMENTS

1  VALUES: UM $20

Hola, Amigo! (Mexico)
#456454
Issued: 1998 • Open
Retail Price: $20

2  VALUES: UM $20

I'd Travel The Highlands To Be With You (Scotland)
#456470
Issued: 1998 • Open
Retail Price: $20

3  VALUES: UM $20

Life Is A Fiesta (Spain)
#456381
Issued: 1998 • Open
Retail Price: $20

4  VALUES: UM $20

Love's Russian Into My Heart (Russia)
#456446
Issued: 1998 • Open
Retail Price: $20

5  VALUES: UM $20

My Love Will Stand Guard Over You (England)
#456934
Issued: 1998 • Open
Retail Price: $20

6  VALUES: UM $20

Our Friendship Is Always In Bloom (Japan)
#456926
Issued: 1998 • Open
Retail Price: $20

7  VALUES: UM $20

Sure Would Love To Squeeze You (Germany)
#456896
Issued: 1998 • Open
Retail Price: $20

8  VALUES: UM $20

You Are A Dutch-ess To Me (Holland)
#456373
Issued: 1998 • Open
Retail Price: $20

9  VALUES: UM $20

You Are My Amour (France)
#456918
Issued: 1998 • Open
Retail Price: $20

10  VALUES: UM $20

You Can't Beat The Red, White And Blue (United States)
#456411
Issued: 1998 • Open
Retail Price: $20

International Collection

	Price Paid	Value
1.		
2.		
3.		
4.		
5.		
6.		
7.		
8.		
9.		
10.		
Totals		

KEY: NM *Pre-1981* ▲ 1981 Ⅱ 1982 ◄ 1983 ✝ 1984 ✔ 1985 ♪ 1986 ▲ 1987 ✤ 1988 ♉ 1989 ✦ 1990 ♣ 1991 ♠ 1992 ♀ 1993 ⚘ 1994 △ 1995 ♡ 1996 ✝ 1997 ∞ 1998 ★ 1999 ◎ 2000 UM *Unmarked*

Value Guide — PRECIOUS MOMENTS®

1 VALUES: UM $20

All Things Grow With Love
#139505
Issued: 1996 • Open
Retail Price: $20

2 VALUES: UM $20

**Birthday Wishes With
Hugs And Kisses**
#139556
Issued: 1996 • Open
Retail Price: $20

3 VALUES: UM $20

Bless Your Little Tutu
261173
Issued: 1997 • Open
Retail Price: $20

4 VALUES: UM $20

**Holiday Wishes, Sweety Pie!
(w/scented potpourri pie)**
#312444
Issued: 1998 • Open
Retail Price: $20

5 VALUES: UM $20

**It's Ruff To Always
Be Cheery**
#272639
Issued: 1997 • Open
Retail Price: $20

6 VALUES: UM $20

**Just The Facts . . .
You're Terrific**
#320668
Issued: 1997 • Open
Retail Price: $20

7 VALUES: UM $20

Loving Is Caring
#320579
Issued: 1997 • Open
Retail Price: $20

8 VALUES: UM $20

Loving Is Caring
#320595
Issued: 1997 • Open
Retail Price: $20

9 VALUES: UM $22

**Soap Bubbles, Soap
Bubbles, All Is Soap
Bubbles**
Avon Figurine
#490342
Issued: 1999 • Closed: 1999
Retail Price: $19.99

10 VALUES: UM $23

PHOTO
UNAVAILABLE

**Thank You For The
Time We Share**
Avon Figurine
#384836 / #070-843
Issued: 1998 • Closed: 1998
Retail Price: $19.99

General Figurines

	Price Paid	Value
1.		
2.		
3.		
4.		
5.		
6.		
7.		
8.		
9.		
10.		

Totals

KEY: NM *Pre-1981* ▲ 1981 ▥ 1982 ◀ 1983 ✦ 1984 ♡ 1985 ✎ 1986 ▲ 1987 ✦ 1988 ♛ 1989 ★ 1990
🍸 1991 ⚘ 1992 ⚘ 1993 ⚐ 1994 △ 1995 ♡ 1996 ♱ 1997 ⚭ 1998 ★ 1999 ◌ 2000 UM *Unmarked*

149

VALUES: UM $25

What Would I Do Without You?
#320714
Issued: 1997 • Open
Retail Price: $25

VALUES: UM $20

Where Would I Be Without You?
#139491
Issued: 1996 • Open
Retail Price: $20

VALUES: UM $25

You Have Such A Special Way Of Caring Each And Every Day
#320706
Issued: 1997 • Open
Retail Price: $25

VALUES: UM $20

You Make My Spirit Soar
#139564
Issued: 1996 • Open
Retail Price: $20

VALUES: UM $20

You Make The World A Sweeter Place
#139521
Issued: 1996 • Open
Retail Price: $20

VALUES: UM $20

You Set My Heart Ablaze
#320625
Issued: 1997 • Open
Retail Price: $20

General Figurines

Price Paid	Value
1.	
2.	
3.	
4.	
5.	
6.	
7.	
8.	
9.	
10.	
Totals	

VALUES: UM $20

You Will Always Be A Winner To Me
#272612
Issued: 1997 • Open
Retail Price: $20

VALUES: UM $20

You Will Always Be A Winner To Me
#283460
Issued: 1997 • Open
Retail Price: $20

VALUES: UM $25

You're Forever In My Heart
#139548
Issued: 1996 • Open
Retail Price: $25

VALUES: UM $25

You're Just Perfect In My Book
#320560
Issued: 1997 • Open
Retail Price: $25

1   VALUES: UM $20

You're The Berry Best
#139513
Issued: 1997 • Open
Retail Price: $20

2   VALUES: UM $20

World's Best Helper
#491608
Issued: 1999 • Open
Retail Price: $20

3   VALUES: UM $20

World's Greatest Student
#491586
Issued: 1999 • Open
Retail Price: $20

4   VALUES: UM $20

World's Greatest Student
#491616
Issued: 1999 • Open
Retail Price: $20

5   VALUES: UM $20

World's Sweetest Girl
#491594
Issued: 1999 • Open
Retail Price: $20

6   VALUES: UM $20

You're No. 1
#491624
Issued: 1999 • Open
Retail Price: $20

7   VALUES: UM $20

You're No. 1
#491640
Issued: 1999 • Open
Retail Price: $20

General Figurines

	Price Paid	Value
1.		

Trophies

2.		
3.		
4.		
5.		
6.		
7.		

Totals

KEY: NM *Pre-1981*   ▲ 1981   ✖ 1982   ◄ 1983   ✝ 1984   ❦ 1985   ✗ 1986   ▲ 1987   ✦ 1988   ✤ 1989   ★ 1990   ♠ 1991   ♣ 1992   ✿ 1993   ✎ 1994   △ 1995   ♡ 1996   ✝ 1997   ♊ 1998   ★ 1999   ◐ 2000   UM *Unmarked*

151

Ornament Series

This section consists of six series, including the popular *Annual Christmas Ornaments*. PRECIOUS MOMENTS ornaments, whether from the series or general line, make the perfect keep-sakes of Christmases past. In addition to the annual ornaments, there are plenty of special pieces that are available year after year, bringing holiday joy to collectors old and new.

1   VALUES: ▲ $255

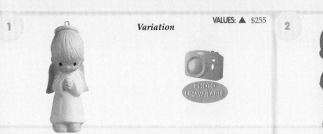

Variation

Let The Heavens Rejoice (Dated 1981)
#E5629
Issued: 1981 • Closed: 1981
Retail Price: $6
Variation: Missing decal – $285

2   VALUES: ✗ $99

I'll Play My Drum For Him (Dated 1982)
#E2359
Issued: 1982 • Closed: 1982
Retail Price: $9

3   VALUES: ◄ $70

Surround Us With Joy (Dated 1983)
#E0513
Issued: 1983 • Closed: 1983
Retail Price: $9

4   VALUES: ✝ $40

Wishing You A Merry Christmas (Dated 1984)
#E5387
Issued: 1984 • Closed: 1984
Retail Price: $10

5   VALUES: ✎ $33

God Sent His Love (Dated 1985)
#15768
Issued: 1985 • Closed: 1985
Retail Price: $10

6   VALUES: ♫ $42

Wishing You A Cozy Christmas (Dated 1986)
#102326
Issued: 1986 • Closed: 1986
Retail Price: $10

Annual Christmas Ornaments

	Price Paid	Value
1.		
2.		
3.		
4.		
5.		
6.		
Totals		

Ornament Series

1 VALUES: 🌲 $47

Love Is The Best Gift Of All (Dated 1987)
#109770
Issued: 1987 • Closed: 1987
Retail Price: $11

2 VALUES: ❖ $50

Time To Wish You A Merry Christmas (Dated 1988)
#115320
Issued: 1988 • Closed: 1988
Retail Price: $13

3 VALUES: ⊕ $35

Oh Holy Night (Dated 1989)
#522848
Issued: 1989 • Closed: 1989
Retail Price: $13.50

4 VALUES: ★ $35

Once Upon A Holy Night (Dated 1990)
#523852
Issued: 1990 • Closed: 1990
Retail Price: $15

5 VALUES: 🌢 $36

May Your Christmas Be Merry (Dated 1991)
#524174
Issued: 1991 • Closed: 1991
Retail Price: $15

6 VALUES: ♪ $46

But The Greatest Of These Is Love (Dated 1992)
#527696
Issued: 1992 • Closed: 1992
Retail Price: $15

7 VALUES: ♋ $40

Wishing You The Sweetest Christmas (Dated 1993)
#530212
Issued: 1993 • Closed: 1993
Retail Price: $15

8 VALUES: ⌐ $35

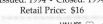

You're As Pretty As A Christmas Tree (Dated 1994)
#530395
Issued: 1994 • Closed: 1994
Retail Price: $16

9 VALUES: △ $35

He Covers The Earth With His Beauty (Dated 1995)
#142662
Issued: 1995 • Closed: 1995
Retail Price: $17

10 VALUES: ♡ $30

Peace On Earth . . . Anyway (Dated 1996)
#183369
Issued: 1996 • Closed: 1996
Retail Price: $18.50

Annual Christmas Ornaments

	Price Paid	Value
1.		
2.		
3.		
4.		
5.		
6.		
7.		
8.		
9.		
10.		
Totals		

KEY: NM *Pre-1981* ▲ 1981 Ⅱ 1982 ◄ 1983 ♈ 1984 ♣ 1985 ♪ 1986 ♠ 1987 ✦ 1988 ⊕ 1989 ★ 1990 ♦ 1991 ♪ 1992 ♋ 1993 ⌐ 1994 △ 1995 ♡ 1996 ♈ 1997 ∽ 1998 ★ 1999 ◐ 2000 UM *Unmarked*

153

Ornament Series

1 — VALUES: † $26

Cane You Join Us For A
Merry Christmas
(Dated 1997)
#272698
Issued: 1997 • Closed: 1997
Retail Price: $18.50

2 — VALUES: 6∂ $20

I'm Sending You A Merry
Christmas (Dated 1998)
#455628
Issued: 1998 • Closed: 1998
Retail Price: $18.50

3 — VALUES: ★ $21

Slide Into The Next
Millennium With Joy
(Dated 1999)
#587788
Issued: 1999 • Closed: 1999
Retail Price: $20

4 — VALUES: ♦ $38
May Your Christmas Be
Merry (set/2, Dated 1991)
The Masterpiece Series
#526940
Issued: 1991 • Closed: 1991
Retail Price: $30

5 — VALUES: ♂ $42
But The Greatest Of These
Is Love (set/2, Dated 1992)
#527734
Issued: 1992 • Closed: 1992
Retail Price: $30

6 — VALUES: ♀ $42
Wishing You The
Sweetest Christmas
(set/2, Dated 1993)
#530190
Issued: 1993 • Closed: 1993
Retail Price: $30

7 — VALUES: ⊷ $44
You're As Pretty As
A Christmas Tree
(set/2, Dated 1994)
#530387
Issued: 1994 • Closed: 1994
Retail Price: $30

8 — VALUES: ⚘ $40
He Covers The Earth
With His Beauty
(set/2, Dated 1995)
#142689
Issued: 1995 • Closed: 1995
Retail Price: $30

9 — VALUES: ♡ $40
Peace On Earth . . . Anyway
(set/2, Dated 1996)
#183350
Issued: 1996 • Closed: 1996
Retail Price: $30

10 — VALUES: † $33

Cane You Join Us For
A Merry Christmas
(set/2, Dated 1997)
#272728
Issued: 1997 • Closed: 1997
Retail Price: $30

Annual Christmas Ornaments

	Price Paid	Value
1.		
2.		
3.		

Annual Christmas Ball Ornaments

	Price Paid	Value
4.		
5.		
6.		
7.		
8.		
9.		
10.		
Totals		

KEY: NM *Pre-1981* ▲ 1981 ◪ 1982 ◁ 1983 † 1984 ◢ 1985 ♪ 1986 ♣ 1987 ✿ 1988 ϑ 1989 ⚘ 1990 ♦ 1991 ♂ 1992 ♀ 1993 ⊷ 1994 ⚘ 1995 ♡ 1996 † 1997 6∂ 1998 ★ 1999 ◌ 2000 UM *Unmarked*

VALUES: ⚞ $188

1

Reindeer (Dated 1986)
#102466
Issued: 1986 • Closed: 1986
Retail Price: $11

VALUES: ⚑ $25

2

Bear The Good News Of Christmas (Dated 1987)
#104515
Issued: 1987 • Closed: 1987
Retail Price: $12.50

VALUES: ⚒ $33

3

Hang On For The Holly Days (Dated 1988)
#520292
Issued: 1988 • Closed: 1988
Retail Price: $13

VALUES: ⚘ $40

4

Christmas Is Ruff Without You (Dated 1989)
#520462
Issued: 1989 • Closed: 1989
Retail Price: $13

VALUES: ⚒ $36

5

Wishing You A Purr-fect Holiday (Dated 1990)
#520497
Issued: 1990 • Closed: 1990
Retail Price: $15

VALUES: ⚲ $35

6

Sno-Bunny Falls For You Like I Do (Dated 1991)
#520438
Issued: 1991 • Closed: 1991
Retail Price: $15

VALUES: ⚵ $25

7

I'm Nuts About You (Dated 1992)
#520411
Issued: 1992 • Closed: 1992
Retail Price: $16

VALUES: ⚖ $29

8

Slow Down And Enjoy The Holidays (Dated 1993)
#520489
Issued: 1993 • Closed: 1993
Retail Price: $16

VALUES: ⚞ $26

9

You Are Always In My Heart (Dated 1994)
#530972
Issued: 1994 • Closed: 1994
Retail Price: $16

VALUES: △ $30

10

Hippo Holly Days (Dated 1995)
#520403
Issued: 1995 • Closed: 1995
Retail Price: $17

Birthday Series Ornaments

	Price Paid	Value
1.		
2.		
3.		
4.		
5.		
6.		
7.		
8.		
9.		
10.		

Totals

KEY: NM Pre-1981 ▲ 1981 ✖ 1982 ◄ 1983 ✝ 1984 ✦ 1985 ⚞ 1986 ⚑ 1987 ⚒ 1988 ⚘ 1989 ⚵ 1990 ⚲ 1991 ⚖ 1992 ⚖ 1993 ⚒ 1994 △ 1995 ♡ 1996 ✝ 1997 ◔ 1998 ★ 1999 ⏾ 2000 UM Unmarked

155

Ornament Series

1 VALUES: ♡ $27

Owl Be Home For Christmas (Dated 1996)
#128708
Issued: 1996 • Closed: 1996
Retail Price: $18.50

2 VALUES: ♱ $25

Slow Down For The Holidays (Dated 1997)
#272760
Issued: 1997 • Closed: 1997
Retail Price: $18.50

3 VALUES: ᴔ $15
★ $15
⏱ $15

May Your Christmas Be Warm (Baby)
#470279
Issued: 1998 • Open
Retail Price: $15

4 VALUES: ᴔ $15
★ $15
⏱ $15

Merry Christmas, Little Lamb (Age 1)
#521078
Issued: 1998 • Open
Retail Price: $15

5 VALUES: ᴔ $15
★ $15
⏱ $15

God Bless You This Christmas (Age 2)
#521094
Issued: 1998 • Open
Retail Price: $15

6 VALUES: ᴔ $15
★ $15
⏱ $15

Heaven Bless Your Special Christmas (Age 3)
#521086
Issued: 1998 • Open
Retail Price: $15

7 VALUES: ᴔ $15
★ $15
⏱ $15

May Your Christmas Be Gigantic (Age 4)
#521108
Issued: 1998 • Open
Retail Price: $15

8 VALUES: ᴔ $15
★ $15
⏱ $15

Christmas Is Something To Roar About (Age 5)
#521116
Issued: 1998 • Open
Retail Price: $15

9 VALUES: ᴔ $15
★ $15
⏱ $15

Christmas Keeps Looking Up (Age 6)
#521124
Issued: 1998 • Open
Retail Price: $15

10 VALUES: UM $12

Always In His Care (Dated 1990)
#225290
Issued: 1990 • Closed: 1990
Retail Price: $8

Birthday Series Ornaments

	Price Paid	Value
1.		
2.		

Birthday Train Series Ornaments

3.		
4.		
5.		
6.		
7.		
8.		
9.		

Easter Seals Commemorative Ornaments

10.		

Totals

KEY: NM *Pre-1981* ▲ 1981 Ⅹ 1982 ◀ 1983 ♱ 1984 ✦ 1985 ♪ 1986 ♣ 1987 ✦ 1988 ♁ 1989 ★ 1990 ❀ 1991 ❀ 1992 ❀ 1993 ☜ 1994 ⚠ 1995 ♡ 1996 ♱ 1997 ᴔ 1998 ★ 1999 ❂ 2000 UM *Unmarked*

1   VALUES: UM $10

Sharing A Gift Of Love
(Dated 1991)
#233196
Issued: 1991 • Closed: 1991
Retail Price: $8

2   VALUES: UM $12

A Universal Love
(Dated 1992)
#238899
Issued: 1992 • Closed: 1992
Retail Price: $8

3   VALUES: UM $12

You're My Number One
Friend (Dated 1993)
#250112
Issued: 1993 • Closed: 1993
Retail Price: $8

4   VALUES: UM $10

It Is No Secret What God
Can Do (Dated 1994)
#244570
Issued: 1994 • Closed: 1994
Retail Price: $6.50

5   VALUES: UM $12

Take Time To Smell The
Roses (Dated 1995)
#128899
Issued: 1995 • Closed: 1995
Retail Price: $7.50

6   VALUES: UM $9

You Can Always Count On
Me (Dated 1996)
#152579
Issued: 1995 • Closed: 1996
Retail Price: $6.50

7   VALUES: UM $9

Give Ability A Chance
(Dated 1997)
#192384
Issued: 1996 • Closed: 1997
Retail Price: $6

8   VALUES: UM $8

Somebody Cares
(Dated 1998)
#272922
Issued: 1997 • Closed: 1998
Retail Price: $6.50

9   VALUES: UM $7

Heaven Bless You Easter
Seal (Dated 1999)
#475076
Issued: 1998 • Closed: 1999
Retail Price: $6.50

Easter Seals Commemorative Ornaments

	Price Paid	Value
1.		
2.		
3.		
4.		
5.		
6.		
7.		
8.		
9.		

Totals

KEY: NM *Pre-1981*   ▲ 1981   Ⅱ 1982   ◄ 1983   ✝ 1984   ✿ 1985   ⚹ 1986   ♣ 1987   ✧ 1988   ⊕ 1989   ★ 1990
  ♦ 1991   ∮ 1992   ♈ 1993   ⊟ 1994   △ 1995   ♡ 1996   ✝ 1997   ↶ 1998   ★ 1999   ◌ 2000   UM *Unmarked*

157

1 VALUES: 6∂ $20 / ★ $20 / ◐ $20

My True Love Gave To Me
1st Day Of Christmas
#455989
Issued: 1998 • Open
Retail Price: $20

2 VALUES: 6∂ $20 / ★ $20 / ◐ $20

We're Two Of A Kind
2nd Day Of Christmas
#455997
Issued: 1998 • Open
Retail Price: $20

3 VALUES: 6∂ $20 / ★ $20 / ◐ $20

Saying "Oui" To Our Love
3rd Day Of Christmas
#456004
Issued: 1998 • Open
Retail Price: $20

4 VALUES: 6∂ $20 / ★ $20 / ◐ $20

Ringing In The Season
4th Day Of Christmas
#456012
Issued: 1998 • Open
Retail Price: $20

5 VALUES: ★ $20 / ◐ $20

The Golden Rings Of Friendship
5th Day Of Christmas
#456020
Issued: 1999 • Open
Retail Price: $20

6 VALUES: ★ $20 / ◐ $20

Hatching The Perfect Holiday
6th Day Of Christmas
#456039
Issued: 1999 • Open
Retail Price: $20

7 VALUES: ★ $20 / ◐ $20

Swimming Into Your Heart
7th Day Of Christmas
#456047
Issued: 1999 • Open
Retail Price: $20

8 VALUES: ★ $20 / ◐ $20

Eight Mice A Milking
8th Day Of Christmas
#456055
Issued: 1999 • Open
Retail Price: $20

Twelve Days Of Christmas Series Ornaments

	Price Paid	Value
1.		
2.		
3.		
4.		
5.		
6.		
7.		
8.		
Totals		

KEY: NM *Pre*-1981 ▲ 1981 ✖ 1982 ◄ 1983 ✝ 1984 ✦ 1985 ♪ 1986 ♠ 1987 ⬧ 1988 ✝ 1989 ✦ 1990 ♣ 1991 ♪ 1992 ♕ 1993 ✇ 1994 △ 1995 ♡ 1996 ✝ 1997 6∂ 1998 ★ 1999 ◐ 2000 UM *Unmarked*

General Ornaments

Since the first ornament introductions in 1981, more than 160 general ornaments have been released. Through the years, many of the ornaments have only been made available as exclusives through special events or select retailers – making them highly coveted. Regardless of how they were made available, PRECIOUS MOMENTS ornaments have proved to be a year round favorite!

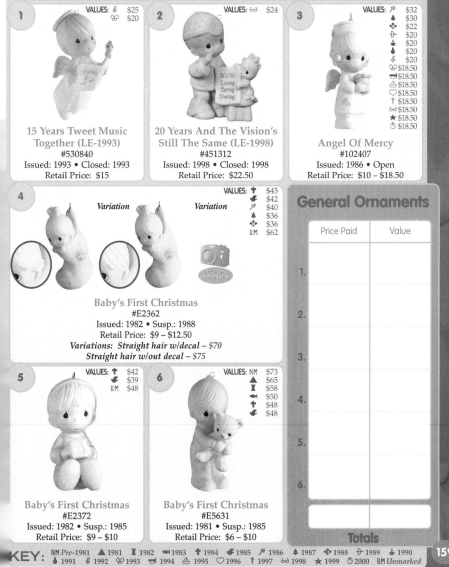

1 VALUES: $25 / $20

15 Years Tweet Music Together (LE-1993)
#530840
Issued: 1993 • Closed: 1993
Retail Price: $15

2 VALUES: $24

20 Years And The Vision's Still The Same (LE-1998)
#451312
Issued: 1998 • Closed: 1998
Retail Price: $22.50

3 VALUES: $32 / $30 / $22 / $20 / $20 / $20 / $20 / $18.50 / $18.50 / $18.50 / $18.50 / $18.50 / $18.50 / $18.50

Angel Of Mercy
#102407
Issued: 1986 • Open
Retail Price: $10 – $18.50

4 VALUES: $45 / $42 / $40 / $36 / $36 / UM $62

Variation *Variation*

Baby's First Christmas
#E2362
Issued: 1982 • Susp.: 1988
Retail Price: $9 – $12.50
Variations: Straight hair w/decal – $70
Straight hair w/out decal – $75

5 VALUES: $42 / $39 / UM $48

Baby's First Christmas
#E2372
Issued: 1982 • Susp.: 1985
Retail Price: $9 – $10

6 VALUES: NM $73 / $65 / $58 / $50 / $48 / $48

Baby's First Christmas
#E5631
Issued: 1981 • Susp.: 1985
Retail Price: $6 – $10

General Ornaments

	Price Paid	Value
1.		
2.		
3.		
4.		
5.		
6.		
Totals		

Value Guide — PRECIOUS MOMENTS®

General Ornaments

1 VALUES: NM $80 / ▲ $70 / Ⅰ $62 / ◀ $57 / ✝ $54 / ✿ $52

Baby's First Christmas
#E5632
Issued: 1981 • Susp.: 1985
Retail Price: $6 – $10

2 VALUES: ✿ $50

**Baby's First Christmas
(Dated 1985)**
#15903
Issued: 1985 • Closed: 1985
Retail Price: $10

3 VALUES: ✿ $45

**Baby's First Christmas
(Dated 1985)**
#15911
Issued: 1985 • Closed: 1985
Retail Price: $10

4 VALUES: ⅍ $30

**Baby's First Christmas
(Dated 1986)**
#102504
Issued: 1986 • Closed: 1986
Retail Price: $10

5 VALUES: ⅍ $30

**Baby's First Christmas
(Dated 1986)**
#102512
Issued: 1986 • Closed: 1986
Retail Price: $10

6 VALUES: ▲ $46

**Baby's First Christmas
(Dated 1987)**
#109401
Issued: 1987 • Closed: 1987
Retail Price: $12

7 VALUES: ▲ $46

**Baby's First Christmas
(Dated 1987)**
#109428
Issued: 1987 • Closed: 1987
Retail Price: $12

8 VALUES: ✤ $26

**Baby's First Christmas
(Dated 1988)**
#115282
Issued: 1988 • Closed: 1988
Retail Price: $15

9 VALUES: ⚓ $28

**Baby's First Christmas
(Dated 1988)**
#520241
Issued: 1988 • Closed: 1988
Retail Price: $15

10 VALUES: ÷ $27

**Baby's First Christmas
(Dated 1989)**
#523194
Issued: 1989 • Closed: 1989
Retail Price: $15

General Ornaments

	Price Paid	Value
1.		
2.		
3.		
4.		
5.		
6.		
7.		
8.		
9.		
10.		
Totals		

KEY: NM *Pre*-1981 ▲1981 Ⅰ1982 ◀1983 ✝1984 ✿1985 ⅍1986 ▲1987 ✤1988 ÷1989 ★1990 ♦1991 ✟1992 ♈1993 ⊟1994 △1995 ♡1996 ↑1997 ∂1998 ★1999 ◐2000 UM *Unmarked*

Value Guide — PRECIOUS MOMENTS®

1 — VALUES: Đ– $32

Baby's First Christmas
(Dated 1989)
#523208
Issued: 1989 • Closed: 1989
Retail Price: $15

2 — VALUES: ★ $32

Baby's First Christmas
(Dated 1990)
#523771
Issued: 1990 • Closed: 1990
Retail Price: $15

3 — VALUES: ★ $28

Baby's First Christmas
(Dated 1990)
#523798
Issued: 1990 • Closed: 1990
Retail Price: $15

4 — VALUES: ♦ $30

Baby's First Christmas
(Dated 1991)
#527084
Issued: 1991 • Closed: 1991
Retail Price: $15

5 — VALUES: ♦ $30

Baby's First Christmas
(Dated 1991)
#527092
Issued: 1991 • Closed: 1991
Retail Price: $15

6 — VALUES: ₤ $30

Baby's First Christmas
(Dated 1992)
#527475
Issued: 1992 • Closed: 1992
Retail Price: $15

7 — VALUES: ₤ $27

Baby's First Christmas
(Dated 1992)
#527483
Issued: 1992 • Closed: 1992
Retail Price: $15

8 — VALUES: ♋ $28

Baby's First Christmas
(Dated 1993)
#530859
Issued: 1993 • Closed: 1993
Retail Price: $15

9 — VALUES: ♋ $30
Baby's First Christmas
(Dated 1993)
#530867
Issued: 1993 • Closed: 1993
Retail Price: $15

10 — VALUES: ⊖ $30

Baby's First Christmas
(Dated 1994)
#530255
Issued: 1994 • Closed: 1994
Retail Price: $16

General Ornaments

	Price Paid	Value
1.		
2.		
3.		
4.		
5.		
6.		
7.		
8.		
9.		
10.		
Totals		

General Ornaments

1 VALUES: 🖐 $30

Baby's First Christmas
(Dated 1994)
#530263
Issued: 1994 • Closed: 1994
Retail Price: $16

2 VALUES: △ $30

Baby's First Christmas
(Dated 1995)
#142719
Issued: 1995 • Closed: 1995
Retail Price: $17.50

3 VALUES: △ $30

Baby's First Christmas
(Dated 1995)
#142727
Issued: 1995 • Closed: 1995
Retail Price: $17.50

4 VALUES: ♡ $26

Baby's First Christmas
(Dated 1996)
#183938
Issued: 1996 • Closed: 1996
Retail Price: $17.50

5 VALUES: ♡ $26

Baby's First Christmas
(Dated 1996)
#183946
Issued: 1996 • Closed: 1996
Retail Price: $17.50

6 VALUES: † $23

Baby's First Christmas
(Dated 1997)
#272744
Issued: 1997 • Closed: 1997
Retail Price: $18.50

7 VALUES: † $23

Baby's First Christmas
(Dated 1997)
#272752
Issued: 1997 • Closed: 1997
Retail Price: $18.50

8 VALUES: 👓 $20

Baby's First Christmas
(Dated 1998)
#455644
Issued: 1998 • Closed: 1998
Retail Price: $18.50

9 VALUES: 👓 $20

Baby's First Christmas
(Dated 1998)
#455652
Issued: 1998 • Closed: 1998
Retail Price: $18.50

10 VALUES: ★ $20

Baby's First Christmas
(Dated 1999)
#587826
Issued: 1999 • Closed: 1999
Retail Price: $18.50

General Ornaments

	Price Paid	Value
1.		
2.		
3.		
4.		
5.		
6.		
7.		
8.		
9.		
10.		
Totals		

KEY: NM *Pre-1981* ▲1981 ▥1982 ◀1983 †1984 ◀1985 ✗1986 ♠1987 ✿1988 ⅃1989 ★1990 ♦1991 ✿1992 ⚇1993 ◅1994 △1995 ♡1996 †1997 👓1998 ★1999 ◯2000 UM *Unmarked*

Value Guide — PRECIOUS MOMENTS®

1 VALUES: ★ $20

**Baby's First Christmas
(Dated 1999)**
#587834
Issued: 1999 • Closed: 1999
Retail Price: $18.50

2 VALUES: ⤢ $44

**Blessed Are The Pure In
Heart (Dated 1983)**
#E0518
Issued: 1983 • Closed: 1983
Retail Price: $9

3 VALUES: † $39

**Blessed Are The Pure In
Heart (Dated 1984)**
#E5392
Issued: 1984 • Closed: 1984
Retail Price: $10

4 VALUES: ⚸ $22
△ $18.50
♡ $18.50
† $18.50
6∂ $18.50

**Bringing You A Merry
Christmas**
#528226
Issued: 1994 • Retired: 1998
Retail Price: $16 – $18.50

5 VALUES: ⚓ $30

Bundles Of Joy (LE-1990)
#525057
Issued: 1990 • Closed: 1990
Retail Price: $15

6 VALUES: NM $116
Ⅱ $108
Ⅰ $100
⤢ $95
† $90
⚶ $84

But Love Goes On Forever
#E5627
Issued: 1981 • Susp.: 1985
Retail Price: $6 – $10

7 VALUES: NM $130
▲ $125
Ⅰ $115
⤢ $105
† $100
⚶ $100

But Love Goes On Forever
#E5628
Issued: 1981 • Susp.: 1985
Retail Price: $6 – $10

8 VALUES: Ⅰ $90
⤢ $83
† $75
UM $105

**Camel, Cow And Donkey
(set/3)**
#E2386
Issued: 1982 • Susp.: 1984
Retail Price: $25 – $27.50

General Ornaments

	Price Paid	Value
1.		
2.		
3.		
4.		
5.		
6.		
7.		
8.		
9.		
10.		

Totals

9 VALUES: ⚜ $35
⚘ $33
⚖ $32
⚬ $30

Cheers To The Leader
#113999
Issued: 1988 • Susp.: 1991
Retail Price: $13.50 – $15

10 VALUES: NM $158
▲ $150
Ⅰ $144
⤢ $134
† $127

**Come Let Us Adore
Him (set/4)**
#E5633
Issued: 1981 • Susp.: 1984
Retail Price: $20 – $31.50

KEY: NM *Pre-1981* ▲ 1981 Ⅰ 1982 ⤢1983 † 1984 ⚶ 1985 ♪ 1986 ▲ 1987 ⚜ 1988 ⚘ 1989 ⚖ 1990
⚸ 1991 ⚬ 1992 ♀ 1993 ⚓ 1994 △ 1995 ♡ 1996 † 1997 6∂ 1998 ★ 1999 ○ 2000 UM *Unmarked*

163

General Ornaments

VALUES: ⚓ $39 / ⚑ $34 / ⚐ $30 / ♧ $28 / $27

Dashing Through The Snow
#521574
Issued: 1990 • Susp.: 1994
Retail Price: $15 – $16

VALUES: ⚓ $46 / ⚑ $42 / ⚐ $38 / ♧ $36 / $32

Don't Let The Holidays Get You Down
#521590
Issued: 1990 • Retired: 1994
Retail Price: $15 – $16

VALUES: Ⅱ $60 / $56 / ✝ $52 / $50 / $47 / UM $65

Dropping In For Christmas
#E2369
Issued: 1982 • Retired: 1986
Retail Price: $9 – $10

VALUES: Ⅱ $60 / $50 / ✝ $45 / $42

Dropping Over For Christmas
#E2376
Issued: 1982 • Retired: 1985
Retail Price: $9 – $10

VALUES: 6∂ $35

Even The Heavens Shall Praise Him (LE-1998)
Century Circle Ornament
#475084
Issued: 1998 • Closed: 1998
Retail Price: $30

VALUES: △ $72

An Event Filled With Sunshine And Smiles (set/2, LE-1995)
Regional Conference Ornament
#160334 (A-G)
Issued: 1995 • Closed: 1995
Retail Price: $35

General Ornaments

	Price Paid	Value
1.		
2.		
3.		
4.		
5.		
6.		
7.		
8.		
9.		
10.		
Totals		

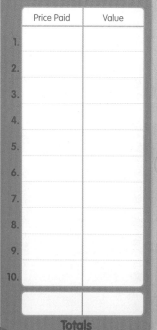

VALUES: ♀ $25

An Event For All Seasons (LE-1993)
Special Event Ornament
#529974
Issued: 1993 • Closed: 1993
Retail Price: $15

VALUES: 🛷 $100

An Event Showered With Love (set/2, LE-1994)
Regional Conference Ornament
#128295 (A, C & D)
Issued: 1994 • Closed: 1994
Retail Price: $30

VALUES: Ⅱ $75 / $70 / ✝ $65

The First Noël
#E2367
Issued: 1982 • Susp.: 1984
Retail Price: $9 – $10

VALUES: Ⅱ $73 / $55 / ✝ $48

The First Noël
#E2368
Issued: 1982 • Retired: 1984
Retail Price: $9 – $10

KEY: NM *Pre-1981* ▲1981 Ⅱ1982 1983 ✝1984 1985 1986 ▲1987 1988 1989 1990 1991 1992 ♀1993 1994 △1995 ♡1996 1997 6∂1998 ★1999 ◯2000 UM *Unmarked*

Value Guide — PRECIOUS MOMENTS®

General Ornaments

1

VALUES: 🕯 $45
$40
$37
$35
$32
$30

Friends Never Drift Apart
#522937
Issued: 1990 • Retired: 1995
Retail Price: $17.50 – $18.50

2

VALUES: 🕯 $40
$35
$30

Glide Through The Holidays
#521566
Issued: 1990 • Retired: 1992
Retail Price: $13.50

3

VALUES: ✤ $40
$36
$33
$32

God Sent You Just In Time
#113972
Issued: 1988 • Susp.: 1991
Retail Price: $13.50 – $15

4
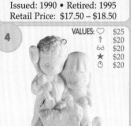
VALUES: ♡ $25
$20
$20
$20
$20

God's Precious Gift
#183881
Issued: 1996 • Open
Retail Price: $20

5

VALUES: $37
$32
$30
$30
$30

Good Friends Are For Always
#524131
Issued: 1992 • Retired: 1997
Retail Price: $15 – $18.50

6

VALUES: $34
$28
$25

The Good Lord Always Delivers
#527165
Issued: 1991 • Susp.: 1993
Retail Price: $15

7

VALUES: $43
$38
$35
$34
$33

Happiness Is The Lord
#15830
Issued: 1985 • Susp.: 1989
Retail Price: $10 – $13.50

8

VALUES: $18.50
★ $18.50
$18.50

Happy Holidaze
#520454
Issued: 1998 • Open
Retail Price: $17.50 – $18.50

9

VALUES: $39
$35
$32
$30

Happy Trails Is Trusting Jesus
#523224
Issued: 1991 • Susp.: 1994
Retail Price: $15 – $16

10

VALUES: $35
$30
$25
$23
$23
$23
$23
$22
$21
$21
$21
$21
$21

Have A Heavenly Christmas
#12416
Issued: 1985 • Susp.: 1998
Retail Price: $12 – $20

General Ornaments

	Price Paid	Value
1.		
2.		
3.		
4.		
5.		
6.		
7.		
8.		
9.		
10.		
Totals		

KEY: NM *Pre-1981* ▲ 1981 ✕ 1982 ◄ 1983 ✝ 1984 🐚 1985 ♫ 1986 ♣ 1987 ✤ 1988 ♪ 1989 ★ 1990 🕯 1991 ⑤ 1992 ✿ 1993 ⊟ 1994 ⚠ 1995 ♡ 1996 ✝ 1997 ⊖ 1998 ★ 1999 🕐 2000 UM *Unmarked*

General Ornaments

1
VALUES: ♠ $34
⬥ $28
🦆 $24
☘ $22
❦ $21
🌸 $20
🌼 $20
⛵ $18.50
⛰ $18.50
♡ $18.50
† $18.50
👓 $18.50
★ $18.50

He Cleansed My Soul
#112380
Issued: 1987 • Retired: 1999
Retail Price: $12 – $18.50

2
VALUES: 🦆 $39
🌿 $36
♠ $34
🦆 $33
⬥ $33
☘ $32
❦ $32
🌸 $30
🌼 $30

Honk If You Love Jesus
#15857
Issued: 1985 • Susp.: 1993
Retail Price: $10 – $15

3
VALUES: 👓 $24.95
★ $24.95
🕐 $24.95

House (personalized)
#150231
Issued: 1998 • Open
Retail Price: $24.95

4
VALUES: † $25
👓 $25
★ $25
🕐 $25

How Can Two Work Together Except They Agree
Care-A-Van Exclusive
#456268
Issued: 1998 • Open
Retail Price: $25

5
VALUES: ⬥ $45
☘ $40
☘ $37
❦ $35
🌸 $32
⛵ $32

I Believe In The Old Rugged Cross
#522953
Issued: 1989 • Susp.: 1994
Retail Price: $15 – $16

6
VALUES: 👓 $19

I'll Be Dog-ged It's That Season Again (Dated 1998)
#455660
Issued: 1998 • Closed: 1998
Retail Price: $18.50

7
VALUES: ♠ $40
🦆 $38
⬥ $35
★ $32

I'm A Possibility
#111120
Issued: 1987 • Susp.: 1990
Retail Price: $11 – $15

8
VALUES: ⛵ $18.50
★ $18.50
🕐 $18.50

I'm Just Nutty About The Holidays
#455776
Issued: 1998 • Open
Retail Price: $17.50 – $18.50

9
VALUES: ♠ $38
🦆 $35
⬥ $35
☘ $32
☘ $30
❦ $28

I'm Sending You A White Christmas
#112372
Issued: 1987 • Susp.: 1992
Retail Price: $11 – $15

10
VALUES: † $60

In God's Beautiful Garden Of Love
Century Circle Ornament
#261599
Issued: 1997 • Closed: 1997
Retail Price: $50

General Ornaments

	Price Paid	Value
1.		
2.		
3.		
4.		
5.		
6.		
7.		
8.		
9.		
10.		
Totals		

KEY: NM *Pre-1981* ▲1981 Ⅱ1982 ◄1983 †1984 ◄1985 🌿1986 ♠1987 🦆1988 ⬥1989 ★1990 ❦1991 ☘1992 🌼1993 ⛵1994 ⛰1995 ♡1996 †1997 👓1998 ★1999 🕐2000 UM *Unmarked*

Value Guide — PRECIOUS MOMENTS®

1
VALUES: ♪ $33 / ♠ $30 / ⚓ $27 / ♁ $25

It's A Perfect Boy
#102415
Issued: 1986 • Susp.: 1989
Retail Price: $10 – $13.50

2
VALUES: ♉ $24 / ♋ $20 / △ $18.50 / ♡ $18.50 / † $18.50 / ᬝ $18.50 / ★ $18.50

It's So Uplifting To Have A Friend Like You
#528846
Issued: 1993 • Retired: 1999
Retail Price: $16 – $18.50

3
VALUES: ✝ $75 / † $67 / ♄ $62

Jesus Is The Light That Shines
#E0537
Issued: 1983 • Susp.: 1985
Retail Price: $9 – $10

4
VALUES: △ $24 / ♡ $20 / † $18.50 / ᬝ $18.50 / ★ $18.50 / ◔ $18.50

Joy From Head To Mistletoe
#150126
Issued: 1995 • Open
Retail Price: $17 – $18.50

5
VALUES: ✝ $60 / † $57 / ♪ $53 / ♠ $49 / ⚓ $44 / UM $70

Joy To The World
#E2343
Issued: 1982 • Susp.: 1988
Retail Price: $9 – $12.50

6
VALUES: ✝ $52 / † $50 / ♪ $47 / ♠ $45

Joy To The World
#E5388
Issued: 1984 • Retired: 1987
Retail Price: $10 – $11

7
VALUES: △ $25 / ♡ $22 / † $20 / ᬝ $20 / ★ $20

Joy To The World
#150320
Issued: 1995 • Retired: 1999
Retail Price: $20

8
VALUES: ♡ $23 / † $20 / ᬝ $20 / ★ $20

Joy To The World
#153338
Issued: 1996 • Retired: 1999
Retail Price: $20

9
VALUES: † $20 / ᬝ $20 / ★ $20

Joy To The World
#272566
Issued: 1997 • Retired: 1999
Retail Price: $20

10
VALUES: ✝ $58 / † $50 / ♥ $45 / ♪ $38

Let Heaven And Nature Sing
#E0532
Issued: 1983 • Retired: 1986
Retail Price: $9 – $10

General Ornaments

	Price Paid	Value
1.		
2.		
3.		
4.		
5.		
6.		
7.		
8.		
9.		
10.		
Totals		

Value Guide — PRECIOUS MOMENTS®

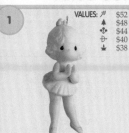

1 VALUES:
⚹	$52
▲	$48
⬧	$44
⊕	$40
⚓	$38

Lord, Keep Me On My Toes
#102423
Issued: 1986 • Retired: 1990
Retail Price: $10 – $15

2 VALUES:
♂	$26
⚘	$23
⊟	$20
♡	$18.50
†	$18.50
👓	$18.50
★	$18.50
⏲	$18.50

Lord, Keep Me On My Toes
#525332
Issued: 1992 • Open
Retail Price: $15 – $18.50

3 VALUES:
✝	$39
⊕	$35
⚹	$34
▲	$32
⬧	$32
⊕	$29

Love Is Kind
#E5391
Issued: 1984 • Susp.: 1989
Retail Price: $10 – $13.50

4 VALUES:
✝	$65
⚘	$60
⚘	$55
⚹	$50

Love Is Patient
#E0535
Issued: 1983 • Susp.: 1986
Retail Price: $9 – $10

5 VALUES:
✝	$73
⚘	$67
⚘	$63
⚹	$60

Love Is Patient
#E0536
Issued: 1983 • Susp.: 1986
Retail Price: $9 – $10

6 VALUES: ♡ $40

Love Makes The World Go 'Round (LE-1996)
Century Circle Ornament
#184209
Issued: 1996 • Closed: 1996
Retail Price: $22.50

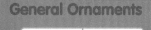

General Ornaments

	Price Paid	Value
1.		
2.		
3.		
4.		
5.		
6.		
7.		
8.		
9.		
Totals		

7 VALUES:
⊕	$30
▲	$28
⚓	$25
♂	$22
⚘	$22
⊟	$20
⛄	$20
♡	$20
†	$20
👓	$20
★	$20
⏲	$20

Love One Another
#522929
Issued: 1989 • Open
Retail Price: $17.50 – $20

8 VALUES:
⚹	$30
▲	$24
⬧	$22
⊕	$22
⚓	$20
♂	$18.50
⚘	$18.50
⊟	$18.50
⛄	$18.50
†	$18.50
👓	$18.50
★	$18.50
⏲	$18.50

Love Rescued Me
#102385
Issued: 1986 • Open
Retail Price: $10 – $18.50

9 VALUES: ♂ $28

The Magic Starts With You (LE-1992)
Special Event Ornament
#529648
Issued: 1992 • Closed: 1992
Retail Price: $16

KEY: NM *Pre-1981* ▲ 1981 ⚹ 1982 ◄1983 † 1984 ⚘ 1985 ⚹ 1986 ▲ 1987 ⬧ 1988 ⊕ 1989 ⚓ 1990 ♂ 1991 ⚓ 1992 ⚘ 1993 ⛄ 1994 ⊟ 1995 ♡ 1996 † 1997 👓 1998 ★ 1999 ⏲ 2000 ∪M *Unmarked*

Value Guide — PRECIOUS MOMENTS®

1

⚓	$42
✚	$38
▼	$35
⚜	$33
✣	$30
⚓	$30
△	$28
♡	$25

Make A Joyful Noise
#522910
Issued: 1989 • Susp.: 1996
Retail Price: $15 – $18.50

2

⚓	$39
✚	$35
▼	$34
⚜	$33
✣	$30
⚓	$30

May All Your Christmases Be White
#521302
Issued: 1989 • Susp.: 1994
Retail Price: $13.50 – $16

3 ★ $23

May All Your Christmases Be White (LE-1999)
#521302R
Issued: 1999 • Closed: 1999
Retail Price: $20

4

✝	$36
✠	$32
♪	$32
✣	$30
⚓	$28
⚓	$26

May God Bless You With A Perfect Holiday Season
#E5390
Issued: 1984 • Susp.: 1989
Retail Price: $10 – $13.50

5 ★ $32

Variation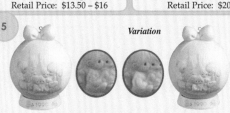

May Your Christmas Be A Happy Home
(set/2, Dated 1990)
The Masterpiece Series
#523704
Issued: 1990 • Closed: 1990
Retail Price: $27.50
Variation: Yellow shirt – $60

6

✿	$44
♪	$37
▼	$35
✣	$33
⚓	$30
✚	$30
✣	$30
⚜	$30
⚓	$30

May Your Christmas Be Delightful
#15849
Issued: 1985 • Susp.: 1993
Retail Price: $10 – $15

7 ★ $21

May Your Christmas Be Delightful (LE-1999)
#15849R
Issued: 1999 • Closed: 1999
Retail Price: $20

8 ★ $22

May Your Christmas Be Delightful (LE-1999)
#587931
Issued: 1999 • Closed: 1999
Retail Price: $20

9

✿	$50
♪	$45
▼	$40
✣	$40
⚓	$40

May Your Christmas Be Happy
#15822
Issued: 1985 • Susp.: 1989
Retail Price: $10 – $13.50

General Ornaments

	Price Paid	Value
1.		
2.		
3.		
4.		
5.		
6.		
7.		
8.		
9.		

Totals

KEY: NM *Pre-1981* ▲ 1981 ✖ 1982 ◄ 1983 ✝ 1984 ✿ 1985 ♪ 1986 ▲ 1987 ✣ 1988 ⚓ 1989 ⚓ 1990 ✣ 1991 ⚜ 1992 ✿ 1993 ⊲ 1994 △ 1995 ♡ 1996 ✝ 1997 ♊ 1998 ★ 1999 ○ 2000 UM *Unmarked*

169

1 VALUES: ★ $22

**May Your Wishes For Peace
Take Wing (Dated 1999)**
#587818
Issued: 1999 • Closed: 1999
Retail Price: $20

2 VALUES: ⬠ $33

Merry Christmoose (LE-1995)
Special Event Ornament
#150134
Issued: 1995 • Closed: 1995
Retail Price: $17

3 VALUES: ★ $24

Merry Giftness (LE-1999)
*Distinguished Service
Retailer Ornament*
#532223
Issued: 1999 • Closed: 1999
Retail Price: $20

4 VALUES: ♡ $35

**The Most Precious Gift
Of All (LE-1996)**
#212520
Issued: 1996 • Closed: 1996
Retail Price: $20

5 VALUES:

✝	$37
✿	$30
♫	$30
▲	$27
⬥	$26
⬥	$26
✝	$23
⚜	$22
⬥	$22
⚖	$20
⬥	$20
⊟	$18.50
△	$18.50
♡	$18.50
✝	$18.50
6ð	$18.50
★	$18.50
⏱	$18.50

Mother Sew Dear
#E0514
Issued: 1983 • Open
Retail Price: $9 – $18.50

6 VALUES:

Ⅱ	$125
✝	$115
✝	$108

Mouse With Cheese
#E2381
Issued: 1982 • Susp.: 1984
Retail Price: $9 – $10

7 VALUES:

✝	$24
6ð	$24

**My Love Will Keep
You Warm**
Catalog Ornament
#272965
Issued: 1998 • Closed: 1998
Retail Price: $20

8 VALUES:

⬥	$40
ᚦ	$36
★	$33
⚖	$30

**My Love Will Never
Let You Go**
#114006
Issued: 1988 • Susp.: 1991
Retail Price: $13.50 – $15

9 VALUES:

✿	$65
✝	$60
✦	$56
♫	$52

O Come, All Ye Faithful
#E0531
Issued: 1983 • Susp.: 1986
Retail Price: $9 – $10

10 VALUES:

⊟	$23
△	$20
♡	$18.50
✝	$18.50
6ð	$18.50
★	$18.50
⏱	$18.50

Onward Christmas Soldiers
#527327
Issued: 1994 • Open
Retail Price: $16 – $18.50

Value Guide — PRECIOUS MOMENTS®

1 VALUES: 🦃 $37 / 📖 $32 / ♡ $30 / † $30 / 👓 $30 / ★ $30 / 🕐 $30

Ornament Enhancer
#603171
Issued: 1994 • Open
Retail Price: $30

2 VALUES: 𝕀 $60 / 🍷 $50 / † $43 / 𝄞 $40 / 🎺 $37 / ⚓ $35 / 🦢 $35 / ⌐ $33 / ☘ $30 / ☘ $30

Our First Christmas
Together
#E2385
Issued: 1982 • Susp.: 1991
Retail Price: $9 – $15

3 VALUES: 𝄞 $35

Our First Christmas
Together (Dated 1986)
#102350
Issued: 1986 • Closed: 1986
Retail Price: $10

4 VALUES: ⚓ $38

Our First Christmas
Together (Dated 1987)
#112399
Issued: 1987 • Closed: 1987
Retail Price: $11

5 VALUES: ☘ $26

Our First Christmas
Together (Dated 1988)
#520233
Issued: 1988 • Closed: 1988
Retail Price: $13

6 VALUES: ⌐ $36

Our First Christmas
Together (Dated 1989)
#521558
Issued: 1989 • Closed: 1989
Retail Price: $17.50

7 VALUES: ☘ $28

Our First Christmas
Together (Dated 1990)
#525324
Issued: 1990 • Closed: 1990
Retail Price: $17.50

8 VALUES: 🍷 $32

Our First Christmas
Together (Dated 1991)
#522945
Issued: 1991 • Closed: 1991
Retail Price: $17.50

9 VALUES: 🎵 $32

Our First Christmas
Together (Dated 1992)
#528870
Issued: 1992 • Closed: 1992
Retail Price: $17.50

10 VALUES: ⚘ $27

Our First Christmas
Together (Dated 1993)
#530506
Issued: 1993 • Closed: 1993
Retail Price: $17.50

General Ornaments

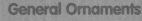

	Price Paid	Value
1.		
2.		
3.		
4.		
5.		
6.		
7.		
8.		
9.		
10.		
Totals		

KEY: NM *Pre-1981* ▲ 1981 𝕀 1982 ◄ 1983 † 1984 ☘ 1985 𝄞 1986 ⚓ 1987 ☘ 1988 ⌐ 1989 ☘ 1990 🍷 1991 🎵 1992 ⚘ 1993 ☜ 1994 📖 1995 ♡ 1996 † 1997 👓 1998 ★ 1999 🕐 2000 UM *Unmarked*

171

General Ornaments

1
VALUES: 🦴 $28

Our First Christmas Together (Dated 1994)
#529206
Issued: 1994 • Closed: 1994
Retail Price: $18.50

2
VALUES: △ $28

Our First Christmas Together (Dated 1995)
#142700
Issued: 1995 • Closed: 1995
Retail Price: $18.50

3
VALUES: ♡ $30

Our First Christmas Together (Dated 1996)
#183911
Issued: 1996 • Closed: 1996
Retail Price: $22.50

4
VALUES: † $28

Our First Christmas Together (Dated 1997)
#272736
Issued: 1997 • Closed: 1997
Retail Price: $20

5
VALUES: 6ð $27

Our First Christmas Together (Dated 1998)
#455636
Issued: 1998 • Closed: 1998
Retail Price: $25

6
VALUES: ★ $26

Our First Christmas Together (Dated 1999)
#587796
Issued: 1999 • Closed: 1999
Retail Price: $25

General Ornaments

	Price Paid	Value
1.		
2.		
3.		
4.		
5.		
6.		
7.		
8.		
9.		
10.		

Totals

7
VALUES: † $28

Pack Your Trunk For The Holidays (LE-1,050)
Special Event Ornament
#272949
Issued: 1997 • Closed: 1997
Retail Price: $20

8
VALUES: † $46
    ✝ $40
    ♫ $37

Peace On Earth
#E5389
Issued: 1984 • Susp.: 1986
Retail Price: $10

9
VALUES: △ $42

Peace On Earth (Dated 1995, LE-15,000)
Century Circle Ornament
#177091
Issued: 1995 • Closed: 1995
Retail Price: $25

10
VALUES: Ð $75

Peace On Earth (set/2, Dated 1989)
The Masterpiece Series
#523062
Issued: 1989 • Closed: 1989
Retail Price: $25

KEY: NM *Pre-1981* ▲1981 𝕀1982 ◄1983 †1984 ✔1985 ♫1986 ▲1987 ♣1988 Ð1989 ▲1990 ♦1991 ♣1992 ♀1993 ◄1994 △1995 ♡1996 †1997 6ð1998 ★1999 ☉2000 UM *Unmarked*

1 VALUES:
- ♱ $50
- ✤ $40
- ☙ $38
- ♪ $36
- ▲ $36
- ✧ $34
- ⚓ $34
- ★ $32

The Perfect Grandpa
#E0517
Issued: 1983 • Susp.: 1990
Retail Price: $9 – $15

2 VALUES: ★ $23

Pretty As A Christmas Princess (LE-1999)
#587958
Issued: 1999 • Closed: 1999
Retail Price: $20

3 VALUES:
- ♱ $23
- 6∂ $18.50
- ★ $18.50
- ☉ $18.50

Puppies On Sled
#272892
Issued: 1997 • Open
Retail Price: $18.50

4 VALUES:
- ♱ $40
- ✤ $30
- ☙ $25
- ♪ $25
- ▲ $24
- ✧ $22
- ⚓ $22
- ✦ $22
- ❦ $22
- ☙ $20
- ✿ $20
- ⚘ $20
- ⛄ $18.50
- ♡ $18.50
- ♱ $18.50
- 6∂ $18.50
- ★ $18.50
- ☉ $18.50

The Purr-fect Grandma
#E0516
Issued: 1983 • Open
Retail Price: $9 – $18.50

5 VALUES:
- ✧ $48
- ⚓ $44
- ★ $40
- ❦ $36

Rejoice O Earth
#113980
Issued: 1988 • Retired: 1991
Retail Price: $13.50 – $15

6 VALUES:
- ♪ $39
- ▲ $34
- ✧ $33
- ⚓ $31
- ★ $27
- ❦ $27

Rocking Horse
#102474
Issued: 1986 • Susp.: 1991
Retail Price: $10 – $15

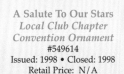

7 VALUES: 6∂ N/E

A Salute To Our Stars
Local Club Chapter Convention Ornament
#549614
Issued: 1998 • Closed: 1998
Retail Price: N/A

8 VALUES:
- ✿ $18.50
- ⛄ $18.50
- ♡ $18.50
- ♱ $18.50
- 6∂ $18.50
- ★ $18.50
- ☉ $18.50

Sending You A White Christmas
#528218
Issued: 1994 • Open
Retail Price: $16 – $18.50

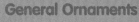

9 VALUES:
- ♪ $30
- ▲ $26
- ⚓ $24

Serve With A Smile
#102431
Issued: 1986 • Susp.: 1988
Retail Price: $10 – $12.50

10 VALUES:
- ♪ $39
- ▲ $35
- ⚓ $29

Serve With A Smile
#102458
Issued: 1986 • Susp.: 1988
Retail Price: $10 – $12.50

General Ornaments

	Price Paid	Value
1.		
2.		
3.		
4.		
5.		
6.		
7.		
8.		
9.		
10.		

Totals

KEY: NM *Pre-1981* ▲ 1981 ⅠⅠ 1982 ◀ 1983 ♱ 1984 🍃 1985 ♪ 1986 ▲ 1987 ✧ 1988 ⚓ 1989 ★ 1990 ❦ 1991 ⚘ 1992 ♥♥ 1993 ✿ 1994 ⛄ 1995 ♡ 1996 ♱ 1997 6∂ 1998 ★ 1999 ☉ 2000 UM *Unmarked*

173

General Ornaments

1
VALUES: 🐝 $24
🐚 $20
△ $18.50
♡ $18.50
✝ $18.50
👓 $18.50
★ $18.50
🕐 $18.50

Share In The Warmth Of Christmas
#527211
Issued: 1993 • Open
Retail Price: $15 – $18.50

2
VALUES: 🎠 $45
▲ $38
🔱 $35
🕊 $32
🕯 $32
🍶 $30
🐝 $27
🐚 $25

Shepherd Of Love
#102288
Issued: 1986 • Susp.: 1993
Retail Price: $10 – $15

3
VALUES: 🔱 $42
🕊 $37
🕯 $34
🍶 $34
🐝 $30
🐚 $26

Smile Along The Way
#113964
Issued: 1988 • Susp.: 1993
Retail Price: $15 – $17.50

4
VALUES: ♡ N/E

Sweet 16 (LE-1996)
Local Club Chapter Convention Ornament
#266841
Issued: 1996 • Closed: 1996
Retail Price: N/A

5
VALUES: 🍶 $26

Take A Bow Cuz You're My Christmas Star (LE-1994)
Special Event Ornament
#520470
Issued: 1994 • Closed: 1994
Retail Price: $16

6
VALUES: 🍶 $68
✝ $62
🎠 $57
🦋 $55
▲ $50
🔱 $50

Tell Me The Story Of Jesus
#E0533
Issued: 1983 • Susp.: 1988
Retail Price: $9 – $12.50

General Ornaments

	Price Paid	Value
1.		
2.		
3.		
4.		
5.		
6.		
7.		
8.		
9.		
10.		
Totals		

7
VALUES: 🍶 $59
✝ $57
🦋 $54
🎠 $52
▲ $52
🔱 $52

To A Special Dad
#E0515
Issued: 1983 • Susp.: 1988
Retail Price: $9 – $12.50

8
VALUES: 🔱 $42
🕊 $30
🕯 $26
🍶 $24
🍶 $22
🐝 $20
🍶 $20
△ $20
♡ $20
✝ $20
👓 $20
★ $20

To My Forever Friend
#113956
Issued: 1988 • Retired: 1999
Retail Price: $16 – $20

9
VALUES: 🍶 $60
✝ $54
🔱 $50
🦋 $48
▲ $45
🕊 $40
🕯 $35

To Thee With Love
#E0534
Issued: 1983 • Retired: 1989
Retail Price: $9 – $13.50

10
VALUES: 🦋 $29
▲ $27
🔱 $25
🕊 $22
🕯 $20
🍶 $20
🍶 $20
🐝 $18.50
🍶 $18.50
△ $18.50
♡ $18.50
✝ $18.50
👓 $18.50
★ $18.50
🕐 $18.50

Trust And Obey
#102377
Issued: 1986 • Open
Retail Price: $10 – $18.50

KEY: NM *Pre-1981* ▲ 1981 ▆ 1982 ◀ 1983 ✝ 1984 🦋 1985 🦋 1986 ▲ 1987 🔱 1988 🕊 1989 ★ 1990 🍶 1991 🍶 1992 🐝 1993 🍶 1994 △ 1995 ♡ 1996 ✝ 1997 👓 1998 ★ 1999 🕐 2000 UM *Unmarked*

Value Guide — PRECIOUS MOMENTS®

1

VALUES:
I	$62
⚓	$62
✝	$60
🌿	$55
⚜	$53
▲	$50
⚓	$50
UM	$65

Unicorn
#E2371
Issued: 1982 • Retired: 1988
Retail Price: $9 – $13

2

VALUES:
NM	$77
▲	$67
I	$60
✝	$57
✝	$55
⚓	$55

Unto Us A Child Is Born
#E5630
Issued: 1981 • Susp.: 1985
Retail Price: $6 – $10

3

VALUES:
⚜	$35
⚓	$25
⊕	$22
⚓	$20
⚜	$20
⚜	$20
♋	$18.50
⟿	$18.50
△	$18.50
♡	$18.50
✝	$18.50
⬂	$18.50
★	$18.50

Waddle I Do Without You
#112364
Issued: 1987 • Retired: 1999
Retail Price: $11 – $18.50

4

VALUES:
NM	$80
▲	$70
I	$66
✝	$63
⚓	$55

We Have Seen His Star
#E6120
Issued: 1981 • Retired: 1984
Retail Price: $6 – $10

5

VALUES:
NM	$150
▲	$145
I	$138
⚓	$130
✝	$125

Wee Three Kings (set/3)
#E5634
Issued: 1981 • Susp.: 1984
Retail Price: $19 – $27.50

6

VALUES:
♡	$22
✝	$18.50
⬂	$18.50
★	$18.50
◔	$18.50

**When The Skating's Ruff,
Try Prayer**
#183903
Issued: 1996 • Open
Retail Price: $18.50

7

VALUES: ♡ $30

**Wishing You A Bear-ie
Merry Christmas (LE-1996)**
Special Event Ornament
#531200
Issued: 1996 • Closed: 1996
Retail Price: $17.50

8

VALUES: ⚓ $22

**You Are My Gift Come True
(Dated 1988)**
#520276
Issued: 1988 • Closed: 1988
Retail Price: $12.50

9

VALUES:
⚜	$45
⚓	$40
⊕	$34
⚓	$34
⚜	$33
⚜	$33
♋	$32
⟿	$32
△	$30
♡	$30

**You Have Touched
So Many Hearts**
#112356
Issued: 1987 • Retired: 1997
Retail Price: $11 – $18.50

10

VALUES:
△	$25
♡	$20
✝	$18.50
⬂	$18.50
★	$18.50
◔	$18.50

**You're "A" Number One In
My Book, Teacher**
#150142
Issued: 1995 • Open
Retail Price: $17 – $18.50

General Ornaments

	Price Paid	Value
1.		
2.		
3.		
4.		
5.		
6.		
7.		
8.		
9.		
10.		

Totals

KEY: NM *Pre-1981* ▲ *1981* I *1982* ◄ *1983* ✝ *1984* ⚜ *1985* ♪ *1986* ⚜ *1987* ⚜ *1988* ⊕ *1989* ★ *1990* ⚓ *1991* ⚜ *1992* ♋ *1993* ⟿ *1994* △ *1995* ♡ *1996* ✝ *1997* ⬂ *1998* ★ *1999* ◔ *2000* UM *Unmarked*

175

OTHER PRECIOUS MOMENTS® PIECES

Beautiful bells, plates, picture frames and musicals are only a few of the products that are available to complement the PRECIOUS MOMENTS figurine and ornament collections. This year collectors can look forward to a new plush series called *Hugs For The Soul* which makes its debut with seven adorable dressed bears.

1
VALUES: UM $215

Let The Heavens Rejoice
(Dated 1981)
#E5622
Issued: 1981 • Closed: 1981
Retail Price: $15

2
VALUES: UM $65

I'll Play My Drum For Him
(Dated 1982)
#E2358
Issued: 1982 • Closed: 1982
Retail Price: $17

3
VALUES: ✒ $65
UM $70

Surrounded With Joy
(Dated 1983)
#E0522
Issued: 1983 • Closed: 1983
Retail Price: $18

4
VALUES: ✝ $44

Wishing You A Merry Christmas (Dated 1984)
#E5393
Issued: 1984 • Closed: 1984
Retail Price: $19

5
VALUES: ✿ $38

God Sent His Love
(Dated 1985)
#15873
Issued: 1985 • Closed: 1985
Retail Price: $19

6
VALUES: ♪ $36

Wishing You A Cozy Christmas (Dated 1986)
#102318
Issued: 1986 • Closed: 1986
Retail Price: $20

7
VALUES: ▲ $44

Love Is The Best Gift Of All
(Dated 1987)
#109835
Issued: 1987 • Closed: 1987
Retail Price: $22.50

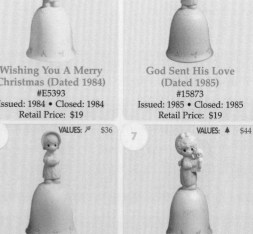

Bells

	Price Paid	Value
1.		
2.		
3.		
4.		
5.		
6.		
7.		
Totals		

KEY: NM *Pre-1981* ▲ 1981 ✕ 1982 ◄ 1983 ✝ 1984 ✿ 1985 ♪ 1986 ▲ 1987 ✤ 1988 ꝯ 1989 ↓ 1990
♠ 1991 ⚑ 1992 ❀ 1993 ⊟ 1994 ⚘ 1995 ♡ 1996 ✝ 1997 ∞ 1998 ★ 1999 ◐ 2000 UM *Unmarked*

Other PRECIOUS MOMENTS® Pieces

1 VALUES: ❧ $40

Time To Wish You A Merry
Christmas (Dated 1988)
#115304
Issued: 1988 • Closed: 1988
Retail Price: $25

2 VALUES: ⊅ $38

Oh Holy Night (Dated 1989)
#522821
Issued: 1989 • Closed: 1989
Retail Price: $25

3 VALUES: ↓ $38

Once Upon A Holy Night
(Dated 1990)
#523828
Issued: 1990 • Closed: 1990
Retail Price: $25

4 VALUES: ♦ $40

May Your Christmas Be
Merry (Dated 1991)
#524182
Issued: 1991 • Closed: 1991
Retail Price: $25

5 VALUES: ♒ $36

But The Greatest Of These
Is Love (Dated 1992)
#527726
Issued: 1992 • Closed: 1992
Retail Price: $25

6 VALUES: ॐ $38

Wishing You The Sweetest
Christmas (Dated 1993)
#530174
Issued: 1993 • Closed: 1993
Retail Price: $25

7 VALUES: ⌐ $34

You're As Pretty As A
Christmas Tree (Dated 1994)
#604216
Issued: 1994 • Closed: 1994
Retail Price: $27.50

8 VALUES: ✝ $47
       UM $49

God Understands
#E5211
Issued: 1981 • Retired: 1984
Retail Price: $15 – $19

9 VALUES: ✝ $49
       UM $62

Jesus Is Born
#E5623
Issued: 1981 • Susp.: 1984
Retail Price: $15 – $19

10 VALUES: ✝ $50
       ♣ $46
       UM $60

Jesus Loves Me
#E5208
Issued: 1981 • Susp.: 1985
Retail Price: $15 – $19

Bells

	Price Paid	Value
1.		
2.		
3.		
4.		
5.		
6.		
7.		
8.		
9.		
10.		
Totals		

KEY: NM *Pre-1981* ▲ 1981 ✗ 1982 ◄⊓ 1983 ✝ 1984 ✔ 1985 ╱ 1986 ▲ 1987 ❧ 1988 ⊅ 1989 ↓ 1990
♦ 1991 ♒ 1992 ॐ 1993 ⌐ 1994 ⚖ 1995 ♡ 1996 ↑ 1997 ∞ 1998 ★ 1999 ◐ 2000 UM *Unmarked*

177

Other PRECIOUS MOMENTS® Pieces

1 VALUES: ✝ $55 • 🍃 $51 • UM $60

Jesus Loves Me
#E5209
Issued: 1981 • Susp.: 1985
Retail Price: $15 – $19

2 VALUES: ✝ $40 • 🍃 $37 • UM $46

The Lord Bless You And Keep You
#E7175
Issued: 1982 • Susp.: 1985
Retail Price: $17 – $19

3 VALUES: ✝ $62 • 🍃 $55 • UM $68

The Lord Bless You And Keep You
#E7176
Issued: 1982 • Susp.: 1985
Retail Price: $17 – $19

4 VALUES: ✝ $65 • 🍃 $62 • ♫ $62 • ▲ $60 • ◈ $59 • ♃ $57 • ★ $57 • ♠ $55 • ♧ $55 • ♋ $55 • UM $68

The Lord Bless You And Keep You
#E7179
Issued: 1982 • Susp.: 1993
Retail Price: $22.50 – $35

5 VALUES: ✝ $48 • 🍃 $44 • ♫ $38 • ▲ $36 • ◈ $35 • UM $53

Mother Sew Dear
#E7181
Issued: 1982 • Susp.: 1988
Retail Price: $17 – $22.50

6 VALUES: ✝ $50 • UM $60

Prayer Changes Things
#E5210
Issued: 1981 • Susp.: 1984
Retail Price: $15 – $19

7 VALUES: ✝ $48 • 🍃 $45 • ♫ $43 • ▲ $43 • ◈ $38 • UM $56

The Purr-fect Grandma
#E7183
Issued: 1982 • Susp.: 1988
Retail Price: $17 – $22.50

8 VALUES: ✝ $45 • 🍃 $44 • UM $58

We Have Seen His Star
#E5620
Issued: 1981 • Susp.: 1985
Retail Price: $15 – $19

9 VALUES: ◀ $103 • ✝ $98 • 🍃 $95 • ♫ $90 • ▲ $86 • ◈ $84 • UM $115

But Love Goes On Forever (set/2)
#E6118
Issued: 1981 • Susp.: 1988
Retail Price: $14 – $25

10 VALUES: ✝ $107 • 🍃 $100 • UM $125

Joy To The World (set/2)
#E2344
Issued: 1982 • Susp.: 1985
Retail Price: $20 – $22.50

Bells

	Price Paid	Value
1.		
2.		
3.		
4.		
5.		
6.		
7.		
8.		

Candle Climbers

9.		
10.		

Totals

KEY: NM *Pre-1981* ▲ 1981 ✕ 1982 ◀ 1983 ✝ 1984 🍃 1985 ♫ 1986 ▲ 1987 ◈ 1988 ♃ 1989 ★ 1990 ♠ 1991 ♧ 1992 ♋ 1993 ▬ 1994 ⚖ 1995 ♡ 1996 ✝ 1997 ⊛ 1998 ★ 1999 ⊘ 2000 UM *Unmarked*

1

VALUES: 𝕀 $115
🐟 $108
✝ $90
⚓ $83

Forever Friends (set/2)
#E9283
Issued: 1983 • Susp.: 1984
Retail Price: $15 – $17

2

VALUES: 🐟 $55
✝ $50
◀ $50
⁄⁒ $46
▲ $45
✧ $42
UM $60

**I'm Falling For Some Bunny/
Our Love Is Heaven-scent
(set/2)**
#E9266
Issued: 1983 • Susp.: 1988
Retail Price: $13.50 – $18.50

3

VALUES: 𝕀 $55
✝ $50
✝ $48
⚓ $47

Jesus Loves Me
#E9280
Issued: 1983 • Susp.: 1985
Retail Price: $17.50 – $19

4

VALUES: 𝕀 $72
✝ $68
✝ $63
⚓ $60

Jesus Loves Me
#E9281
Issued: 1983 • Susp.: 1985
Retail Price: $17.50 – $19

5

VALUES: 🐟 $67
✝ $63
✝ $57
⚓ $50

**The Lord Bless You
And Keep You**
#E7167
Issued: 1982 • Susp.: 1985
Retail Price: $22.50 – $25

6

VALUES: UM $30

Care-A-Van Truck
Care-A-Van Exclusive
#475041
Issued: 1998 • Open
Retail Price: $30

7

VALUES: ✿ $155
⁄⁒ $145

Aaron
#12424
Issued: 1985 • Susp.: 1986
Retail Price: $135

8

VALUES: ▲ $285

**Angie, The Angel Of Mercy
(LE-12,500)**
#12491
Issued: 1987 • Closed: 1987
Retail Price: $160

Covered Boxes

	Price Paid	Value
1.		
2.		
3.		
4.		
5.		

Die-Cast Metal

6.		

Dolls

7.		
8.		
9.		
10.		

9

VALUES: ⚓ $156
🔔 $156

**Autumn's Praise
(LE-1990/1991)**
#408808
Issued: 1990 • Closed: 1991
Retail Price: $150

10

VALUES: ✿ $155
⁄⁒ $145

Bethany
#12432
Issued: 1985 • Susp.: 1986
Retail Price: $135

Totals

KEY: NM *Pre-1981* ▲ 1981 𝕀 1982 ◀ 1983 ✝ 1984 🐟 1985 ⁄⁒ 1986 ▲ 1987 ✧ 1988 ⊕ 1989 ✿ 1990 🔔 1991 ⛁ 1992 ❀ 1993 ✇ 1994 ⛲ 1995 ♡ 1996 ✝ 1997 ∞ 1998 ★ 1999 🕙 2000 UM *Unmarked*

179

Other PRECIOUS MOMENTS® Pieces

1 VALUES: ♪ $275

Bong Bong (LE-12,000)
#100455
Issued: 1986 • Closed: 1986
Retail Price: $150

2 VALUES: ♪ $295

Candy (LE-12,000)
#100463
Issued: 1986 • Closed: 1986
Retail Price: $150

3 VALUES: ♪ $265

Connie (LE-7,500)
#102253
Issued: 1986 • Closed: 1986
Retail Price: $160

4 VALUES: UM $480

Cubby (LE-5,000)
#E7267B
Issued: 1982 • Closed: 1982
Retail Price: $200

5 VALUES: ♣ $240
♠ $230
♣ $225
UM $260

Debbie
#E6214G
Issued: 1981 • Susp.: 1985
Retail Price: $175 – $200

6 VALUES: ♣ $75
♠ $68
♣ $68
♥ $68
♣ $68

**The Eyes Of The Lord
Are Upon You**
♪ *"Brahms' Lullaby"*
#429570
Issued: 1991 • Susp.: 1994
Retail Price: $65

7 VALUES: ♣ $75
♠ $68
♣ $68
♥ $68
♣ $68

**The Eyes Of The Lord
Are Upon You**
♪ *"Brahms' Lullaby"*
#429589
Issued: 1991 • Susp.: 1994
Retail Price: $65

8 VALUES: ♣ $185
♠ $180
♣ $180
♪ $175
⚓ $175
♣ $175
UM $195

Katie Lynne
#E0539
Issued: 1983 • Susp.: 1988
Retail Price: $150 – $175

9 VALUES: ♠ $188
♣ $180
♪ $175
⚓ $175
♣ $175
♦ $175

Kristy
#E2851
Issued: 1984 • Susp.: 1989
Retail Price: $150 – $170

10 VALUES: ♣ $155
♠ $155
♣ $155

**May You Have An Old
Fashioned Christmas
(LE-1991/1992)**
#417785
Issued: 1991 • Closed: 1992
Retail Price: $150

Dolls

	Price Paid	Value
1.		
2.		
3.		
4.		
5.		
6.		
7.		
8.		
9.		
10.		
Totals		

KEY: NM *Pre-1981* ▲ 1981 Ⅱ 1982 ◄1983 ♣ 1984 ◢ 1985 ♪ 1986 ♠ 1987 ✦ 1988 ♦ 1989 ♣ 1990 ♠ 1991 ♣ 1992 ♥ 1993 ⛫ 1994 ⌂ 1995 ♡ 1996 ♣ 1997 ↻ 1998 ★ 1999 ○ 2000 UM *Unmarked*

1
VALUES: ✝ $225
✝ $220
🍂 $210
UM $255

Mikey
#E6214B
Issued: 1981 • Susp.: 1985
Retail Price: $175 – $200

2
VALUES: ✝ $360
🍂 $355
UM $355

Mother Sew Dear
#E2850
Issued: 1984 • Retired: 1985
Retail Price: $350

3
VALUES: 🍂 $75
♪ $70
UM $79

P.D.
#12475
Issued: 1985 • Susp.: 1986
Retail Price: $50

4
VALUES: ⚓ $155
🍂 $155

Summer's Joy (LE-1990/1991)
#408794
Issued: 1990 • Closed: 1991
Retail Price: $150

5
VALUES: UM $565

Tammy (LE-5,000)
#E7267G
Issued: 1982 • Closed: 1982
Retail Price: $300

6
VALUES: ✝ $165
✝ $158
♪ $155
▲ $155
⚓ $155
⊕ $155
⚓ $155
🍂 $155

Timmy
#E5397
Issued: 1984 • Susp.: 1991
Retail Price: $125 – $150

7
VALUES: 🍂 $86
♪ $78
UM $92

Trish
#12483
Issued: 1985 • Susp.: 1986
Retail Price: $50

8
VALUES: ⚓ $155
🍂 $155

The Voice Of Spring
(LE-1990/1991)
#408786
Issued: 1990 • Closed: 1991
Retail Price: $150

Dolls

	Price Paid	Value
1.		
2.		
3.		
4.		
5.		
6.		
7.		
8.		
9.		
10.		
Totals		

9
VALUES: ⚓ $160
🍂 $160

Winter's Song (LE-1990/1991)
#408816
Issued: 1990 • Closed: 1991
Retail Price: $150

10
VALUES: ⚓ $95
🍂 $95
🍂 $95

You Have Touched So Many
Hearts (LE-1991/1992)
#427527
Issued: 1991 • Closed: 1992
Retail Price: $90

KEY: NM *Pre-1981* ▲ 1981 ✠ 1982 ◀ 1983 ✝ 1984 🍂 1985 ♪ 1986 ▲ 1987 ✣ 1988 ⊕ 1989 ⚓ 1990 🍂 1991 ✦ 1992 ❀ 1993 ◀ 1994 ⚒ 1995 ♡ 1996 ✝ 1997 ∞ 1998 ★ 1999 ◌ 2000 UM *Unmarked*

181

1 VALUES: ⚹ $44 / ♦ $37

I Will Cherish The Old Rugged Cross
(set/2, Dated 1991)
#523534
Issued: 1991 • Closed: 1991
Retail Price: $27.50

2 VALUES: ♒ $38 / ♋ $32

Make A Joyful Noise
(set/2, Dated 1993)
#528617
Issued: 1993 • Closed: 1993
Retail Price: $27.50

3 VALUES: ♒ $37 / ⊶ $32

A Reflection Of His Love
(set/2, Dated 1994)
#529095
Issued: 1994 • Closed: 1994
Retail Price: $27.50

4 VALUES: ♦ $35 / ♋ $32

We Are God's Workmanship
(set/2, Dated 1992)
#525960
Issued: 1992 • Closed: 1992
Retail Price: $27.50

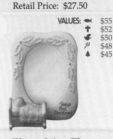

5 VALUES: ⊷ $55 / ✝ $52 / ♣ $50 / ♪ $48 / ▲ $45

Blessed Are The Pure In Heart
#E0521
Issued: 1983 • Susp.: 1987
Retail Price: $18 – $21

6 VALUES: ✝ $120 / ⊷ $112 / ♪ $92 / ▲ $80

God's Precious Gift
#12033
Issued: 1985 • Susp.: 1987
Retail Price: $19 – $20

7 VALUES: ✝ $68 / ⊷ $65 / ♪ $60 / ▲ $57 / ♣ $55 / ⊶ $52 / ♣ $52 / ♦ $48 / ♋ $45

God's Precious Gift
#12041
Issued: 1985 • Susp.: 1992
Retail Price: $19 – $27.50

8 VALUES: Ⅱ $66 / ⊷ $60 / ✝ $57 / ♣ $57

Jesus Loves Me
#E7170
Issued: 1982 • Susp.: 1985
Retail Price: $17 – $19

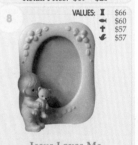

9 VALUES: Ⅱ $75 / ⊷ $68 / ✝ $64 / ♣ $62

Jesus Loves Me
#E7171
Issued: 1982 • Susp.: 1985
Retail Price: $17 – $19

10 VALUES: Ⅱ $70 / ✝ $64 / ⊷ $60 / ♣ $60 / ♪ $56 / ▲ $56 / ⊷ $54 / ♣ $54 / ⚹ $52 / ♦ $50 / ♋ $48 / ♒ $46

The Lord Bless You And Keep You
#E7166
Issued: 1982 • Susp.: 1993
Retail Price: $22.50 – $32.50

Eggs

	Price Paid	Value
1.		
2.		
3.		
4.		

Frames

5.		
6.		
7.		
8.		
9.		
10.		

Totals

KEY: NM *Pre-1981* ▲ 1981 Ⅱ 1982 ⊷ 1983 ✝ 1984 ♣ 1985 ♪ 1986 ▲ 1987 ✤ 1988 ⊕ 1989 ⚹ 1990 ♦ 1991 ♋ 1992 ♒ 1993 ⊷ 1994 △ 1995 ♡ 1996 ✝ 1997 ⊶ 1998 ★ 1999 ○ 2000 UM *Unmarked*

1 VALUES:
- ✠ $55
- ✠ $50
- ✝ $45
- ♫ $45
- ♪ $42
- ▲ $40

**The Lord Bless
You And Keep You**
#E7177
Issued: 1982 • Susp.: 1987
Retail Price: $18 – $20

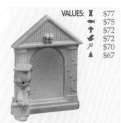

2 VALUES:
- ✠ $77
- ✠ $75
- ✝ $72
- ♫ $72
- ♪ $70
- ▲ $67

**The Lord Bless
You And Keep You**
#E7178
Issued: 1982 • Susp.: 1987
Retail Price: $18 – $20

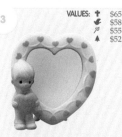

3 VALUES:
- ✝ $65
- ✠ $58
- ♫ $55
- ▲ $52

Loving You
#12017
Issued: 1985 • Susp.: 1987
Retail Price: $19 – $20

4 VALUES:
- ✝ $67
- ✠ $62
- ♫ $57
- ▲ $55

Loving You
#12025
Issued: 1985 • Susp.: 1987
Retail Price: $19 – $20

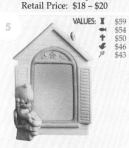

5 VALUES:
- ✠ $59
- ✠ $54
- ✝ $50
- ♫ $46
- ♪ $43

Mother Sew Dear
#E7241
Issued: 1982 • Susp.: 1986
Retail Price: $18 – $19

6 VALUES:
- ✠ $75
- ✠ $68
- ✝ $65

My Guardian Angel
#E7168
Issued: 1982 • Susp.: 1984
Retail Price: $18 – $19

7 VALUES:
- ✠ $85
- ✠ $73
- ✝ $70

My Guardian Angel
#E7169
Issued: 1982 • Susp.: 1984
Retail Price: $18 – $19

8 VALUES:
- ✠ $55
- ✠ $50
- ✝ $50
- ✠ $50
- ♫ $45
- ▲ $43
- ⚓ $43

The Purr-fect Grandma
#E7242
Issued: 1982 • Susp.: 1988
Retail Price: $18 – $22.50

9 VALUES:
- ∞ $25
- ★ $25
- ⏲ $25

**Garnet – Color Of Boldness
(January)**
Birthstone Collection
#335533
Issued: 1998 • Open
Retail Price: $25

10 VALUES:
- ∞ $25
- ★ $25
- ⏲ $25

**Amethyst – Color Of Faith
(February)**
Birthstone Collection
#335541
Issued: 1998 • Open
Retail Price: $25

Frames

	Price Paid	Value
1.		
2.		
3.		
4.		
5.		
6.		
7.		
8.		

Hinged Boxes

9.		
10.		

Totals

KEY: NM *Pre-1981* ▲ 1981 ✠ 1982 ◀ 1983 ✝ 1984 ✎ 1985 ♪ 1986 ♫ 1987 ✢ 1988 ✥ 1989 ★ 1990
♦ 1991 ✦ 1992 ✿ 1993 ☞ 1994 △ 1995 ♡ 1996 ✝ 1997 ∞ 1998 ★ 1999 ⏲ 2000 UM *Unmarked*

183

1 VALUES: 👓 $25
★ $25
🕐 $25

Aquamarine – Color Of Kindness (March)
Birthstone Collection
#335568
Issued: 1998 • Open
Retail Price: $25

2 VALUES: 👓 $25
★ $25
🕐 $25

Diamond – Color Of Purity (April)
Birthstone Collection
#335576
Issued: 1998 • Open
Retail Price: $25

3 VALUES: 👓 $25
★ $25
🕐 $25

Emerald – Color Of Patience (May)
Birthstone Collection
#335584
Issued: 1998 • Open
Retail Price: $25

4 VALUES: 👓 $25
★ $25
🕐 $25

Pearl – Color Of Love (June)
Birthstone Collection
#335592
Issued: 1998 • Open
Retail Price: $25

5 VALUES: 👓 $25
★ $25
🕐 $25

Ruby – Color Of Joy (July)
Birthstone Collection
#335606
Issued: 1998 • Open
Retail Price: $25

6 VALUES: 👓 $25
★ $25
🕐 $25

Peridot – Color Of Pride (August)
Birthstone Collection
#335614
Issued: 1998 • Open
Retail Price: $25

7 VALUES: 👓 $25
★ $25
🕐 $25

Sapphire – Color Of Confidence (September)
Birthstone Collection
#335622
Issued: 1998 • Open
Retail Price: $25

8 VALUES: 👓 $25
★ $25
🕐 $25

Opal – Color Of Happiness (October)
Birthstone Collection
#335657
Issued: 1998 • Open
Retail Price: $25

9 VALUES: 👓 $25
★ $25
🕐 $25

Topaz – Color Of Truth (November)
Birthstone Collection
#335665
Issued: 1998 • Open
Retail Price: $25

10 VALUES: 👓 $25
★ $25
🕐 $25

Turquoise – Color Of Loyalty (December)
Birthstone Collection
#335673
Issued: 1998 • Open
Retail Price: $25

Hinged Boxes

	Price Paid	Value
1.		
2.		
3.		
4.		
5.		
6.		
7.		
8.		
9.		
10.		
Totals		

KEY: NM *Pre-1981* ▲ 1981 𝕀 1982 ◀1983 ✝ 1984 🍃 1985 ✒ 1986 ✿ 1987 ✤ 1988 ⊕ 1989 ✚ 1990 ✤ 1991 ⚘ 1992 ✾1993 ⊶ 1994 △ 1995 ♡1996 ✝ 1997 👓 1998 ★ 1999 🕐 2000 UM *Unmarked*

Other PRECIOUS MOMENTS® Pieces

1

VALUES: 6ᵈ $25 / ★ $25 / ⏱ $25

His Burden Is Light
"Original 21" Collection
#488429
Issued: 1999 • Open
Retail Price: $25

2

VALUES: 6ᵈ $25 / ★ $25 / ⏱ $25

Jesus Is The Light
"Original 21" Collection
#488437
Issued: 1999 • Open
Retail Price: $25

3

VALUES: 6ᵈ $25 / ★ $25 / ⏱ $25

Jesus Loves Me
"Original 21" Collection
#488380
Issued: 1999 • Open
Retail Price: $25

4

VALUES: 6ᵈ $25 / ★ $25 / ⏱ $25

Jesus Loves Me
"Original 21" Collection
#488399
Issued: 1999 • Open
Retail Price: $25

5

VALUES: 6ᵈ $25 / ★ $25 / ⏱ $25

Love One Another
"Original 21" Collection
#488410
Issued: 1999 • Open
Retail Price: $25

6

VALUES: 6ᵈ $25 / ★ $25 / ⏱ $25

Make A Joyful Noise
"Original 21" Collection
#488402
Issued: 1999 • Open
Retail Price: $25

7

VALUES: $204 / $204

Autumn's Praise
(LE-1990/1991)
♪ *"Autumn Leaves"*
#408751
Issued: 1990 • Closed: 1991
Retail Price: $200

8

VALUES: $208 / $208

May You Have An Old Fashioned Christmas
(LE-1991/1992)
♪ *"Have Yourself A Merry Little Christmas"*
#417777
Issued: 1991 • Closed: 1992
Retail Price: $200

9

VALUES: $205 / $205

Summer's Joy (LE-1990/1991)
♪ *"You Are My Sunshine"*
#408743
Issued: 1990 • Closed: 1991
Retail Price: $200

10

VALUES: $205 / $205

The Voice Of Spring
(LE-1990/1991)
♪ *"April Love"*
#408735
Issued: 1990 • Closed: 1991
Retail Price: $200

Hinged Boxes

	Price Paid	Value
1.		
2.		
3.		
4.		
5.		
6.		

Jack-In-The-Boxes

7.		
8.		
9.		
10.		

Totals

KEY: NM Pre-1981 ▲1981 ✠1982 ◀1983 ✿1984 ✦1985 ♩1986 ♣1987 ✚1988 ⊕1989 ⚓1990 ♦1991 ⚘1992 ♋1993 ⬟1994 △1995 ♡1996 ✝1997 6ᵈ1998 ★1999 ⏱2000 UM *Unmarked*

185

Other PRECIOUS MOMENTS® Pieces

1

VALUES: ♨ $208
＆ $208

Winter's Song (LE-1990/1991)
♪"Through The Eyes
Of Love"
#408778
Issued: 1990 • Closed: 1991
Retail Price: $200

2

VALUES: ♨ $180
＆ $180
＄ $180

You Have Touched So Many
Hearts (LE-1991/1992)
♪"Everybody Loves
Somebody"
#422282
Issued: 1991 • Closed: 1992
Retail Price: $175

3 
VALUES: �llM $72

15 Years Tweet Music
Together (LE-1993)
PRECIOUS MOMENTS
Collection 15th Anniversary
Convention Medallion
#529087
Issued: 1993 • Closed: 1993
Retail Price: N/A

4 
VALUES: �llM $645

Friends Never Drift Apart
(LE-1993)
PRECIOUS MOMENTS
Collection 15th Anniversary
Cruise Medallion
#529079
Issued: 1993 • Closed: 1993
Retail Price: N/A

5

VALUES: �llM N/E

Make A Joyful Noise
(LE-1988)
Enesco Orient Tour
Medallion
#PM030
Issued: 1988 • Closed: 1988
Retail Price: N/A

6 
VALUES: △ $355

A Perfect Display Of 15
Happy Years
PRECIOUS MOMENTS
Collection 15th Anniversary
Convention Medallion
#177083
Issued: 1995 • Closed: 1995
Retail Price: N/A

Jack-In-The-Boxes

	Price Paid	Value
1.		
2.		

Medallions

3.		
4.		
5.		
6.		

Musicals

7.		
8.		
9.		

Totals

7

VALUES: NM $182
▲ $170
Ⅱ $160
◄ $157
✝ $150

Christmas Is A Time
To Share
♪"Away In A Manger"
#E2806
Issued: 1980 • Retired: 1984
Retail Price: $35 – $50

8

VALUES: NM $165
▲ $148
Ⅱ $140
◄ $135
✝ $129
🍃 $120
♪ $118
▲ $118
⚓ $118
Ð $118
↓ $112
＆ $112
＄ $112
♀ $112

Come Let Us
Adore Him
♪"Joy To The World"
#E2810
Issued: 1980 • Susp.: 1993
Retail Price: $60 – $100

9

VALUES: NM $140
▲ $130
Ⅱ $122
◄ $116
✝ $105

Crown Him Lord Of All
♪"O Come, All Ye Faithful"
#E2807
Issued: 1980 • Susp.: 1984
Retail Price: $35 – $50

186

Other PRECIOUS MOMENTS® Pieces

1
VALUES: $99 / $92 / $88

Do Not Open 'Til Christmas
♪"Toyland"
#522244
Issued: 1992 • Susp.: 1994
Retail Price: $75

2
VALUES: $126 / $115 / $108 / $102 / $100

God Sent You Just In Time
♪"We Wish You A Merry Christmas"
#15504
Issued: 1985 • Retired: 1989
Retail Price: $45 – $60

3
VALUES: NM $112 / $93 / $82 / $77 / $75 / $70 / $67 / $65 / $65 / $63 / $63 / $63 / $62 / $62 / $62 / $60 / $60 / $60 / $60 / $60

The Hand That Rocks The Future
♪"Mozart's Lullaby"
#E5204
Issued: 1981 • Open
Retail Price: $30 – $60

4
VALUES: $115 / $92 / $85 / $80 / $80 / $80 / $77 / $75 / $75

Heaven Bless You
♪"Brahms' Lullaby"
#100285
Issued: 1986 • Susp.: 1993
Retail Price: $45 – $60

5
VALUES: $210 / $200 / $180

I'll Play My Drum For Him
♪"The Little Drummer Boy"
#E2355
Issued: 1982 • Susp.: 1984
Retail Price: $45 – $50

6
VALUES: $150 / $135 / $125 / $125 / $125 / $120 / $115

I'm Sending You A White Christmas
♪"White Christmas"
#112402
Issued: 1987 • Retired: 1993
Retail Price: $55 – $75

7
VALUES: NM $160 / $137 / $135 / $135 / $130 / $130

Jesus Is Born
♪"Hark, The Herald Angels Sing"
#E2809
Issued: 1980 • Susp.: 1985
Retail Price: $35 – $50

8
VALUES: $165 / $155 / $145 / $137 / $130 / $130 / $125 / $125 / UM $180

Let Heaven And Nature Sing
♪"Joy To The World"
#E2346
Issued: 1982 • Susp.: 1989
Retail Price: $50 – $75

9
VALUES: $160 / $135 / $132 / $132 / $122 / UM $170

Let The Whole World Know
♪"What A Friend We Have In Jesus"
#E7186
Issued: 1982 • Susp.: 1986
Retail Price: $60 – $65

10
VALUES: $125 / $110 / $105 / $102 / $98 / $96 / $93 / $93 / $90 / $90 / $90 / $90 / $90 / $90

Let's Keep In Touch
♪"Be A Clown"
#102520
Issued: 1986 • Retired: 1999
Retail Price: $65 – $90

Musicals

	Price Paid	Value
1.		
2.		
3.		
4.		
5.		
6.		
7.		
8.		
9.		
10.		
Totals		

Other PRECIOUS MOMENTS® Pieces

1

VALUES:
꒨ $94
★ $82
✿ $79
☝ $76
⚘ $74
⊟ $72
♡ $70
✝ $70
୪ $70
★ $70

**The Light Of
The World Is Jesus**
♪ *"White Christmas"*
#521507
Issued: 1989 • Retired: 1999
Retail Price: $60 – $70

2

VALUES:
✠ $110
▲ $106
✝ $102
⚘ $95
✿ $92
⚓ $90
⚓ $90
⊟ $88
★ $85
✿ $85
⊜ $85
△ $85
✝ $85
☝ $85
★ $85
ⓢ $85
UM $135

**The Lord Bless You
And Keep You**
♪ *"Wedding March
By Mendelssohn"*
#E7180
Issued: 1982 • Open
Retail Price: $55 – $85

3

VALUES:
⚘ $94
✿ $87
♀ $82

**Lord, Keep My Life
In Balance**
♪ *"Music Box Dancer"*
#520691
Issued: 1991 • Susp.: 1993
Retail Price: $60 – $65

4

VALUES:
✿ $155
✿ $140
▲ $135
⚓ $130
⊟ $125

**Lord, Keep My Life In
Tune (set/2)**
Rejoice In The Lord Band Series
♪ *"Amazing Grace"*
#12165
Issued: 1985 • Susp.: 1989
Retail Price: $37.50 – $50

5

VALUES:
✿ $285
⚘ $268
⚓ $258
⊟ $250
★ $230

**Lord, Keep My Life In
Tune (set/2)**
Rejoice In The Lord Band Series
♪ *"I'd Like To Teach The
World To Sing"*
#12580
Issued: 1987 • Susp.: 1990
Retail Price: $37.50 – $55

6

VALUES:
✠ $195
▲ $182
✝ $168
✿ $162

Love Is Sharing
♪ *"School Days"*
#E7185
Issued: 1982 • Retired: 1985
Retail Price: $40 – $45

Musicals

	Price Paid	Value
1.		
2.		
3.		
4.		
5.		
6.		
7.		
8.		
9.		
10.		
Totals		

7

VALUES:
✝ $83
✿ $78
▲ $70
▲ $70
⊟ $67
⊟ $65
✿ $65
✿ $65
⚘ $65
⊜ $65
✝ $65
୪ $65
★ $65
ⓢ $65
UM $105

Mother Sew Dear
♪ *"You Light Up
My Life"*
#E7182
Issued: 1982 • Open
Retail Price: $35 – $65

8

VALUES:
NM $125
▲ $110
✠ $100
⚓ $98
✝ $95
✿ $92

My Guardian Angel
♪ *"Brahms' Lullaby"*
#E5205
Issued: 1981 • Susp.: 1985
Retail Price: $22.50 – $27.50

9

VALUES:
NM $125
▲ $110
✠ $96
⚓ $93
✝ $90
⊟ $88
⚘ $86
▲ $82
⚓ $82

My Guardian Angel
♪ *"Brahms' Lullaby"*
#E5206
Issued: 1981 • Susp.: 1988
Retail Price: $22.50 – $33

10

VALUES:
✠ $150
▲ $140
✝ $137
UM $178

O Come All Ye Faithful
♪ *"O Come, All Ye Faithful"*
#E2352
Issued: 1982 • Susp.: 1984
Retail Price: $45 – $50

KEY: NM *Pre-1981* ▲ 1981 ✠ 1982 ◀ 1983 ✝ 1984 ✿ 1985 ⚘ 1986 ▲ 1987 ⚓ 1988 ⊟ 1989 ★ 1990 ⚘ 1991 ✿ 1992 ♀ 1993 ◀ 1994 △ 1995 ♡ 1996 ✝ 1997 ୪ 1998 ★ 1999 ⓢ 2000 UM *Unmarked*

1

VALUES: ♪ $128
▲ $120
✤ $115
✈ $110
☀ $108
● $100
₰ $100

Our First Christmas Together
♪ *"We Wish You A Merry Christmas"*
#101702
Issued: 1986 • Retired: 1992
Retail Price: $50 – $70

2

VALUES: NM $155
▲ $136
✕ $132
◄ $125
✝ $120

Peace On Earth
♪ *"Jesus Loves Me"*
#E4726
Issued: 1981 • Susp.: 1984
Retail Price: $45 – $50

3

VALUES: ▲ $165
✤ $150
✈ $150
☀ $142
☂ $140
₰ $140
∞ $135

Peace On Earth
♪ *"Hark, The Herald Angels Sing"*
#109746
Issued: 1988 • Susp.: 1993
Retail Price: $100 – $130

4

VALUES: ✝ $95
☂ $91
♪ $89
▲ $85
✤ $80
✈ $78
☀ $72
☂ $70
₰ $68
∞ $65
UM $100

The Purr-fect Grandma
♪ *"Always In My Heart"*
#E7184
Issued: 1982 • Susp.: 1993
Retail Price: $35 – $60

5

VALUES: NM $145
▲ $135
✕ $125
✤ $115
✝ $110
✦ $98
♪ $95
▲ $88
✤ $85

Rejoice O Earth
♪ *"Joy To The World"*
#E5645
Issued: 1981 • Retired: 1988
Retail Price: $35 – $55

6

VALUES: ◄ $175
✝ $160
☂ $152
♪ $140

Sharing Our Season Together
♪ *"Winter Wonderland"*
#E0519
Issued: 1983 • Retired: 1986
Retail Price: $70

7

VALUES: NM $400
▲ $390
✕ $380
◄ $375
✝ $370
✦ $350

Silent Knight
♪ *"Silent Night"*
#E5642
Issued: 1981 • Susp.: 1985
Retail Price: $45 – $60

8

VALUES: ✦ $112
◄ $105
▲ $97
✤ $94
✈ $90
☀ $88
☂ $88
₰ $85

Silent Night
Family Christmas Series
♪ *"Silent Night"*
#15814
Issued: 1985 • Susp.: 1992
Retail Price: $37.50 – $55

Musicals

	Price Paid	Value
1.		
2.		
3.		
4.		
5.		
6.		
7.		
8.		
9.		
10.		

Totals

9

VALUES: ☂ $83
₰ $72
∞ $68
⊶ $67
⚏ $65
♡ $65
✝ $65
๛ $65
★ $65
○ $65

This Day Has Been Made In Heaven
♪ *"Amazing Grace"*
#523682
Issued: 1992 • Open
Retail Price: $60 – $65

10

VALUES: NM $150
▲ $125
✕ $117
✤ $110
✝ $105

Unto Us A Child Is Born
♪ *"Jesus Loves Me"*
#E2808
Issued: 1981 • Susp.: 1984
Retail Price: $35 – $50

KEY: NM *Pre-1981* ▲ 1981 ✕ 1982 ◄ 1983 ✝ 1984 ✦ 1985 ♪ 1986 ▲ 1987 ✤ 1988 ✈ 1989 ☀ 1990 ● 1991 ₰ 1992 ∞ 1993 ⊶ 1994 ⚏ 1995 ♡ 1996 ✝ 1997 ๛ 1998 ★ 1999 ○ 2000 UM *Unmarked*

189

Other PRECIOUS MOMENTS® Pieces

1
VALUES: 🕊 $135
🎵 $124
🔺 $120

We Saw A Star (set/3)
♪ *"Joy To The World"*
#12408
Issued: 1985 • Susp.: 1987
Retail Price: $50 – $55

2
VALUES: ➳ $142
✝ $136
🔺 $129
🎵 $122

Wee Three Kings
♪ *"We Three Kings*
Of Orient Are"
#E0520
Issued: 1983 • Susp.: 1986
Retail Price: $60

3
VALUES: ✝ $130
🔺 $122
🎵 $110

Wishing You A Merry Christmas
♪ *"We Wish You A Merry Christmas"*
#E5394
Issued: 1984 • Susp.: 1986
Retail Price: $55

4
VALUES: 🕊 $137
🔺 $115
🎵 $112
🔺 $108
♡ $105
✝ $105
🔺 $105

Wishing You Were Here
♪ *"When You Wish*
Upon A Star"
#526916
Issued: 1993 • Susp.: 1998
Retail Price: $100

5
VALUES: 🔺 $110
🔺 $104
🔺 $98
🔺 $94
🔺 $90
🔺 $90
🔺 $88
🔺 $85
🔺 $80
♡ $80

You Have Touched So Many Hearts
♪ *"Everybody Loves Somebody"*
#112577
Issued: 1988 • Susp.: 1996
Retail Price: $50 – $65

6
VALUES: 🕊 $125
🎵 $115
🔺 $110
🔺 $103
🎵 $99

God Bless You With Rainbows
#16020
Issued: 1986 • Susp.: 1989
Retail Price: $45 – $57.50

7
VALUES: 🔺 $190
UM $255

My Guardian Angel
#E5207
Issued: 1981 • Susp.: 1984
Retail Price: $30 – $37.50

8
VALUES: 🔺 $55

But The Greatest Of These Is Love (Annual, Dated 1992)
Christmas Blessings Series
#527742
Issued: 1992 • Closed: 1992
Retail Price: $50

9
VALUES: 🎵 $55

Wishing You The Sweetest Christmas
(Annual, Dated 1993)
Christmas Blessings Series
#530204
Issued: 1993 • Closed: 1993
Retail Price: $50

10
VALUES: ➳ $55

You're As Pretty As A Christmas Tree
(Annual, Dated 1994)
The Beauty Of Christmas Series
#530409
Issued: 1994 • Closed: 1994
Retail Price: $50

Musicals

	Price Paid	Value
1.		
2.		
3.		
4.		
5.		

Night Lights

6.		
7.		

Plates

8.		
9.		
10.		

Totals

KEY: NM *Pre-1981* 🔺 *1981* 🔺 *1982* ➳ *1983* ✝ *1984* 🕊 *1985* 🎵 *1986* 🔺 *1987* 🔺 *1988* 🔺 *1989* ⭐ *1990*
🔺 *1991* 🔺 *1992* 🎵 *1993* ➳ *1994* 🔺 *1995* ♡ *1996* ✝ *1997* 6d *1998* ★ *1999* ○ *2000* UM *Unmarked*

1
VALUES: ⚠ $58

He Covers The Earth With His Beauty
(Annual, Dated 1995)
The Beauty Of Christmas Series
#142670
Issued: 1995 • Closed: 1995
Retail Price: $50

2
VALUES: ♡ $53

Peace On Earth . . . Anyway
(Annual, Dated 1996)
The Beauty Of Christmas Series
#183377
Issued: 1996 • Closed: 1996
Retail Price: $50

3
VALUES: † $55

Cane You Join Us For A Merry Christmas
(Annual, Dated 1997)
The Beauty Of Christmas Series
#272701
Issued: 1997 • Closed: 1997
Retail Price: $50

4
VALUES: 6ð $52

I'm Sending You A Merry Christmas
(Annual, Dated 1998)
#469327
Issued: 1998 • Closed: 1998
Retail Price: $50

5
VALUES: ★ $62

Wishing You A Yummy Christmas (Dated 1990)
Christmas Blessings Plate Series
#523801
Issued: 1990 • Closed: 1990
Retail Price: $50

6
VALUES: ⚫ $55

Blessings From Me To Thee (Dated 1991)
Christmas Blessings Plate Series
#523860
Issued: 1991 • Closed: 1991
Retail Price: $50

7
VALUES: UM $49

Come Let Us Adore Him (LE-15,000)
Christmas Collection Plate Series
#E5646
Issued: 1981 • Closed: 1981
Retail Price: $40

8
VALUES: UM $48

Let Heaven And Nature Sing (LE-15,000)
Christmas Collection Plate Series
#E2347
Issued: 1982 • Closed: 1982
Retail Price: $45

9
VALUES: UM $48

Wee Three Kings (LE-15,000)
Christmas Collection Plate Series
#E0538
Issued: 1983 • Closed: 1983
Retail Price: $45

Plates

	Price Paid	Value
1.		
2.		
3.		
4.		
5.		
6.		
7.		
8.		
9.		

Totals

Other PRECIOUS MOMENTS® Pieces

---

1 VALUES: ✝ $45
UM $50

Unto Us A Child Is Born
(LE-15,000)
Christmas Collection Plate
Series
#E5395
Issued: 1984 • Closed: 1984
Retail Price: $40

---

2 VALUES: 🎵 $62

I'm Sending You A White
Christmas (Dated 1986)
Christmas Love Plate Series
#101834
Issued: 1986 • Closed: 1986
Retail Price: $45

---

3 VALUES: ▲ $70

My Peace I Give Unto Thee
(Dated 1987)
Christmas Love Plate Series
#102954
Issued: 1987 • Closed: 1987
Retail Price: $45

---

4 VALUES: ⚓ $60

Merry Christmas Deer
(Dated 1988)
Christmas Love Plate Series
#520284
Issued: 1988 • Closed: 1988
Retail Price: $50

---

5 VALUES: Ð $56

May Your Christmas Be A
Happy Home (Dated 1989)
Christmas Love Plate Series
#523003
Issued: 1989 • Closed: 1989
Retail Price: $50

---

6 VALUES: ✝ $106
🕯 $92

The Voice Of Spring
(LE-1985)
Four Seasons Plate Series
#12106
Issued: 1985 • Closed: 1985
Retail Price: $40

---

7 VALUES: ✝ $87
🕯 $82

Summer's Joy (LE-1985)
Four Seasons Plate Series
#12114
Issued: 1985 • Closed: 1985
Retail Price: $40

---

8 VALUES: 🎵 $78

Autumn's Praise (LE-1986)
Four Seasons Plate Series
#12122
Issued: 1986 • Closed: 1986
Retail Price: $40

---

9 VALUES: 🕯 $60
🎵 $45

Winter's Song (LE-1986)
Four Seasons Plate Series
#12130
Issued: 1986 • Closed: 1986
Retail Price: $40

Plates

	Price Paid	Value
1.		
2.		
3.		
4.		
5.		
6.		
7.		
8.		
9.		

Totals

KEY: NM *Pre-1981* ▲ 1981 ✕ 1982 ◄ 1983 ✝ 1984 🕯 1985 🎵 1986 ▲ 1987 ⚓ 1988 Ð 1989 ↟ 1990 ↓ 1991 🔔 1992 ❀ 1993 ◄ 1994 ⌂ 1995 ♡ 1996 ↑ 1997 ♋ 1998 ★ 1999 ◯ 2000 UM *Unmarked*

Other PRECIOUS MOMENTS® Pieces

1 VALUES: UM $57

Love One Another
(LE-15,000)
Inspired Thoughts Plate Series
#E5215
Issued: 1981 • Closed: 1981
Retail Price: $40

2 VALUES: UM $46

Make A Joyful Noise
(LE-15,000)
IInspired Thoughts Plate Series
#E7174
Issued: 1982 • Closed: 1982
Retail Price: $40

3 VALUES: UM $40

I Believe In Miracles
(LE-15,000)
Inspired Thoughts Plate Series
#E9257
Issued: 1983 • Closed: 1983
Retail Price: $40

4 VALUES: 🐟 $47
🕯 $42
UM $50

Love Is Kind (LE-15,000)
Inspired Thoughts Plate Series
#E2847
Issued: 1984 • Closed: 1984
Retail Price: $40

5 VALUES: UM $70

I'll Play My Drum For Him
(Dated 1982)
Joy Of Christmas Plate Series
#E2357
Issued: 1982 • Closed: 1982
Retail Price: $40

6 VALUES: UM $80

Christmastime Is For
Sharing (Dated 1983)
Joy Of Christmas Plate Series
#E0505
Issued: 1983 • Closed: 1983
Retail Price: $40

7 VALUES: 🕯 $50

The Wonder Of Christmas
(Dated 1984)
Joy Of Christmas Plate Series
#E5396
Issued: 1984 • Closed: 1984
Retail Price: $40

8 VALUES: 🐟 $80

Tell Me The Story Of Jesus
(Dated 1985)
Joy Of Christmas Plate Series
#15237
Issued: 1985 • Closed: 1985
Retail Price: $40

9 VALUES: 🔨 $57
🥄 $52

Thinking Of You Is What
I Really Like To Do
(Dated 1994)
Mother's Day Plate Series
#531766
Issued: 1994 • Closed: 1994
Retail Price: $50

10 VALUES: 🔺 $52

He Hath Made Every Thing
Beautiful In His Time
(Dated 1995)
Mother's Day Plate Series
#129151
Issued: 1995 • Closed: 1995
Retail Price: $50

Plates

	Price Paid	Value
1.		
2.		
3.		
4.		
5.		
6.		
7.		
8.		
9.		
10.		

Totals

KEY: NM *Pre-1981* ▲ 1981 ▮ 1982 ◀ 1983 🕯 1984 🐟 1985 🖊 1986 ♣ 1987 ✤ 1988 ⊕ 1989 ⊥ 1990
🔨 1991 🍃 1992 ☯ 1993 ⊷ 1994 🔺 1995 ♡ 1996 ↑ 1997 ∞ 1998 ★ 1999 ○ 2000 UM *Unmarked*

193

Other PRECIOUS MOMENTS® Pieces

1 VALUES: ♡ $50

Of All The Mothers I Have Known There's None As Precious As My Own (Dated 1996)
Mother's Day Plate Series
#163716
Issued: 1996 • Closed: 1996
Retail Price: $50

2 VALUES: UM $50

Mother Sew Dear (LE-15,000)
Mother's Love Plate Series
#E5217
Issued: 1981 • Closed: 1981
Retail Price: $40

3 VALUES: UM $45

The Purr-fect Grandma (LE-15,000)
Mother's Love Plate Series
#E7173
Issued: 1982 • Closed: 1982
Retail Price: $40

4 VALUES: UM $42

The Hand That Rocks The Future (LE-15,000)
Mother's Love Plate Series
#E9256
Issued: 1983 • Closed: 1983
Retail Price: $40

5 VALUES: ✝ $42

Loving Thy Neighbor (LE-15,000)
Mother's Love Plate Series
#E2848
Issued: 1984 • Closed: 1984
Retail Price: $40

6 VALUES: ♀ $57
♙ $52

Bring The Little Ones To Jesus (Dated 1994)
Child Evangelism Fellowship Plate
#531359
Issued: 1994 • Closed: 1994
Retail Price: $50

Plates

	Price Paid	Value
1.		
2.		
3.		
4.		
5.		
6.		
7.		
8.		
9.		
10.		
Totals		

7 VALUES: ⇌ $40
✝ $38
UM $50

Jesus Loves Me
#E9275
Issued: 1983 • Susp.: 1984
Retail Price: $30

8 VALUES: ⇌ $40
✝ $38
UM $50

Jesus Loves Me
#E9276
Issued: 1983 • Susp.: 1984
Retail Price: $30

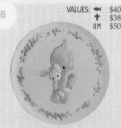

9 VALUES: ✝ $40
✿ $40
♫ $40
♠ $38
UM $48

The Lord Bless You And Keep You
#E5216
Issued: 1981 • Susp.: 1987
Retail Price: $30 – 37.50

10 VALUES: ✝ $40
✿ $35
UM $46

Our First Christmas Together
#E2378
Issued: 1982 • Susp.: 1985
Retail Price: $30

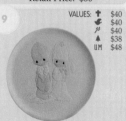

1 VALUES: ✝ $35   🐚 $33   UM $40

Rejoicing With You
#E7172
Issued: 1982 • Susp.: 1985
Retail Price: $30

2 VALUES: PE $35   OE $35

New!

Friendship Hits The Spot
Hugs For The Soul
#729167
Issued: 2000 • Open
Retail Price: $35

3 VALUES: PE $35   OE $35

New!

**God Loveth A
Cheerful Giver**
Hugs For The Soul
#729205
Issued: 2000 • Open
Retail Price: $35

4 VALUES: PE $35   OE $35

New!

Lord, Keep Me On My Toes
Hugs For The Soul
#729191
Issued: 2000 • Open
Retail Price: $35

5 VALUES: UM $70

New!

Love One Another (set/2)
Century Circle Plush
#729213
Issued: 2000 • Open
Retail Price: $70

6 VALUES: PE $35   OE $35

New!

Put On A Happy Face
Hugs For The Soul
#729183
Issued: 2000 • Open
Retail Price: $35

7 VALUES: PE $35   OE $35

New!

Tell It To Jesus
Hugs For The Soul
#729221
Issued: 2000 • Open
Retail Price: $35

8 VALUES: PE $35   OE $35

New!

**You Have Touched So
Many Hearts**
Hugs For The Soul
#729175
Issued: 2000 • Open
Retail Price: $35

9 VALUES: 🐚 $57

**God Sent His Love
(Dated 1985)**
#15865
Issued: 1985 • Closed: 1985
Retail Price: $5.50

10 VALUES: ⌐ $26

**Wishing You A Cozy
Christmas (Dated 1986)**
#102334
Issued: 1986 • Closed: 1986
Retail Price: $5.50

General Plates

	Price Paid	Value
1.		

Plush

2.		
3.		
4.		
5.		
6.		
7.		
8.		

Annual Christmas Thimbles

9.		
10.		

Totals

KEY: NM *Pre-1981*   ▲ *1981*   ▥ *1982*   ◄ *1983*   ✝ *1984*   🐚 *1985*   ♪ *1986*   ▲ *1987*   ✣ *1988*   ♄ *1989*   ⚓ *1990*
  ♨ *1991*   ✿ *1992*   ♀ *1993*   ⚒ *1994*   △ *1995*   ♡ *1996*   ↑ *1997*   ∞ *1998*   ★ *1999*   ☉ *2000*   UM *Unmarked*

195

Other PRECIOUS MOMENTS® Pieces

1 VALUES: ♠ $38

Love Is The Best Gift Of All (Dated 1987)
#109843
Issued: 1987 • Closed: 1987
Retail Price: $6

2 VALUES: ⊕ $57

Time To Wish You A Merry Christmas (Dated 1988)
#115312
Issued: 1988 • Closed: 1988
Retail Price: $7

3 VALUES: ঌ $27

Oh Holy Night (Dated 1989)
#522554
Issued: 1989 • Closed: 1989
Retail Price: $7.50

4 VALUES: ↓ $25

Once Upon A Holy Night (Dated 1990)
#523844
Issued: 1990 • Closed: 1990
Retail Price: $8

5 VALUES: ♦ $25

May Your Christmas Be Merry (Dated 1991)
#524190
Issued: 1991 • Closed: 1991
Retail Price: $8

6 VALUES: ♮ $23

But The Greatest Of These Is Love (Dated 1992)
#527718
Issued: 1992 • Closed: 1992
Retail Price: $8

7 VALUES: ♚♚ $18

Wishing You The Sweetest Christmas (Dated 1993)
#530182
Issued: 1993 • Closed: 1993
Retail Price: $8

8 VALUES: ⋟ $45
♠ $40
⊕ $38

Clowns (set/2)
#100668
Issued: 1986 • Susp.: 1988
Retail Price: $11 – $14

9 VALUES: ⋟ $98

Four Seasons (set/4, LE-1986)
#100641
Issued: 1986 • Closed: 1986
Retail Price: $20

Annual Christmas Thimbles

	Price Paid	Value
1.		
2.		
3.		
4.		
5.		
6.		
7.		

General Thimbles

	Price Paid	Value
8.		
9.		
Totals		

KEY: NM Pre-1981 ▲1981 ⊞1982 ◄1983 ♱1984 ☙1985 ✿1986 ♠1987 ⊕1988 ঌ1989 ↓1990 ♦1991 ♮1992 ♚♚1993 ◄1994 △1995 ♡1996 ♱1997 ൭1998 ★1999 ☉2000 UM Unmarked

1

VALUES: 🍃 $28
📅 $23
▲ $20
✠ $16
Ᏸ $16

God Is Love, Dear Valentine
#100625
Issued: 1986 • Susp.: 1989
Retail Price: $5.50 – $8

2

VALUES: 🍃 $25
📅 $25
▲ $22
✠ $20
Ᏸ $20
★ $18
🍶 $15

The Lord Bless You And Keep You
#100633
Issued: 1986 • Susp.: 1991
Retail Price: $5.50 – $8

3

VALUES: ✝ $26
🍃 $22
📅 $20
▲ $18
Ᏸ $16
Ᏸ $15
🍶 $14
★ $14

Love Covers All
#12254
Issued: 1985 • Susp.: 1990
Retail Price: $5.50 – $8

4

VALUES: ✝ $21
📅 $19
🍃 $18
▲ $15
✠ $15
Ᏸ $14
🍶 $14
🍶 $12
🐚 $11
⚲ $11
🗝 $9
🗝 $9
♡ $9
✝ $8
👓 $8
★ $8
$8

Mother Sew Dear
#13293
Issued: 1985 • Retired: 1999
Retail Price: $5.50 – $8

5

VALUES: ✝ $22
🍃 $21
📅 $19
▲ $17
✠ $15
Ᏸ $14
🍶 $13
🍶 $13
🐚 $12
⚲ $11
🗝 $9
🗝 $9
♡ $9
✝ $8
👓 $8
★ $8
$8

The Purr-fect Grandma
#13307
Issued: 1985 • Retired: 1999
Retail Price: $5.50 – $8

6

VALUES: ★ $140

Rejoice O Earth
♪ "Hark, The Herald Angels Sing"
#617334
Issued: 1990 • Retired: 1991
Retail Price: $125

7

VALUES: ♡ $135
✝ $125
👓 $125
★ $125

Sing In Excelsis Deo
#183830
Issued: 1996 • Retired: 1999
Retail Price: $125

General Thimbles

	Price Paid	Value
1.		
2.		
3.		
4.		
5.		

Tree Toppers

6.		
7.		

Totals

KEY: NM *Pre-1981* ▲ 1981 Ⅱ 1982 ◄ 1983 ✝ 1984 🍃 1985 📅 1986 ▲ 1987 ✠ 1988 Ᏸ 1989 ★ 1990
🍶 1991 🐚 1992 ⚲ 1993 🗝 1994 △ 1995 ♡ 1996 ✝ 1997 👓 1998 ★ 1999 🕐 2000 UM *Unmarked*

197

TENDER TAILS

The TENDER TAILS line was introduced in 1997. This year the *Hugs For You* collection makes its debut, with 10 pieces. *Limited Edition* TENDER TAILS are the only pieces in the line to have year marks, making them a little different from the rest of the pack. (At press time, the 2000 year mark was set to be a three-petal flower, but actual artwork was not yet available.)

1 VALUES: UM $9.99

Ascension Of Jesus
#657018
Issued: 1999 • Open
Retail Price: $9.99

2 VALUES: UM $9.99

God Made The World
#657069
Issued: 1999 • Open
Retail Price: $9.99

3 VALUES: UM $9.99

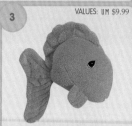

**Jesus Feeds
The 5,000 People**
#657042
Issued: 1999 • Open
Retail Price: $9.99

4 VALUES: UM $9.99

Jesus And The Children
#657026
Issued: 1999 • Open
Retail Price: $9.99

5 VALUES: UM $9.99

Noah's Ark
#657050
Issued: 1999 • Open
Retail Price: $9.99

6 VALUES: UM $9.99

The Ten Commandments
#660604
Issued: 1999 • Open
Retail Price: $9.99

Bible Stories

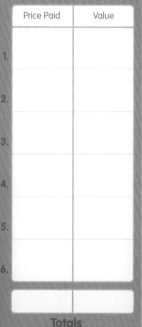

	Price Paid	Value
1.		
2.		
3.		
4.		
5.		
6.		
Totals		

Value Guide — PRECIOUS MOMENTS®

1 VALUES: IIM $7

Baby Bear
#610011
Issued: 1999 • Open
Retail Price: $7

2 VALUES: IIM $7

Age 1
#600156
Issued: 1999 • Open
Retail Price: $7

3 VALUES: IIM $7

Age 2
#600164
Issued: 1999 • Open
Retail Price: $7

4 VALUES: IIM $7

Age 3
#600172
Issued: 1999 • Open
Retail Price: $7

5 VALUES: IIM $7

Age 4
#600180
Issued: 1999 • Open
Retail Price: $7

6 VALUES: IIM $7

Age 5
#600199
Issued: 1999 • Open
Retail Price: $7

7 VALUES: IIM $7

Age 6
#600210
Issued: 1999 • Open
Retail Price: $7

8 VALUES: IIM $10

Circus Clown
#648221
Issued: 1999 • Open
Retail Price: $10

9 VALUES: IIM $10

Display
#648213
Issued: 1999 • Open
Retail Price: $10

Birthday Train

	Price Paid	Value
1.		
2.		
3.		
4.		
5.		
6.		
7.		
8.		
9.		
Totals		

VALUES: IM $6.99

Billy Goat
#476102
Issued: 1998 • Open
Retail Price: $6.99

VALUES: IM $6.99

Brown Cow
#540560
Issued: 1998 • Open
Retail Price: $6.99

VALUES: IM $6.99

Horse
#540609
Issued: 1998 • Open
Retail Price: $6.99

VALUES: IM $6.99

Peach Pig
#540579
Issued: 1998 • Open
Retail Price: $6.99

VALUES: IM $6.99

Rooster
#540617
Issued: 1998 • Open
Retail Price: $6.99

VALUES: IM $6.99

White Duck
#540587
Issued: 1998 • Open
Retail Price: $6.99

COUNTRY LANE

	Price Paid	Value
1.		
2.		
3.		
4.		
5.		
6.		
Totals		

1 · VALUES: UM · $7

Chipmunk
#473979
Issued: 1999 • Open
Retail Price: $7

2 · VALUES: UM · $7

Crow
#534285
Issued: 1999 • Open
Retail Price: $7

3 · VALUES: UM · $7

Field Mouse
#547115
Issued: 1999 • Open
Retail Price: $7

4 · VALUES: UM · $7

Skunk
#473960
Issued: 1999 • Open
Retail Price: $7

5 · VALUES: UM · $7

Squirrel
#476099
Issued: 1999 • Open
Retail Price: $7

6 · VALUES: UM · $7

Turkey
#534315
Issued: 1999 • Open
Retail Price: $7

Grandma Ethel's Farm

	Price Paid	Value
1.		
2.		
3.		
4.		
5.		
6.		

Totals

TENDER TAILS

1   VALUES: ЦМ $7

Camel
#533963
Issued: 1999 • Open
Retail Price: $7

2   VALUES: ЦМ $7

Donkey
#533971
Issued: 1999 • Open
Retail Price: $7

3   VALUES: ЦМ $7

Gray Lamb
#963151
Issued: 1999 • Open
Retail Price: $7

4   VALUES: ЦМ $22.50

Mary/Jesus/Joseph (set/3)
#963135
Issued: 1999 • Open
Retail Price: $22.50

5   VALUES: ЦМ $7

Nativity Cow
#540668
Issued: 1999 • Open
Retail Price: $7

6   VALUES: ЦМ $10

Nativity Quilt Display
#540676
Issued: 1999 • Open
Retail Price: $10

Nativity

	Price Paid	Value
1.		
2.		
3.		
4.		
5.		
6.		
7.		

General Plush

8.		
9.		

Totals

7   VALUES: ЦМ $10

Palm Tree
#963208
Issued: 1999 • Open
Retail Price: $10

8   VALUES: ♥ $7
           ЦМ $7

**20th Anniversary Bear
(LE-1998)**
Care-A-Van Exclusive
#462829
Issued: 1998 • Closed: 1998
Retail Price: $6.99

9   VALUES: ЦМ $9.99

Ant
Bug Series
#656917
Issued: 1999 • Open
Retail Price: $9.99

Value Guide — PRECIOUS MOMENTS®

1   VALUES: UM $15

Bear
#358274
Issued: 1997 • Retired: 1998
Retail Price: $6.99

2   VALUES: UM $20

Bear Couple
(w/ornament, "Our First
Christmas Together")
#966771
Issued: 1998 • Open
Retail Price: $20

3   VALUES: UM $3.99

Bear Cub
*Collect Your Own
Family Series*
#661481
Issued: 1999 • Open
Retail Price: $3.99

4   VALUES: UM $10.99

Bear With Cub
*Collect Your Own
Family Series*
#661406
Issued: 1999 • Open
Retail Price: $10.99

5   VALUES: ❀ $6.99
(Can.)

New!

Beaver
Exclusive To Canada
#536369
Issued: 2000 • Open
Retail Price: $6.99

6   VALUES: UM $7

Bee
#464295
Issued: 1999 • Open
Retail Price: $7

7   VALUES: UM $6.99

Beetle
Bug Series
#656887
Issued: 1999 • Open
Retail Price: $6.99

8   VALUES: UM $12

Blue Bird
#382531
Issued: 1998 • Retired: 1998
Retail Price: $6.99

9   VALUES: UM $15

Boy Bear (w/ornament,
"Baby's First Christmas")
#966755
Issued: 1998 • Open
Retail Price: $15

General Plush

	Price Paid	Value
1.		
2.		
3.		
4.		
5.		
6.		
7.		
8.		
9.		
Totals		

Value Guide — PRECIOUS MOMENTS®

1 VALUES: ∐M $6.99

Brontosaurus
#686808
Issued: 1999 • Open
Retail Price: $6.99

2 VALUES: ∐M $14

Brown Bunny
#464422
Issued: 1998 • Retired: 1999
Retail Price: $6.99

3 VALUES: ★ $6.99
00 $6.99

**Bunny
(6", Dated 2000)**
#649120
Issued: 1999 • Open
Retail Price: $6.99

4 VALUES: ∐M $14

Bunny
*Collect Your Own
Family Series*
#661449
Issued: 1999 • Open
Retail Price: $3.99

5 VALUES: ★ $20
00 $20

**Bunny
(12", Dated 2000)**
#670197
Issued: 1999 • Open
Retail Price: $20

6 VALUES: ∐M $10.99

Bunny With Baby
*Collect Your Own
Family Series*
#661309
Issued: 1999 • Open
Retail Price: $10.99

General Plush

	Price Paid	Value
1.		
2.		
3.		
4.		
5.		
6.		
7.		
8.		
9.		
Totals		

7 VALUES: ∐M $7

Butterfly
#482234
Issued: 1999 • Open
Retail Price: $7

8 VALUES: ∐M $9

Cardinal
#471909
Issued: 1998 • Retired: 1999
Retail Price: $6.99

9 VALUES: ∐M $11

Cat
#382256
Issued: 1998 • Retired: 1999
Retail Price: $6.99

1 VALUES: ★ N/E

Cat
Chapel Licensee
Show Plush
#676497
Issued: 1999 • Closed: 1999
Retail Price: N/A

2 VALUES: UM $10.99

Cat With Kitten
Collect Your Own
Family Series
#661333
Issued: 1999 • Open
Retail Price: $10.99

3 VALUES: UM $6.99

Caterpillar
Bug Series
#656941
Issued: 1999 • Open
Retail Price: $6.99

4 VALUES: UM $9.99

Caveman
#686735
Issued: 1999 • Open
Retail Price: $9.99

5 VALUES: UM $9.99

Cavewoman
#686743
Issued: 1999 • Open
Retail Price: $9.99

6 VALUES: UM $10

Cow
#475890
Issued: 1998 • Retired: 1999
Retail Price: $6.99

7 VALUES: UM $6.99

Diplodocus
#688061
Issued: 1999 • Retired: 1999
Retail Price: $6.99

8 VALUES: UM $6.99

Dolphin
#535192
Issued: 1999 • Open
Retail Price: $6.99

9 VALUES: UM $6.99

Dragon Fly
Bug Series
#656976
Issued: 1999 • Open
Retail Price: $6.99

General Plush

	Price Paid	Value
1.		
2.		
3.		
4.		
5.		
6.		
7.		
8.		
9.		

Totals

TENDER TAILS

1 VALUES: IIM $9

Duck
#382515
Issued: 1998 • Retired: 1998
Retail Price: $6.99

2 VALUES: IIM $6.99

New!

Eagle
*I'm Proud To Be An
American Series*
#648248
Issued: 2000 • Open
Retail Price: $6.99

3 VALUES: IIM $13

Elephant
#358320
Issued: 1997 • Retired: 1998
Retail Price: $6.99

4 VALUES: ★ $7

Elephant
Special Event Plush
#609692
Issued: 1999 • Closed: 1999
Retail Price: $7

5 VALUES: IIM $15

Girl Bear (w/ornament,
"Baby's First Christmas")
#966763
Issued: 1998 • Open
Retail Price: $15

6 VALUES: IIM $7

Goose
#473952
Issued: 1999 • Open
Retail Price: $7

General Plush

	Price Paid	Value
1.		
2.		
3.		
4.		
5.		
6.		
7.		
8.		
9.		
Totals		

7 VALUES: IIM N/E

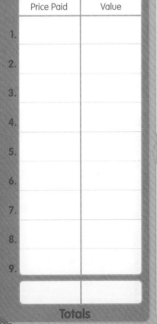

Gorilla
*Local Club Chapter
Convention Plush*
#480355
Issued: 1998 • Closed: 1998
Retail Price: N/A

8 VALUES: IIM $6.99

Graduation Bear
#534595
Issued: 1999 • Open
Retail Price: $6.99

9 VALUES: ★ $6.99
00 $6.99

Graduation Bear
(Dated 2000)
#750816
Issued: 1999 • Open
Retail Price: $6.99

1 VALUES: UM $6.99

Grasshopper
Bug Series
#656933
Issued: 1999 • Open
Retail Price: $6.99

2 VALUES: UM $9

Harp Seal
#382086
Issued: 1998 • Retired: 1999
Retail Price: $6.99

3 VALUES: UM $6.99

Hippo
#475912
Issued: 1998 • Open
Retail Price: $6.99

4 VALUES: UM $12

Horse
#358290
Issued: 1997 • Retired: 1998
Retail Price: $6.99

5 VALUES: UM $6.99

Iguariandon
#686824
Issued: 1999 • Open
Retail Price: $6.99

6 VALUES: UM $3.99

Kangaroo
*Collect Your Own
Family Series*
#661457
Issued: 1999 • Open
Retail Price: $3.99

7 VALUES: UM $10.99

Kangaroo With Baby
*Collect Your Own
Family Series*
#661325
Issued: 1999 • Open
Retail Price: $10.99

8 VALUES: UM $3.99

Kitten
*Collect Your Own
Family Series*
#661465
Issued: 1999 • Open
Retail Price: $3.99

9 VALUES: ★ $10

Koala (LE-1999)
Catalog Plush
#535141
Issued: 1999 • Closed: 1999
Retail Price: $7

General Plush

	Price Paid	Value
1.		
2.		
3.		
4.		
5.		
6.		
7.		
8.		
9.		
Totals		

1 VALUES: UM $11

Ladybug
#476080
Issued: 1999 • Retired: 1999
Retail Price: $7

2 VALUES: UM $9

Lamb
#463299
Issued: 1998 • Retired: 1999
Retail Price: $6.99

3 VALUES: UM $12.99

Lamb (12")
#477192
Issued: 1999 • Open
Retail Price: $12.99

4 VALUES: UM $20

Lamb (16")
#544094
Issued: 1999 • Open
Retail Price: $20

5 VALUES: ★ $6.99
00 $6.99

Lavender Bear With Kiss
(LE-2000)
#670200
Issued: 1999 • To Be Closed: 2000
Retail Price: $6.99

6 VALUES: UM $7

Lavender Bunny
#516597
Issued: 1999 • Open
Retail Price: $7

General Plush

	Price Paid	Value
1.		
2.		
3.		
4.		
5.		
6.		
7.		
8.		
9.		
Totals		

7 VALUES: UM $11

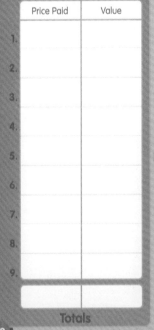

Lion
#358266
Issued: 1997 • Retired: 1998
Retail Price: $6.99

8 VALUES: UM $6.99

Lobster
#750611
Issued: 1999 • Open
Retail Price: $6.99

9 VALUES: ✦ $10
(Can.)

Loon
Exclusive To Canada
#535354
Issued: 1999 • Open
Retail Price: $10 (Canadian)

1 — VALUES: ⅡM $6.99

Monkey
#475939
Issued: 1998 • Open
Retail Price: $6.99

2 — VALUES: ♥ $42

**Monkey Triplets
(set/3, LE-1998)**
Special Event Plush
#537977
Issued: 1998 • Closed: 1998
Retail Price: $14.99

3 — VALUES: ⬜ $10 (Can.)

Moose
Exclusive To Canada
#549509
Issued: 1999 • Open
Retail Price: $10 (Canadian)

4 — VALUES: ⅡM $6.99

Octopus
#750654
Issued: 1999 • Open
Retail Price: $6.99

5 — VALUES: ⅡM $6.99

Owl
#475882
Issued: 1998 • Open
Retail Price: $6.99

6 — VALUES: ♥ N/E
★ N/E

Panda Bear (LE-1999)
Care-A-Van Exclusive
#600873
Issued: 1999 • Closed: 1999
Retail Price: $7

7 — VALUES: ★ N/E

Parrot (LE-1999)
#480371
Issued: 1999 • Closed: 1999
Retail Price: $7

8 — VALUES: ⅡM $6.99

Penguin
#471917
Issued: 1998 • Open
Retail Price: $6.99

9 — VALUES: ⅡM $14

Pink Bunny
#464414
Issued: 1998 • Retired: 1999
Retail Price: $6.99

General Plush

	Price Paid	Value
1.		
2.		
3.		
4.		
5.		
6.		
7.		
8.		
9.		
Totals		

Value Guide — PRECIOUS MOMENTS®

TENDER TAILS

VALUES: ♥ $15

Pink Flamingo (LE-1998)
#482889
Issued: 1998 • Closed: 1998
Retail Price: $6.99

VALUES: ⊔M $12.99

Pink Flamingo (12")
N/A
Issued: 1999 • Open
Retail Price: $12.99

VALUES: ⊔M $6.99

Polar Bear
#382027
Issued: 1998 • Open
Retail Price: $6.99

VALUES: ⊔M $6.99

Pterodactyl
#686794
Issued: 1999 • Open
Retail Price: $6.99

VALUES: ⊔M $7

Pumpkin (available in three colors)
#547131
Issued: 1999 • Open
Retail Price: $7

General Plush

	Price Paid	Value
1.		
2.		
3.		
4.		
5.		
6.		
7.		
8.		
Totals		

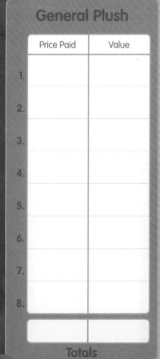

VALUES: ⊔M N/E

Raptor
#686816
Issued: 1999 • Retired: 1999
Retail Price: $6.99

VALUES: ⊔M $6.99

Reindeer
#381969
Issued: 1998 • Open
Retail Price: $6.99

VALUES: ♥ $7

Rosie (LE-1999, available with rose, yellow, green, peach, violet or white ribbon)
Special Event Plush
#486884
Issued: 1999 • Closed: 1999
Retail Price: N/A

Value Guide — PRECIOUS MOMENTS®

1   VALUES: UM $6.99

Seahorse
#535176
Issued: 1999 • Open
Retail Price: $6.99

2   VALUES: ★ N/E

Seal (LE-1999)
Easter Seals
Commemorative Plush
N/A
Issued: 1999 • Closed: 1999
Retail Price: $7

3   VALUES: UM $6.99

Shark
#750646
Issued: 1999 • Open
Retail Price: $6.99

4   VALUES: UM $6.99

Snail
Bug Series
#656968
Issued: 1999 • Open
Retail Price: $6.99

5   VALUES: ★ N/E

Spider
(LE-1999, vibrating)
#656895E
Issued: 1999 • Closed: 1999
Retail Price: $6.99

6   VALUES: UM $6.99

Starfish
#750638
Issued: 1999 • Open
Retail Price: $6.99

7   VALUES: UM $6.99

Stegosaurus
#686778
Issued: 1999 • Open
Retail Price: $6.99

8   VALUES: ♥ $10

Tippy
Special Event Plush
#477869
Issued: 1999 • Closed: 1999
Retail Price: $7

9   VALUES: UM $6.99

T-Rex
#686751
Issued: 1999 • Open
Retail Price: $6.99

10   VALUES: UM $6.99

Triceratops
#686786
Issued: 1999 • Open
Retail Price: $6.99

General Plush

	Price Paid	Value
1.		
2.		
3.		
4.		
5.		
6.		
7.		
8.		
9.		
10.		
Totals		

1 — VALUES: UM $20

Turkey With Sign (12")
#634174
Issued: 1999 • Open
Retail Price: $20

2 — VALUES: UM $13

Turtle
#358339
Issued: 1997 • Retired: 1998
Retail Price: $6.99

3 — VALUES: ★ N/E

Turtle
Chapel Commemorative Plush
#681040
Issued: 1999 • Closed: 1999
Retail Price: $6.99

4 — VALUES: ♥ $16

Unicorn (LE-1998)
#478180
Issued: 1998 • Closed: 1998
Retail Price: $6.99

5 — VALUES: UM $7

Whale
#573639
Issued: 1999 • Open
Retail Price: $7

6 — VALUES: UM $7

Whale
#576115
Issued: 1999 • Open
Retail Price: $7

7 — VALUES: UM $7

Whale
#576131
Issued: 1999 • Open
Retail Price: $7

8 — VALUES: UM $7

Whale
#576956
Issued: 1999 • Open
Retail Price: $7

9 — VALUES: UM $7

Whale
#576964
Issued: 1999 • Open
Retail Price: $7

10 — VALUES: UM $7

Whale
#576980
Issued: 1999 • Open
Retail Price: $7

General Plush

	Price Paid	Value
1.		
2.		
3.		
4.		
5.		
6.		
7.		
8.		
9.		
10.		
Totals		

Value Guide — PRECIOUS MOMENTS®

1   VALUES: UM $7

Whale
#576999
Issued: 1999 • Open
Retail Price: $7

2   VALUES: ♥   N/E

Whale
#577006
Issued: 1999 • Retired: 1999
Retail Price: $7

3   VALUES: UM $9

White Bunny
#382345
Issued: 1998 • Retired: 1999
Retail Price: $6.99

4   VALUES: ♥ $12

White Owl (LE-1998)
Special Event Plush
#504394
Issued 1998 • Closed: 1998
Retail Price: N/A

5   VALUES: ♥ $14
                UM $14

White Rhino (LE-1998)
#358312
Issued: 1998 • Closed: 1998
Retail Price: $6.99

6   VALUES: UM $4

20th Anniversary Bear
#612421
Issued: 1999 • Open
Retail Price: $4

7   VALUES: UM $3.99

Bear
#463256
Issued: 1998 • Open
Retail Price: $3.99

8   VALUES: UM $4

Blue Bird
#478458
Issued: 1999 • Open
Retail Price: $4

9   VALUES: UM $4

Bunny Mini Ornaments
(available in 6 colors)
#649112
Issued: 1999 • Open
Retail Price: $4

10   VALUES: UM $3.99

Cardinal
#463264
Issued: 1998 • Open
Retail Price: $3.99

General Plush

	Price Paid	Value
1.		
2.		
3.		
4.		
5.		

General Ornaments

6.		
7.		
8.		
9.		
10.		

Totals

TENDER TAILS

1 VALUES: UM $3.99

Elephant
#463256
Issued: 1998 • Open
Retail Price: $3.99

2 VALUES: UM $4

Flamingo
#612421
Issued: 1999 • Open
Retail Price: $4

3 VALUES: UM $3.99

Harp Seal
#463264
Issued: 1998 • Open
Retail Price: $3.99

4 VALUES: UM $3.99

Horse
#463256
Issued: 1998 • Open
Retail Price: $3.99

5 VALUES: UM $4

Lamb
#478458
Issued: 1999 • Open
Retail Price: $4

6 VALUES: UM $3.99

Lion
#463256
Issued: 1998 • Open
Retail Price: $3.99

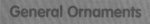

General Ornaments

	Price Paid	Value
1.		
2.		
3.		
4.		
5.		
6.		
7.		
8.		
9.		
Totals		

7 VALUES: UM $4

Monkey
(available in three colors)
#612421
Issued: 1999 • Open
Retail Price: $4

8 VALUES: UM $4

Owl
#612421
Issued: 1999 • Open
Retail Price: $4

9 VALUES: UM $3.99

Pig
#463256
Issued: 1998 • Open
Retail Price: $3.99

Value Guide — PRECIOUS MOMENTS®

1 VALUES: UM $4

Pink Bunny
#478458
Issued: 1999 • Open
Retail Price: $4

2 VALUES: UM $3.99

Polar Bear
#463264
Issued: 1998 • Open
Retail Price: $3.99

3 VALUES: UM $3.99

Reindeer
#463264
Issued: 1998 • Open
Retail Price: $3.99

4 VALUES: UM $4

Rhino
#612421
Issued: 1999 • Open
Retail Price: $4

5 VALUES: UM $4

Rosie
#612421
Issued: 1999 • Open
Retail Price: $4

6 VALUES: UM $4

Tippy
#612421
Issued: 1999 • Open
Retail Price: $4

7 VALUES: UM $3.99

Turtle
#463256
Issued: 1998 • Open
Retail Price: $3.99

8 VALUES: UM $4

Unicorn
#612421
Issued: 1999 • Open
Retail Price: $4

9 VALUES: UM $4

Yellow Duck
#478458
Issued: 1999 • Open
Retail Price: $4

General Ornaments

	Price Paid	Value
1.		
2.		
3.		
4.		
5.		
6.		
7.		
8.		
9.		
Totals		

Value Guide — PRECIOUS MOMENTS®

1 New! VALUES: UM $12.50	

Bear
Hugs For You
#729086
Issued: 2000 • Open
Retail Price: $12.50

Bird
Hugs For You
#729094
Issued: 2000 • Open
Retail Price: $12.50

Bunny
Hugs For You
#729116
Issued: 2000 • Open
Retail Price: $12.50

Cat
Hugs For You
#729051
Issued: 2000 • Open
Retail Price: $12.50

Cow
Hugs For You
#729132
Issued: 2000 • Open
Retail Price: $12.50

Dog
Hugs For You
#729078
Issued: 2000 • Open
Retail Price: $12.50

Elephant
Hugs For You
#729159
Issued: 2000 • Open
Retail Price: $12.50

Lion
Hugs For You
#729140
Issued: 2000 • Open
Retail Price: $12.50

Monkey
Hugs For You
#729124
Issued: 2000 • Open
Retail Price: $12.50

Pig
Hugs For You
#729108
Issued: 2000 • Open
Retail Price: $12.50

VALUES: UM $12.50 (items 1-10)

Other Collectibles

	Price Paid	Value
1.		
2.		
3.		
4.		
5.		
6.		
7.		
8.		
9.		
10.		
Totals		

CHAPEL EXCLUSIVES

Within this section you'll find both figurines and ornaments that have been made available exclusively through The PRECIOUS MOMENTS Chapel. The Chapel, which is located in Carthage, Missouri, also offers pieces to collectors through their PRECIOUS MOMENTS Chapel catalog. To date, more than 50 pieces have been offered through The Chapel, with many more expected for 2000.

1
VALUES: † $55
68 $55
★ $55
🕐 $55

He Maketh Me Lie Down In Green Pastures (LE-7,500)
#523305
Issued: 1997 • Open
Retail Price: $55

2
VALUES: † $55
68 $55
★ $55
🕐 $55

He Restoreth My Soul (LE-7,500)
#523364
Issued: 1998 • Open
Retail Price: $55

3
VALUES: ★ $55
🕐 $55

I Will Dwell In The House Of The Lord Forever (LE-7,500)
#523410
Issued: 1999 • Open
Retail Price: $55

4
VALUES: 68 $55
$55
★ $55
🕐 $55

The Lord Is My Shepherd I Shall Not Want (LE-7,500)
#523402
Issued: 1997 • Open
Retail Price: $55

5
VALUES: ★ $55
🕐 $55

Thou Anointest My Head With Oil; My Cup Runneth Over (LE-7,500)
#523429
Issued: 1999 • Open
Retail Price: $55

23rd Psalm Window Figurines

	Price Paid	Value
1.		
2.		
3.		
4.		
5.		
6.		
7.		
Totals		

6
VALUES: 68 $55
★ $55
🕐 $55

Thou Preparest A Table Before Me In The Presence Of Mine Enemies (LE-7,500)
#523372
Issued: 1998 • Open
Retail Price: $55

7
VALUES: 68 $55
★ $55
🕐 $55

Yea, Though I Walk Through The Valley Of The Shadow Of Death (LE-7,500)
#523356
Issued: 1998 • Open
Retail Price: $55

Chapel Exclusives

1 VALUES: ⚘ $63

Blessed Are The Meek, For They Shall Inherit The Earth (LE-1993/1994)
#523313
Issued: 1993 • Closed: 1994
Retail Price: $55

2 VALUES: 🍥 $65

Blessed Are The Merciful, For They Shall Obtain Mercy (LE-1994)
#523291
Issued: 1994 • Closed: 1994
Retail Price: $55

3 VALUES: 🍥 $75

Blessed Are The Peacemakers, For They Shall Be Called The Children Of God (LE-1995)
#523348
Issued: 1995 • Closed: 1995
Retail Price: $55

4 VALUES: ⏧ $70

Blessed Are The Poor In Spirit, For Theirs Is The Kingdom Of Heaven (LE-1992)
#523437
Issued: 1992 • Closed: 1992
Retail Price: $55

5 VALUES: 🍥 $75

Blessed Are The Pure In Heart, For They Shall See God (LE-1994/1995)
#523399
Issued: 1994 • Closed: 1995
Retail Price: $55

6 VALUES: ⚘ $65

Blessed Are They That Hunger And Thirst After Righteousness, For They Shall Be Filled (LE-1993)
#523321
Issued: 1993 • Closed: 1993
Retail Price: $55

Beatitudes Window Figurines

	Price Paid	Value
1.		
2.		
3.		
4.		
5.		
6.		
7.		

7 VALUES: ⏧ $70

Blessed Are They That Mourn, For They Shall Be Comforted (LE-1992)
#523380
Issued: 1992 • Closed: 1992
Retail Price: $55

8
VALUES: † $32.50
6∂ $32.50
★ $32.50
🕓 $32.50
UM $38

Coleenia
#204889
Issued: 1996 • Open
Retail Price: $32.50

General Figurines

8.		
9.		
10.		

Totals

9
VALUES: † $35
6∂ $35
★ $35
🕓 $35
UM $42

Crown Him Lord Of All
#261602
Issued: 1997 • Open
Retail Price: $35

10
VALUES: 🍥 $34
⚙ $32
♡ $30
† $30
6∂ $30
★ $30
🕓 $30
UM $45

Death Can't Keep Him In The Ground
#531928
Issued: 1994 • Open
Retail Price: $30

KEY: NM *Pre*-1981 ▲ 1981 Ⅱ 1982 ◄ 1983 † 1984 ◢ 1985 ✻ 1986 ▲ 1987 ✧ 1988 ⏀ 1989 ⚶ 1990 ⏧ 1991 ⏧ 1992 ⚘ 1993 🍥 1994 ⚙ 1995 ♡ 1996 † 1997 6∂ 1998 ★ 1999 🕓 2000 UM *Unmarked*

Value Guide — PRECIOUS MOMENTS®

Chapel Exclusives

1 VALUES: 🕶 $67.50 · ★ $67.50 · ○ $67.50

Feed My Lambs
#543722
Issued: 1998 • Open
Retail Price: $67.50

2 VALUES: ★ $45 · ○ $45 · ᑌᗰ $45

Fountain Of Angels
#384844
Issued: 1998 • Open
Retail Price: $45

3 VALUES: ᑌᗰ $45

Good Night, Sleep Tight
#542636
Issued: 1999 • Open
Retail Price: $45

4 VALUES: △ $125 · ♡ $120 · ✝ $105 · 🕶 $100 · ★ $100 · ○ $100

Grandpa's Island
#129259
Issued: 1995 • Open
Retail Price: $100

5 VALUES: ᑌᗰ N/E

Happy 10th Anniversary
*10th Anniversary
Commemorative Figurine*
#540013
Issued: 1999 • Closed: 1999
Retail Price: $45

6 VALUES: ᑌᗰ $95

He Is My Inspiration
#523038
Issued: 1991 • Open
Retail Price: $60

7 *Variation* VALUES: 🐟 $68 · △ $63 · ♡ $60 · ✝ $60 · ◀ $60 · ★ $60 · ○ $60 · ᑌᗰ $100

HE IS NOT HERE
FOR HE IS RISEN
AS HE SAID.
MATH 28:6

He Is Not Here For He Is Risen As He Said
#527106
Issued: 1993 • Open
Retail Price: $60
Variation: Inscription reads "Math" – $105

8 VALUES: ᑌᗰ $30

**He Is The Bright
Morning Star**
#588067
Issued: 1999 • Open
Retail Price: $30

19 VALUES: ✝ $45 · 🕶 $45 · ★ $45 · ○ $45 · ᑌᗰ $60

Heaven Must Have Sent You
#135992
Issued: 1996 • Open
Retail Price: $45

General Figurines

	Price Paid	Value
1.		
2.		
3.		
4.		
5.		
6.		
7.		
8.		
9.		

Totals

KEY: NM *Pre-1981* ▲ 1981 ⊠ 1982 ◣ 1983 ✝ 1984 ◀ 1985 ✐ 1986 ▲ 1987 ⬦ 1988 ⬠ 1989 ☆ 1990 ▲ 1991 ⬚ 1992 ⊕ 1993 ◀ 1994 △ 1995 ♡ 1996 ✝ 1997 🕶 1998 ★ 1999 ○ 2000 ᑌᗰ *Unmarked*

Chapel Exclusives

1 VALUES: ♡ $28 / † $28 / 6∂ $28

His Presence Is Felt In The Chapel
#163872
Issued: 1996 • Retired: 1998
Retail Price: $25

2 VALUES: ᙀM $50

I'm Gonna Let It Shine
#349852
Issued: 1999 • Open
Retail Price: $50

3 VALUES: ᙀM $45

A King Is Born
#604151
Issued: 1994 • Retired: 1995
Retail Price: $25

4 VALUES: ⏛ $45 / ♡ $36 / † $36 / 6∂ $36

Lighting The Way To A Happy Holiday
#129267
Issued: 1995 • Retired: 1998
Retail Price: $30

5 VALUES: ᙀM $50

The Lord Is Our Chief Inspiration
#204862
Issued: 1996 • Open
Retail Price: $45

6 VALUES: ᙀM $282

The Lord Is Our Chief Inspiration (9", LE-1996/1997)
#204870
Issued: 1996 • Closed: 1997
Retail Price: $250

General Figurines

	Price Paid	Value
1.		
2.		
3.		
4.		
5.		
6.		
7.		
8.		
9.		
10.		
Totals		

7 VALUES: ♡ $52 / † $50 / 6∂ $50 / ᙀM $85

On The Hill Overlooking The Quiet Blue Stream
#603503
Issued: 1994 • Retired: 1998
Retail Price: $45

8 VALUES: ᙀM $90

Our Love Will Flow Eternal
#588059
Issued: 1999 • Open
Retail Price: $90

9 VALUES: ★ $45 / ① $45 / ᙀM $45

A Prayer Warrior's Faith Can Move Mountains
#354406
Issued: 1998 • Open
Retail Price: $45

10 VALUES: 6∂ $259 / ★ $259

A Prayer Warrior's Faith Can Move Mountains (9", LE-1998)
#354414
Issued: 1998 • Closed: 1998
Retail Price: $250

KEY: NM *Pre-*1981 ▲ 1981 ✠ 1982 ◄ 1983 † 1984 ✿ 1985 ✦ 1986 ▲ 1987 ✤ 1988 ৳ 1989 ⟟ 1990 ● 1991 ✦ 1992 ♈ 1993 ᅠ 1994 ⏛ 1995 ♡ 1996 † 1997 6∂ 1998 ★ 1999 ① 2000 ᙀM *Unmarke*

Value Guide — PRECIOUS MOMENTS®

1 VALUES: UM $75

Precious Moments Chapel
Lilliput Lane® Figurine
#L2258
Issued: 1999 • Open
Retail Price: $75

2 VALUES: 6d $30 / ★ $30 / ◷ $30 / UM $46

Seeds Of Love From The Chapel
#271586
Issued: 1997 • Susp.: 1999
Retail Price: $30

3 VALUES: ⊟ $35 / ♡ $33 / ◷ $30 / † $30 / 6d $30 / ★ $30 / ◷ $30 / UM $56

Surrounded With Joy
#531677
Issued: 1993 • Open
Retail Price: $30

4 VALUES: ♦ $70 / ⚘ $64 / ⊟ $60 / △ $58 / UM $105

Variation

There's A Christian Welcome Here
#523011
Issued: 1989 • Susp.: 1995
Retail Price: $45
Variation: Missing right eyebrow – $125

5 VALUES: † $85 / 6d $85 / ★ $85 / ◷ $85 / UM $95

This World Is Not My Home (I'm Just A Passing Thru)
#212547
Issued: 1997 • Retired: 1999
Retail Price: $85

6 VALUES: 6d $40 / ★ $40 / ◷ $40

Toy Maker
#475092
Issued: 1998 • Open
Retail Price: $40

7 VALUES: † $25 / 6d $25 / ★ $25 / ◷ $25 / UM $35

Crown Him Lord Of All
#261610
Issued: 1997 • Open
Retail Price: $25

8 VALUES: UM N/E

Happy 10th Anniversary
10th Anniversary Commemorative Figurine
#588040
Issued: 1999 • Closed: 1999
Retail Price: $20

9 VALUES: † $23 / 6d $23 / UM $28

His Presence Is Felt In The Chapel
#163880
Issued: 1996 • Susp.: 1998
Retail Price: $17.50

General Figurines

	Price Paid	Value
1.		
2.		
3.		
4.		
5.		

Ornaments

6.		
7.		
8.		
9.		

Totals

KEY: NM Pre-1981 ▲1981 ✕1982 ◄1983 †1984 ✔1985 ✦1986 ♣1987 ✦1988 Đ1989 ±1990 ♦1991 ⚘1992 ⚘1993 ⊟1994 △1995 ♡1996 †1997 6d1998 ★1999 ◷2000 UM Unmarked

221

Chapel Exclusives

1
VALUES: UM $20

He Is The Bright Morning Star
#588075
Issued: 1999 • Open
Retail Price: $20

2
VALUES: UM $45

A King Is Born
#532088
Issued: 1994 • Retired: 1995
Retail Price: $17.50

3
VALUES: ⚓ $32
♡ $25
† $20
👓 $20
★ $20
🕐 $20

Lighting The Way To A Happy Holiday
#129275
Issued: 1995 • Susp.: 1999
Retail Price: $20

4
VALUES: ⌘ $22
⚓ $20
♡ $17.50
† $17.50
👓 $17.50
★ $17.50
🕐 $17.50
UM $39

Surrounded With Joy
#531685
Issued: 1993 • Open
Retail Price: $17.50

5
VALUES: ⚲ $27
⛄ $24
⚓ $24
♡ $22.50
† $22.50
👓 $22.50
★ $22.50
🕐 $22.50
UM $35

There's A Christian Welcome Here
#528021
Issued: 1992 • Open
Retail Price: $22.50

6
VALUES: 👓 $20
★ $20
🕐 $20

Toy Maker
#475106
Issued: 1998 • Open
Retail Price: $20

Ornaments

	Price Paid	Value
1.		
2.		
3.		
4.		
5.		
6.		
Totals		

KEY: NM *Pre-1981* ▲ 1981 ✗ 1982 ◄ 1983 † 1984 ◀ 1985 ✒ 1986 ♣ 1987 ✤ 1988 ♃ 1989 ↓ 1990 ♦ 1991 ✦ 1992 ⚲ 1993 ⛴ 1994 ⚓ 1995 ♡ 1996 † 1997 👓 1998 ★ 1999 🕐 2000 UM *Unmarked*

COLLECTORS' CLUB

This section features pieces that are exclusive to club members and is divided into the following sections: *Collectors' Club* pieces, *Birthday Club* pieces and *Fun Club* pieces. For the year 2000, club pieces will have a special year mark, which was not yet determined at press time.

VALUES: NM $195
▲ $160
Ⅱ $160

1

But Love Goes On Forever
(charter member figurine)
#E0001
Issued: 1981 • Closed: 1981
Retail Price: N/A

2 VALUES: ▲ $90
Ⅱ $76
UM $130

But Love Goes On Forever
(charter member plaque)
#E0102
Issued: 1982 • Closed: 1982
Retail Price: N/A

3 *Variation*

VALUES: ▲ $82
Ⅱ $70
UM $120

But Love Goes On Forever
#E0202
Issued: 1982 • Closed: 1982
Retail Price: N/A
Variation: 🍁 *(mistakenly produced and shipped to Canada)* – $122

4 VALUES: Ⅱ $72
$62

Let Us Call The Club
To Order
(charter member figurine)
#E0103
Issued: 1983 • Closed: 1983
Retail Price: N/A

5 VALUES: Ⅱ $66
✝ $58
✝ $55

Let Us Call The Club
To Order
#E0303
Issued: 1983 • Closed: 1983
Retail Price: N/A

6 VALUES: ✎ $66
✝ $54

Join In On The Blessings
(charter member figurine)
#E0104
Issued: 1984 • Closed: 1984
Retail Price: N/A

7 VALUES: ✎ $58
✝ $46

Join In On The Blessings
#E0404
Issued: 1984 • Closed: 1984
Retail Price: N/A

Symbol Of Membership Figurines

	Price Paid	Value
1.		
2.		
3.		
4.		
5.		
6.		
7.		
Totals		

Value Guide — PRECIOUS MOMENTS®

Collectors' Club

1 — VALUES: † $52 / 🕊 $47

Seek And Ye Shall Find
#E0005
Issued: 1985 • Closed: 1985
Retail Price: N/A

2 — VALUES: † $62 / 🕊 $50

Seek And Ye Shall Find
(charter member figurine)
#E0105
Issued: 1985 • Closed: 1985
Retail Price: N/A

3 — VALUES: 🕊 $46 / ♫ $42

Birds Of A Feather
Collect Together
#E0006
Issued: 1986 • Closed: 1986
Retail Price: N/A

4 — VALUES: 🕊 $52 / ♫ $48

Birds Of A Feather
Collect Together
(charter member figurine)
#E0106
Issued: 1986 • Closed: 1986
Retail Price: N/A

5 — VALUES: ♫ $48 / ♠ $36

Sharing Is Universal
#E0007
Issued: 1987 • Closed: 1987
Retail Price: N/A

6 — VALUES: ♫ $53 / ♠ $48

Sharing Is Universal
(charter member figurine)
#E0107
Issued: 1987 • Closed: 1987
Retail Price: N/A

Symbol Of Membership Figurines

	Price Paid	Value
1.		
2.		
3.		
4.		
5.		
6.		
7.		
8.		
9.		
10.		
Totals		

7 — VALUES: ♠ $45 / ✤ $32

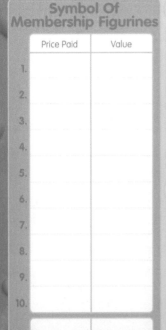

A Growing Love
#E0008
Issued: 1988 • Closed: 1988
Retail Price: N/A

8 — VALUES: ♠ $55 / ✤ $47

A Growing Love
(charter member figurine)
#E0108
Issued: 1988 • Closed: 1988
Retail Price: N/A

9 — VALUES: ✤ $48 / Ð $42 / ★ $37

Always Room For One More
#C0009
Issued: 1989 • Closed: 1989
Retail Price: N/A

10 — VALUES: ✤ $55 / Ð $50

Always Room For One Mor
(charter member figurine)
#C0109
Issued: 1989 • Closed: 1989
Retail Price: N/A

KEY: NM *Pre-1981* ▲ 1981 Ⅱ 1982 ◄1983 † 1984 🕊1985 ♫ 1986 ♠ 1987 ✤1988 Ð 1989 ★ 1990 ❧ 1991 ✿ 1992 ❀ 1993 ❤ 1994 ⚜ 1995 ♡ 1996 ↑ 1997 ∞ 1998 ★ 1999 🕑 2000 UM *Unmarked*

1 VALUES: ♁ $42
♠ $32

My Happiness
#C0010
Issued: 1990 • Closed: 1990
Retail Price: N/A

2 VALUES: ♁ $55
♠ $45

My Happiness
(charter member figurine)
#C0110
Issued: 1990 • Closed: 1990
Retail Price: N/A

3 VALUES: ♣ $43
♦ $32

Sharing The
Good News Together
#C0011
Issued: 1991 • Closed: 1991
Retail Price: N/A

4 VALUES: ♣ $50
♦ $43

Sharing The
Good News Together
(charter member figurine)
#C0111
Issued: 1991 • Closed: 1991
Retail Price: N/A

5 VALUES: ♦ $45
♢ $38

The Club That's Out Of
This World
#C0012
Issued: 1992 • Closed: 1992
Retail Price: N/A

6 VALUES: ♦ $50
♢ $44

The Club That's Out Of
This World
(charter member figurine)
#C0112
Issued: 1992 • Closed: 1992
Retail Price: N/A

7 VALUES: ♢ $42
❀ $37

Loving, Caring, And
Sharing Along The Way
#C0013
Issued: 1993 • Closed: 1993
Retail Price: N/A

8 VALUES: ♢ $50
❀ $45

Loving, Caring, And
Sharing Along The Way
(charter member figurine)
#C0113
Issued: 1993 • Closed: 1993
Retail Price: N/A

9 VALUES: ❀ $42
⊲ $30

You Are The End
Of My Rainbow
#C0014
Issued: 1994 • Closed: 1994
Retail Price: N/A

10 VALUES: ❀ $50
⊲ $45

You Are The End
Of My Rainbow
(charter member figurine)
#C0114
Issued: 1994 • Closed: 1994
Retail Price: N/A

Symbol Of Membership Figurines

	Price Paid	Value
1.		
2.		
3.		
4.		
5.		
6.		
7.		
8.		
9.		
10.		
Totals		

KEY: NM *Pre-1981* ▲ 1981 ☰ 1982 ◀ 1983 ✝ 1984 ❤ 1985 ♪ 1986 ♣ 1987 ♧ 1988 ♁ 1989 ♠ 1990
♦ 1991 ♢ 1992 ❀ 1993 ⊲ 1994 △ 1995 ♡ 1996 ✝ 1997 ∞ 1998 ★ 1999 ◊ 2000 UM *Unmarked*

225

Value Guide — PRECIOUS MOMENTS®

Collectors' Club

1 VALUES: $39 / $30

You're The Sweetest Cookie In The Batch
#C0015
Issued: 1995 • Closed: 1995
Retail Price: N/A

2 VALUES: $45 / $34

You're The Sweetest Cookie In The Batch (charter member figurine)
#C0115
Issued: 1995 • Closed: 1995
Retail Price: N/A

3 VALUES: $34 / $28

You're As Pretty As A Picture
#C0016
Issued: 1996 • Closed: 1996
Retail Price: N/A

4 VALUES: $38 / $30

You're As Pretty As A Picture (charter member figurine)
#C0116
Issued: 1996 • Closed: 1996
Retail Price: N/A

5 VALUES: $38 / $35

A Special Toast To Precious Moments
#C0017
Issued: 1997 • Closed: 1997
Retail Price: N/A

6 VALUES: $40 / $34
A Special Toast To Precious Moments (charter member figurine)
#C0117
Issued: 1997 • Closed: 1997
Retail Price: N/A

Symbol Of Membership Figurines

	Price Paid	Value
1.		
2.		
3.		
4.		
5.		
6.		
7.		
8.		
9.		
10.		
Totals		

7 VALUES: $35 / $27
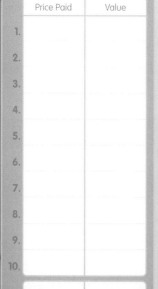
Focusing In On Those Precious Moments
#C0018
Issued: 1998 • Closed: 1998
Retail Price: N/A

8 VALUES: $35 / $27

Focusing In On Those Precious Moments (charter member figurine)
#C0118
Issued: 1998 • Closed: 1998
Retail Price: N/A

9 VALUES: $45 / N/E

Wishing You A World Of Peace
#C0019
Issued: 1999 • Closed: 1999
Retail Price: N/A

10 VALUES: $45 / N/E

Wishing You A World Of Peace (charter member figurine)
#C0119
Issued: 1999 • Closed: 1999
Retail Price: N/A

226 KEY: NM Pre-1981 ▲1981 ⚍1982 ◀1983 ♦1984 ♣1985 ♪1986 ♠1987 ✧1988 ♭1989 ↓1990 ♦1991 ♂1992 ♋1993 ⚊1994 △1995 ♡1996 †1997 ᎙1998 ★1999 ◔2000 UM Unmarked

Value Guide — PRECIOUS MOMENTS®

Collectors' Club

1 VALUES: 00 N/E

Thanks A Bunch
N/A
Issued: 2000 • To Be Closed: 2000
Retail Price: N/A

2 VALUES: 00 N/E
Thanks A Bunch
(charter member figurine)
N/A
Issued: 2000 • To Be Closed: 2000
Retail Price: N/A

3 VALUES: ▲ $455 ▮ $440

Hello, Lord, It's Me Again
#PM811
Issued: 1981 • Closed: 1981
Retail Price: $25

4 VALUES: ▮ $210 ◀ $200

Smile, God Loves You
#PM821
Issued: 1982 • Closed: 1982
Retail Price: $25

5 VALUES: ▮ $225 ◀ $200 ✝ $195

Put On A Happy Face
#PM822
Issued: 1983 • Closed: 1983
Retail Price: $25

6 VALUES: ◀ $78 ✝ $72

Dawn's Early Light
#PM831
Issued: 1983 • Closed: 1983
Retail Price: $27.50

7 VALUES: ◀ $95 ✝ $60 ◢ $50

God's Ray Of Mercy
#PM841
Issued: 1984 • Closed: 1984
Retail Price: $25

8 VALUES: ✝ $66 ◀ $60

Trust In The Lord To The Finish
#PM842
Issued: 1984 • Closed: 1984
Retail Price: $25

9 VALUES: ◢ $82

The Lord Is My Shepherd
#PM851
Issued: 1985 • Closed: 1985
Retail Price: $25

10 VALUES: ◢ $68 ♪ $62

I Love To Tell The Story
#PM852
Issued: 1985 • Closed: 1985
Retail Price: $27.50

Symbol Of Membership Figurines

	Price Paid	Value
1.		
2.		

Members Only Figurines

3.	
4.	
5.	
6.	
7.	
8.	
9.	
10.	

Totals

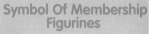

Value Guide — PRECIOUS MOMENTS®

Collectors' Club

1   VALUES: 🍃 $305

God Bless Our Years Together
5th Anniversary
Commerative Figurine
#12440
Issued: 1985 • Closed: 1985
Retail Price: $175

2   VALUES: 🍃 $92
    🎋 $80
    ▲ $76

Grandma's Prayer
#PM861
Issued: 1986 • Closed: 1986
Retail Price: $25

3   VALUES: 🎋 $88

I'm Following Jesus
#PM862
Issued: 1986 • Closed: 1986
Retail Price: $25

4   VALUES: 🎋 $92
    ▲ $65
    ⚓ $58

Feed My Sheep
#PM871
Issued: 1987 • Closed: 1987
Retail Price: $25

5   VALUES: 🎋 $66
    ▲ $58
    ⚓ $55

In His Time
#PM872
Issued: 1987 • Closed: 1987
Retail Price: $25

6   VALUES: 🎋 $48
    ▲ $42
    ⚓ $40

Loving You Dear Valentine
#PM873
Issued: 1987 • Closed: 1987
Retail Price: $25

7   VALUES: 🎋 $50
    ▲ $45
    ⚓ $40

Loving You Dear Valentine
#PM874
Issued: 1987 • Closed: 1987
Retail Price: $25

8   VALUES: ▲ $68
    ⚓ $57
    ⊕ $50

God Bless You For Touching
My Life
#PM881
Issued: 1988 • Closed: 1988
Retail Price: $27.50

9   VALUES: ⚓ $56
    ⊕ $50

You Just Cannot Chuck A
Good Friendship
#PM882
Issued: 1988 • Closed: 1988
Retail Price: $27.50

10   VALUES: ⊕ $50
    ★ $44

You Will Always Be
My Choice
#PM891
Issued: 1989 • Closed: 1989
Retail Price: $27.50

Members Only Figurines

	Price Paid	Value
1.		
2.		
3.		
4.		
5.		
6.		
7.		
8.		
9.		
10.		
Totals		

KEY: NM *Pre-1981*   ▲1981   ▌1982   ◄1983   ✝1984   🍃1985   🎋1986   ▲1987   ⚓1988   ⊕1989   ★1990
     ♣1991   ⚘1992   ⚯1993   ◄1994   △1995   ♡1996   ✝1997   6ð1998   ★1999   ○2000   UM *Unmarked*

1 VALUES: ꝺ $64 / ⭐ $56

Mow Power To Ya
#PM892
Issued: 1989 • Closed: 1989
Retail Price: $27.50

2 VALUES: ⭐ $54 / ꝺ $50

**Ten Years And Still
Going Strong**
#PM901
Issued: 1990 • Closed: 1990
Retail Price: $30

3 VALUES: ⭐ $63 / ꝺ $55

You Are A Blessing To Me
#PM902
Issued: 1990 • Closed: 1990
Retail Price: $27.50

4 VALUES: ꝺ $60 / ꝼ $52

One Step At A Time
#PM911
Issued: 1991 • Closed: 1991
Retail Price: $33

5 VALUES: ꝺ $64 / ꝼ $57

**Lord, Keep Me In Teepee
Top Shape**
#PM912
Issued: 1991 • Closed: 1991
Retail Price: $27.50

6 VALUES: ꝼ $70 / ꝙ $63

**Only Love Can Make
A Home**
#PM921
Issued: 1992 • Closed: 1992
Retail Price: $30

7 VALUES: ꝼ $45 / ꝙ $40

Sowing The Seeds Of Love
#PM922
Issued: 1992 • Closed: 1992
Retail Price: $30

8 VALUES: ꝼ $390

**This Land Is Our Land
(LE-1992)**
#527386
Issued: 1992 • Closed: 1992
Retail Price: $350

9 VALUES: ꝙ $50 / ꝗ $46

His Little Treasure
#PM931
Issued: 1993 • Closed: 1993
Retail Price: $30

10 VALUES: ꝙ $76 / ꝗ $70

Loving
#PM932
Issued: 1993 • Closed: 1993
Retail Price: $30

Members Only Figurines

	Price Paid	Value
1.		
2.		
3.		
4.		
5.		
6.		
7.		
8.		
9.		
10.		

Totals

KEY: NM *Pre-1981* ▲ 1981 ❚ 1982 ◄1983 ✝ 1984 ✿ 1985 ✒ 1986 ▲ 1987 ✦ 1988 ꝺ 1989 ⭐ 1990 ꝺ 1991 ꝼ 1992 ꝙ 1993 ꝗ 1994 △ 1995 ♡ 1996 ✝ 1997 ∞ 1998 ★ 1999 ◎ 2000 UM *Unmarked*

229

Value Guide — PRECIOUS MOMENTS®

1
VALUES: 🎺 $63 · ⛵ $60

Caring
#PM941
Issued: 1994 • Closed: 1994
Retail Price: $35

2
VALUES: 🎺 $63 · ⛵ $60

Sharing
#PM942
Issued: 1994 • Closed: 1994
Retail Price: $35

3
VALUES: 🎺 $85

You Fill The Pages Of My Life (w/book, stock number for figurine is #530980)
#PMB034
Issued: 1994 • Closed: 1995
Retail Price: $67.50

4
VALUES: ⛵ $45

You're One In A Million To Me
#PM951
Issued: 1995 • Closed: 1995
Retail Price: $35

5
VALUES: ⛵ $55

Always Take Time To Pray
#PM952
Issued: 1995 • Closed: 1995
Retail Price: $35

6
VALUES: ⛵ $145

A Perfect Display Of Fifteen Happy Years
15th Anniversary Commemorative Figurine
#127817
Issued: 1995 • Closed: 1995
Retail Price: $100

Members Only Figurines

	Price Paid	Value
1.		
2.		
3.		
4.		
5.		
6.		
7.		
8.		
9.		
Totals		

7
VALUES: ⛵ $60 · ♡ $52

Teach Us To Love One Another
#PM961
Issued: 1996 • Closed: 1996
Retail Price: $40

8
VALUES: ♡ $62

Our Club Is Soda-licious
#PM962
Issued: 1996 • Closed: 1996
Retail Price: $35

9
VALUES: † $55

You Will Always Be A Treasure To Me
#PM971
Issued: 1997 • Closed: 1997
Retail Price: $50

KEY: NM *Pre*-1981 · ▲ 1981 · 1982 · 1983 · 1984 · 1985 · 1986 · 1987 · 1988 · 1989 · 1990 · 1991 · 1992 · 1993 · 1994 · △ 1995 · ♡ 1996 · † 1997 · 1998 · ★ 1999 · 2000 · UM *Unmarked*

Collectors' Club

1 VALUES: † $48

Blessed Are The Merciful
#PM972
Issued: 1997 • Closed: 1997
Retail Price: $40

2 VALUES: † $52
　　　　6ð $52

Happy Trails
#PM981
Issued: 1998 • Closed: 1998
Retail Price: $50

3 VALUES: † $47
　　　　6ð $47

Lord, Please Don't Put Me On Hold
#PM982
Issued: 1998 • Closed: 1998
Retail Price: $40

4 VALUES: 6ð N/E

How Can Two Work Together Except They Agree
20th Anniversary Commemorative Figurine
#PM983
Issued: 1998 • Closed: 1998
Retail Price: $125

5 VALUES: ★ $33

Jumping For Joy
#PM991
Issued: 1999 • Closed: 1999
Retail Price: $30

6 VALUES: ★ $32

God Speed
#PM992
Issued: 1999 • Closed: 1999
Retail Price: $30

7 VALUES: ★ N/E

He Watches Over Us All
Millennium Figurine
#PM993
Issued: 1999 • Closed: 1999
Retail Price: $225

8 VALUES: 00 N/E

New!

Collecting Friends Along The Way
N/A
Issued: 2000 • To Be Closed: 2000
Retail Price: N/A

9 VALUES: 00 N/E

New!

My Collection
N/A
Issued: 2000 • To Be Closed: 2000
Retail Price: N/A

10 VALUES: 00 N/E

New!

Thank You For Your Membering
5 Year Membership Piece
N/A
Issued: 2000 • To Be Closed: 2000
Retail Price: N/A

Members Only Figurines

	Price Paid	Value
1.		
2.		
3.		
4.		
5.		
6.		
7.		
8.		
9.		
10.		

Totals

Collectors' Club

1 — VALUES: 00 N/E

New!

A Club Where Friendship Is Made
10 Year Membership Piece
N/A
Issued: 2000 • To Be Closed: 2000
Retail Price: N/A

2 — VALUES: 00 N/E

New!

A Club Where Fellowship Reigns
15 Year Membership Piece
N/A
Issued: 2000 • To Be Closed: 2000
Retail Price: N/A

3 — VALUES: 00 N/E

New!

Companionship Happens In Our Club
20 Year Membership Piece
N/A
Issued: 2000 • To Be Closed: 2000
Retail Price: N/A

4 — VALUES: UM $20

Blessed Are The Meek, For They Shall Inherit The Earth
#PM390
Issued: 1990 • Closed: 1990
Retail Price: $15

5 — VALUES: UM $20

Blessed Are The Merciful, For They Shall Obtain Mercy
#PM590
Issued: 1990 • Closed: 1990
Retail Price: $15

6 — VALUES: UM $20

Blessed Are The Peacemakers, For They Shall Be Called Sons Of God
#PM790
Issued: 1990 • Closed: 1990
Retail Price: $15

Members Only Figurines

	Price Paid	Value
1.		
2.		
3.		

Members Only Ornaments

4.		
5.		
6.		
7.		
8.		
9.		
10.		
Totals		

7 — VALUES: UM $20

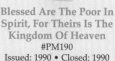

Blessed Are The Poor In Spirit, For Theirs Is The Kingdom Of Heaven
#PM190
Issued: 1990 • Closed: 1990
Retail Price: $15

8 — VALUES: UM $20

Blessed Are The Pure In Heart, For They Shall See God
#PM690
Issued: 1990 • Closed: 1990
Retail Price: $15

9 — VALUES: UM $20

Blessed Are They That Hunger And Thirst, For They Shall Be Filled
#PM490
Issued: 1990 • Closed: 1990
Retail Price: $15

10 — VALUES: UM $20

Blessed Are They That Mourn, For They Shall Be Comforted
#PM290
Issued: 1990 • Closed: 1990
Retail Price: $15

KEY: NM *Pre-1981* ▲ 1981 ✕ 1982 ◄ 1983 ✝ 1984 ✦ 1985 ✗ 1986 ▲ 1987 ✣ 1988 ✞ 1989 ✦ 1990 ♦ 1991 ✿ 1992 ❀ 1993 ◄ 1994 ⚘ 1995 ♡ 1996 ✝ 1997 ∞ 1998 ★ 1999 ○ 2000 UM *Unmarked*

Value Guide — PRECIOUS MOMENTS®

1   VALUES: UM $140

Members' Only Ornaments (set/7)
#PM890
Issued: 1990 • Closed: 1990
Retail Price: $105

2   VALUES: UM $12

**Celebrating A Decade Of
Loving, Caring, And Sharing
(Dated 1990)**
*10th Anniversary
Commemorative Ornament*
#227986
Issued: 1990 • Closed: 1990
Retail Price: $7

3   VALUES: ♋ $37

**Loving, Caring, And
Sharing Along The Way**
#PM040
Issued: 1993 • Closed: 1993
Retail Price: $15

4   VALUES: ⌐ $37

**You Are The End
Of My Rainbow**
#PM041
Issued: 1994 • Closed: 1994
Retail Price: $15

5   VALUES: UM $10

**Giraffe (LE-1998,
gift application club
exclusive, TENDER TAILS)**
#358304
Issued: 1998 • Closed: 1998
Retail Price: N/A

6   VALUES: 6∂   N/E

**God Loveth A Cheerful
Giver (early renewal gift,
hinged box)**
#495891
Issued: 1998 • Closed: 1998
Retail Price: N/A

7   VALUES: UM   N/E

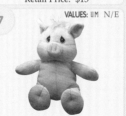

**Pig (early renewal gift,
also available in stores,
TENDER TAILS)**
#358258
Issued: 1998 • Retired: 1998
Retail Price: N/A

8   VALUES: UM $6.99

**Twinkle
(TENDER TAILS)**
#646237
Issued: 1999 • To Be Closed: 2000
Retail Price: $6.99

Members Only Ornaments

	Price Paid	Value
1.		
2.		
3.		
4.		

Members Gifts

5.		
6.		
7.		
8.		

Totals

Collectors' Club

KEY: NM *Pre-1981*   ▲ 1981   ▮ 1982   ◀ 1983   ✝ 1984   ✦ 1985   ♪ 1986   ♣ 1987   ✤ 1988   ♄ 1989   ✦ 1990
      ♦ 1991   ♠ 1992   ♋ 1993   ⌐ 1994   △ 1995   ♡ 1996   ✝ 1997   6∂ 1998   ★ 1999   ◐ 2000   UM *Unmarked*

Collectors' Club

1 VALUES: † $85 6ð $85

Faith Is The Victory
#283592
Issued: 1997 • Closed: 1998
Retail Price: N/A

2 VALUES: † $68 6ð $68

God Bless You With Bouquets Of Victory
#283584
Issued: 1997 • Closed: 1998
Retail Price: N/A

3 VALUES: UM N/E

Lord, It's Hard To Be Humble
N/A
Issued: 1998 • Closed: 1998
Retail Price: N/A

4 VALUES: † $45 6ð $45

Rejoice In The Victory
#283541
Issued: 1997 • Closed: 1998
Retail Price: N/A

5 VALUES: † $115

Precious Moments Last Forever (medallion)
#12246
Issued: 1984 • Closed: 1984
Retail Price: N/A

6 VALUES: ℐ $175

Birds Of A Feather Collect Together (ornament)
#PM864
Issued: 1986 • Closed: 1986
Retail Price: N/A

Precious Rewards Figurines

	Price Paid	Value
1.		
2.		
3.		
4.		

Sharing Season Gifts

5.		
6.		
7.		
8.		
9.		
10.		
Totals		

7 VALUES: ⚜ $70
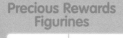
A Growing Love (ornament)
#520349
Issued: 1988 • Closed: 1988
Retail Price: N/A

8 VALUES: Ð $98

Always Room For One More (ornament)
#522961
Issued: 1989 • Closed: 1989
Retail Price: N/A

9 VALUES: ★ $88

My Happiness (ornament)
#PM904
Issued: 1990 • Closed: 1990
Retail Price: N/A

10 VALUES: ⬥ $80

Sharing The Good News Together (ornament)
#PM037
Issued: 1991 • Closed: 1991
Retail Price: N/A

KEY: NM *Pre-1981* ▲1981 𝕀1982 ◀1983 †1984 ✎1985 ℐ1986 ♣1987 ✤1988 Ð1989 ★1990 ⬥1991 ♦1992 ❀1993 ❤1994 △1995 ♡1996 †1997 6ð1998 ★1999 ◐2000 UM *Unmarked*

Value Guide — PRECIOUS MOMENTS®

1 VALUES: 🔥 $78

The Club That's Out Of This World (ornament)
#PM038
Issued: 1992 • Closed: 1992
Retail Price: N/A

2 VALUES: 🐦 $92
🐤 $84
🔥 $78

Our Club Can't Be Beat
#B0001
Issued: 1986 • Closed: 1986
Retail Price: N/A

3 VALUES: ✐ $74
▲ $68
⚓ $60

A Smile's The Cymbal Of Joy
#B0002
Issued: 1987 • Closed: 1987
Retail Price: N/A

4 VALUES: ✐ $80
▲ $75

Variation

A Smile's The Cymbal Of Joy (charter member figurine)
#B0102
Issued: 1987 • Closed: 1987
Retail Price: N/A
Variation: "A Smile's The <u>Symbol</u> Of Joy" – $92

5 VALUES: ♣ $47
⌗ $42

The Sweetest Club Around
#B0003
Issued: 1988 • Closed: 1988
Retail Price: N/A

6 VALUES: ♣ $52
⌗ $45

The Sweetest Club Around (charter member figurine)
#B0103
Issued: 1988 • Closed: 1988
Retail Price: N/A

7 VALUES: ⌗ $38
★ $32

Have A Beary Special Birthday
#B0004
Issued: 1989 • Closed: 1989
Retail Price: N/A

8 VALUES: ♣ $50
⌗ $37
★ $32

Have A Beary Special Birthday (charter member figurine)
#B0104
Issued: 1989 • Closed: 1989
Retail Price: N/A

9 VALUES: ★ $37
🍓 $33

Our Club Is A Tough Act To Follow
#B0005
Issued: 1990 • Closed: 1990
Retail Price: N/A

Sharing Season Gifts

	Price Paid	Value
1.		

Symbol Of Membership Figurines

2.		
3.		
4.		
5.		
6.		
7.		
8.		
9.		
Totals		

Birthday Club

1 VALUES: ⚷ $40 ⚶ $35

Our Club Is A Tough
Act To Follow
(charter member figurine)
#B0105
Issued: 1990 • Closed: 1990
Retail Price: N/A

2 VALUES: ⚶ $37 ⚷ $33

Jest To Let You Know
You're Tops
#B0006
Issued: 1991 • Closed: 1991
Retail Price: N/A

3 VALUES: ⚶ $40 ⚷ $34

Jest To Let You Know
You're Tops
(charter member figurine)
#B0106
Issued: 1991 • Closed: 1991
Retail Price: N/A

4 VALUES: ⚷ $39 ⚸ $33

All Aboard For
Birthday Club Fun
#B0007
Issued: 1992 • Closed: 1992
Retail Price: N/A

5 VALUES: ⚷ $42 ⚸ $35

All Aboard For
Birthday Club Fun
(charter member figurine)
#B0107
Issued: 1992 • Closed: 1992
Retail Price: N/A

6 VALUES: ⚸ $32 ⚹ $28

Happiness Is Belonging
#B0008
Issued: 1993 • Closed: 1993
Retail Price: N/A

Symbol Of Membership Figurines

	Price Paid	Value
1.		
2.		
3.		
4.		
5.		
6.		
7.		
8.		
9.		
10.		

Totals

7 VALUES: ⚸ $37 ⚹ $32

Happiness Is Belonging
(charter member figurine)
#B0108
Issued: 1993 • Closed: 1993
Retail Price: N/A

8 VALUES: ⚹ $33 ⚺ $29

Can't Get Enough
Of Our Club
#B0009
Issued: 1994 • Closed: 1995
Retail Price: N/A

9 VALUES: ⚹ $38 ⚺ $33

Can't Get Enough
Of Our Club
(charter member figurine)
#B0109
Issued: 1994 • Closed: 1995
Retail Price: N/A

10 VALUES: ⚺ $34 ♡ $29

Hoppy Birthday
#B0010
Issued: 1995 • Closed: 1996
Retail Price: N/A

KEY: NM *Pre–1981* ▲ 1981 Ⅱ 1982 ◄ 1983 ♦ 1984 ✿ 1985 ♪ 1986 ♦ 1987 ✿ 1988 ♭ 1989 ⚷ 1990 ⚶ 1991 ⚷ 1992 ⚸ 1993 ⚹ 1994 ⚺ 1995 ♡ 1996 † 1997 ∽ 1998 ★ 1999 ✦ 2000 UM *Unmarked*

1 VALUES: ⬤ $42 / ♡ $35

Hoppy Birthday
(charter member figurine)
#B0110
Issued: 1995 • Closed: 1996
Retail Price: N/A

2 VALUES: ✝ $33 / † $28

Scootin' By Just To Say Hi!
#B0011
Issued: 1996 • Closed: 1997
Retail Price: N/A

3 VALUES: ♡ $36 / † $29

Scootin' By Just To Say Hi!
(charter member figurine)
#B0111
Issued: 1996 • Closed: 1997
Retail Price: N/A

4 VALUES: † $25 / 6d $23

The Fun Starts Here
#B0012
Issued: 1997 • Closed: 1998
Retail Price: N/A

5 VALUES: † $30 / 6d $25

The Fun Starts Here
(charter member figurine)
#B0112
Issued: 1997 • Closed: 1998
Retail Price: N/A

6 VALUES: ⁄ $140 / ▲ $126

Fishing For Friends
#BC861
Issued: 1986 • Closed: 1986
Retail Price: $10

7 VALUES: ▲ $110 / ✤ $97 / ꝺ $90

Hi Sugar
#BC871
Issued: 1987 • Closed: 1987
Retail Price: $11

8 VALUES: ✤ $63 / ꝺ $53

Somebunny Cares
#BC881
Issued: 1988 • Closed: 1988
Retail Price: $13.50

9 VALUES: ꝺ $60 / ★ $54 / ● $50

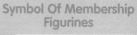

Can't Beehive Myself
Without You
#BC891
Issued: 1989 • Closed: 1989
Retail Price: $13.50

10 VALUES: ★ $38 / ● $34

Collecting Makes
Good Scents
#BC901
Issued: 1990 • Closed: 1990
Retail Price: $15

Symbol Of Membership Figurines

	Price Paid	Value
1.		
2.		
3.		
4.		
5.		

Members Only Figurines

6.		
7.		
8.		
9.		
10.		

Totals

Birthday Club

Value Guide — PRECIOUS MOMENTS®

1 VALUES: ⚓ $40 / ◊ $35

I'm Nuts Over My Collection
#BC902
Issued: 1990 • Closed: 1990
Retail Price: $15

2 VALUES: ◊ $44 / ⚓ $40

Love Pacifies
#BC911
Issued: 1991 • Closed: 1991
Retail Price: $15

3 VALUES: ◊ $45 / ⚓ $40

True Blue Friends
#BC912
Issued: 1991 • Closed: 1991
Retail Price: $15

4 VALUES: ⚓ $38 / ✿ $33

Every Man's House Is His Castle
#BC921
Issued: 1992 • Closed: 1992
Retail Price: $16.50

5 VALUES: ⚓ $40 / ✿ $34

I Got You Under My Skin
#BC922
Issued: 1992 • Closed: 1992
Retail Price: $16

6 VALUES: ✿ $25 / ⊐ $22

Put A Little Punch In Your Birthday
#BC931
Issued: 1993 • Closed: 1993
Retail Price: $15

Members Only Figurines

	Price Paid	Value
1.		
2.		
3.		
4.		
5.		
6.		
7.		
8.		
9.		
10.		
Totals		

7 VALUES: ✿ $32 / ⊐ $28
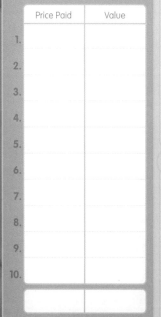
Owl Always Be Your Friend
#BC932
Issued: 1993 • Closed: 1993
Retail Price: $16

8 VALUES: ⊐ $38 / △ $30

God Bless Our Home
#BC941
Issued: 1994 • Closed: 1994
Retail Price: $16

9 VALUES: ⊐ $33 / △ $27

You're A Pel-I-Can Count On
#BC942
Issued: 1994 • Closed: 1994
Retail Price: $16

10 VALUES: △ $38

Making A Point To Say You're Special
#BC951
Issued: 1995 • Closed: 1995
Retail Price: $15

238

KEY: NM *Pre-1981* ▲1981 ✕1982 ◄1983 ✝1984 ✿1985 ✎1986 ♣1987 ✤1988 ✤1989 ★1990 ◊1991 ⚓1992 ✿1993 ⊐1994 △1995 ♡1996 ✝1997 ∞1998 ★1999 ☽2000 UM *Unmarked*

Value Guide — PRECIOUS MOMENTS®

1 VALUES: △ $68

10 Wonderful Years Of Wishes
#BC952
Issued: 1995 • Closed: 1995
Retail Price: $50

2 VALUES: ♡ $25

There's A Spot In My Heart For You
#BC961
Issued: 1996 • Closed: 1996
Retail Price: $15

3 VALUES: ♡ $28 / † $23

You're First In My Heart
#BC962
Issued: 1996 • Closed: 1996
Retail Price: $15

4 VALUES: † $22

Hare's To The Birthday Club
#BC971
Issued: 1997 • Closed: 1997
Retail Price: $16

5 VALUES: † $22

Holy Tweet
#BC972
Issued: 1997 • Closed: 1997
Retail Price: $18.50

6 VALUES: 6∂ $17 / ★ $17

Slide Into The Celebration (LE-1999)
#BC981
Issued: 1998 • Closed: 1999
Retail Price: $15

7 VALUES: 6∂ $20 / ★ N/E

You Are My Mane Inspiration (charter member figurine)
#B0014
Issued: 1999 • Closed: 1999
Retail Price: N/A

8 VALUES: 6∂ $30 / ★ N/E

You Are My Mane Inspiration (double charter member figurine)
#B0114
Issued: 1999 • Closed: 1999
Retail Price: N/A

9 VALUES: 00 N/E

New!

Don't Fret, We'll Get There Yet
N/A
Issued: 2000 • To Be Closed: 2000
Retail Price: N/A

10 VALUES: 00 N/E

New!

Don't Fret, We'll Get There Yet
N/A
Issued: 2000 • To Be Closed: 2000
Retail Price: N/A

Members Only Figurines

	Price Paid	Value
1.		
2.		
3.		
4.		
5.		
6.		

Symbol Of Membership Figurines

7.		
8.		
9.		
10.		

Totals

Fun Club

1 VALUES: UM $10

Chester (TENDER TAILS)
#BC992
Issued: 1999 • Closed: 1999
Retail Price: $7

2 VALUES: ★ $18
Ewe Are So Special To Me
#BC991
Issued: 1999 • Closed: 1999
Retail Price: $15

3 VALUES: 00 N/E
New!
Hold On To The Moment
#FC003
Issued: 2000 • To Be Closed: 2000
Retail Price: N/A

4 VALUES: UM N/E
New!
Reed The Centipede (TENDER TAILS)
#FC002
Issued: 2000 • To Be Closed: 2000
Retail Price: N/A

5 VALUES: UM N/E
New!
Ronnie The Rhino Beetle (TENDER TAILS)
#FC001
Issued: 2000 • To Be Closed: 2000
Retail Price: N/A

6 VALUES: UM $10
Chippie (TENDER TAILS)
#BC993
Issued: 1999 • Closed: 1999
Retail Price: $7

7 VALUES: UM N/E

Gorilla (early renewal gift, TENDER TAILS)
#602361
Issued: 1999 • Closed: 1999
Retail Price: N/A

8 VALUES: UM N/E
Toucan (LE-1999, gift application club exclusive, TENDER TAILS)
#612413
Issued: 1999 • Closed: 1999
Retail Price: N/A

9 VALUES: UM N/E
New!

Iris (TENDER TAILS, transforming animal)
N/A
Issued: 2000 • To Be Closed: 2000
Retail Price: N/A

Members Only Pieces

	Price Paid	Value
1.		
2.		
3.		
4.		
5.		
6.		

Members Gifts

| 7. | | |
| 8. | | |

Club Kit Pieces

| 9. | | |

Totals

KEY: NM *Pre-1981* ▲1981 ✠1982 ◄1983 ✝1984 ✦1985 ♫1986 ♣1987 ✿1988 ✢1989 ★1990 ♦1991 ♣1992 ⊗1993 ⌂1994 ⚖1995 ♡1996 ✝1997 ∞1998 ★1999 ◐2000 UM *Unmarked*

Future Releases

Use this page to record future PRECIOUS MOMENTS releases.

PRECIOUS MOMENTS	Item #	Production Mark	Price Paid	Market Value

	Price Paid	Value
Page Total:		

PRECIOUS MOMENTS	Item #	Production Mark	Price Paid	Market Value

	Price Paid	Value
Page Total:		

Total Value Of My Collection

Add the "Page Totals" together to find the "Grand Total."

PRECIOUS MOMENTS			PRECIOUS MOMENTS		
Page Number	Price Paid	Market Value	Page Number	Price Paid	Market Value
Page 39			Page 64		
Page 40			Page 65		
Page 41			Page 66		
Page 42			Page 67		
Page 43			Page 68		
Page 44			Page 69		
Page 45			Page 70		
Page 46			Page 71		
Page 47			Page 72		
Page 48			Page 73		
Page 49			Page 74		
Page 50			Page 75		
Page 51			Page 76		
Page 52			Page 77		
Page 53			Page 78		
Page 54			Page 79		
Page 55			Page 80		
Page 56			Page 81		
Page 57			Page 82		
Page 58			Page 83		
Page 59			Page 84		
Page 60			Page 85		
Page 61			Page 86		
Page 62			Page 87		
Page 63			Page 88		
Subtotal			Subtotal		

Page Total:	Price Paid	Value

Total Value Of My Collection

PRECIOUS MOMENTS				PRECIOUS MOMENTS		
Page Number	Price Paid	Market Value		Page Number	Price Paid	Market Value
Page 89				Page 114		
Page 90				Page 115		
Page 91				Page 116		
Page 92				Page 117		
Page 93				Page 118		
Page 94				Page 119		
Page 95				Page 120		
Page 96				Page 121		
Page 97				Page 122		
Page 98				Page 123		
Page 99				Page 124		
Page 100				Page 125		
Page 101				Page 126		
Page 102				Page 127		
Page 103				Page 128		
Page 104				Page 129		
Page 105				Page 130		
Page 106				Page 131		
Page 107				Page 132		
Page 108				Page 133		
Page 109				Page 134		
Page 110				Page 135		
Page 111				Page 136		
Page 112				Page 137		
Page 113				Page 138		
Subtotal				Subtotal		

Page Total:	Price Paid	Value

244

PRECIOUS MOMENTS		
Page Number	Price Paid	Market Value
Page 139		
Page 140		
Page 141		
Page 142		
Page 143		
Page 144		
Page 145		
Page 146		
Page 147		
Page 148		
Page 149		
Page 150		
Page 151		
Page 152		
Page 153		
Page 154		
Page 155		
Page 156		
Page 157		
Page 158		
Page 159		
Page 160		
Page 161		
Page 162		
Page 163		
Subtotal		

PRECIOUS MOMENTS		
Page Number	Price Paid	Market Value
Page 164		
Page 165		
Page 166		
Page 167		
Page 168		
Page 169		
Page 170		
Page 171		
Page 172		
Page 173		
Page 174		
Page 175		
Page 176		
Page 177		
Page 178		
Page 179		
Page 180		
Page 181		
Page 182		
Page 183		
Page 184		
Page 185		
Page 186		
Page 187		
Page 188		
Subtotal		

Page Total:	Price Paid	Value

PRECIOUS MOMENTS		
Page Number	Price Paid	Market Value
Page 189		
Page 190		
Page 191		
Page 192		
Page 193		
Page 194		
Page 195		
Page 196		
Page 197		
Page 198		
Page 199		
Page 200		
Page 201		
Page 202		
Page 203		
Page 204		
Page 205		
Page 206		
Page 207		
Page 208		
Page 209		
Page 210		
Page 211		
Page 212		
Page 213		
Page 214		
Subtotal		

PRECIOUS MOMENTS		
Page Number	Price Paid	Market Value
Page 215		
Page 216		
Page 217		
Page 218		
Page 219		
Page 220		
Page 221		
Page 222		
Page 223		
Page 224		
Page 225		
Page 226		
Page 227		
Page 228		
Page 229		
Page 230		
Page 231		
Page 232		
Page 233		
Page 234		
Page 235		
Page 236		
Page 237		
Page 238		
Page 239		
Page 240		
Subtotal		

GRAND TOTAL	Price Paid	

How To Shop
The Secondary Market

*W*hile on vacation, you stumble across a small, out of the way collectibles shop and decide to stop in and browse the PRECIOUS MOMENTS section. And then you see it. You shake your head in disbelief. There before your eyes is one of the most valuable PRECIOUS MOMENTS pieces still marked at retail price! You immediately purchase the piece and walk out of the store, still grinning at your unbelievable luck!

While it isn't likely that this will happen to most collectors, there is a place where you can go to find elusive or long retired pieces . . . the secondary market. The secondary market is an invaluable resource for collectors, as it is here that you can meet nearly all of your collectible needs.

WHAT IS THE SECONDARY MARKET?

A secondary market is formed when a piece is no longer available at retail price, such as when a retirement occurs. When a piece retires, it is no longer produced by the manufacturer, an occasion that is often marked by breaking the production mold of the piece. After stores sell out of their available stock, demand for the piece begins to out-number supply and collectors must find some-where else to obtain the piece. As people are now willing to pay more for the piece, the collectible's value tends to increase, giving way to a secondary market.

RETIRED, SUSPENDED AND CLOSED PIECES

Enesco uses three methods to end production of a PRECIOUS MOMENTS piece. A retirement means that the mold of the piece is broken and it will never be produced again. Retirement usually occurs with no prior warning. This means that the same day that the retire-ment of a piece is announced, production of the piece ceases. Occasionally, Enesco will announce a retirement in advance, giving collectors one last opportunity to purchase the piece at retail before it is no longer available in stores and therefore hits the secondary market.

A second way of stopping production of a PRECIOUS MOMENTS piece is through suspension. When a piece is suspended, it is no longer produced by the manufacturer, but the mold is not broken. This is because suspended pieces can be re-introduced at a later time. However, when a piece that was previously suspended is re-introduced, it will usually undergo design modifications.

Closed pieces often refer to figurines which are limited by either date or number of pieces produced. For instance, if a piece is dated 1999, it is considered to be closed after December 31, 1999. Pieces that are limited in number are considered to be closed after production has reached a specified amount. As demand for limited pieces is often very high, these pieces are often quite valuable on the secondary market.

GETTING THE MOST OUT OF THE SECONDARY MARKET

Other factors which affect a piece's value on the secondary market include condition of both the piece and its packaging. The condition of a piece is one of its most important factors. Of course, pieces in mint, or perfect, condition are the most valuable; while cracked and damaged pieces are worth less. Stray wisps of paint and faded paint can also lessen the value of a piece, so be sure to carefully inspect each piece before you make your purchase. While you can expect to pay less for pieces that are slightly damaged, keep in mind that there is no right or wrong amount to pay. It is up to you to decide how much a piece is worth to you.

Packaging can also make a significant difference in the value of a figurine. Try to keep the original box and packaging with the piece, as many collectors consider a figurine without its packaging to be "incomplete." Boxes are also important for the protection and storage of a piece.

Finally, the production marks also have a large effect on the value of your collectible. Each figurine has a production mark carved into the porcelain, which symbolizes the year in which the piece was produced. As with most collectible lines, older pieces generally fetch a higher price than newly produced editions. See the *Production Mark Chart* on page 37 for more information on this subject.

READY, SET, TRADE!

Now that you've learned the basics, it's time to get out there and explore the secondary market! So where can you go to find it? If you own a computer, you won't have to look any further than your own home. The Internet is one of the largest and most popular arenas for secondary market action. With the touch of a finger, you can access retailers, auction sites and bulletin boards filled with fellow collectors who are looking to buy, sell and trade their PRE-CIOUS MOMENTS collectibles.

Secondary market exchanges are another way to access the secondary market. Exchange services usually provide a regularly updated listing, but also charge a subscription fee. Be aware that some services charge a commission fee on pieces that are sold through their service.

A third way to reach the secondary market is through newspapers and magazines. Many newspapers have a "Swap and Sell" section for antiques and collectibles. Bear in mind, however, that these methods are geared to a local area, and will not reach as wide an audience as other methods.

"Loving, Caring And Sharing" For Your Collection

*T*o keep your PRECIOUS MOMENTS pieces in mint condition, they should be kept somewhere safe, where they will not be at risk of breaking or collecting dust. However, if your favorite pieces do get a little dirty, here's how to clean them.

PRECIOUS MOMENTS manufacturer Enesco suggests hand washing your figurines and TENDER TAILS. Wipe your figurines with a damp cloth, using warm water and mild soap. Place a towel over your work area in case the piece slips and falls. Once clean, gently wipe the piece off and let it air dry.

Collectors often find tags play an important role in the world of plush collectibles. TENDER TAILS come with the option of filling out a name for your animal on its hang tag and submitting the tag to Enesco in exchange for an official "Certificate Of Adoption" and "Love And Care Guide." If you don't want to remove the hang tag, fill out the following information and send it to Enesco:

1. Your name and address.

2. The name you have chosen.

3. Animal type or stock number.

Paperwork and certificates, as well as boxes, can be replaced depending on availability. For more information, the manufacturer call (800) 4-ENESCO.

Variations

$\mathcal{T}$hrough the years not all PRECIOUS MOMENTS figurines with the same name have looked identical, as you might think. When two pieces of the same design differ, the one that varies from the standard or intended version is considered to be a variation.

Some variations occur intentionally, such as when Enesco is unhappy with a design after its production and decides to rework it, or when a piece is reintroduced with slight modifications after a period of suspension.

Variations can also occur as the result of human error. In most cases, no matter what the reason for the change, variations generally consist of text on a figurine being spelled or phrased differently, or parts of the figurine being left unpainted or having subtle changes in color.

PRECIOUS MOMENTS VARIATIONS

The following is a list of variations that have significant value on the secondary market. Their values can be found in the Value Guide section.

Baby's First Christmas (#E2362): This ornament has two variations. In one, the little girl has straight hair instead of curly, while in the second, the girl with curly hair is missing the decal on the bottom of the piece.

Be Not Weary In Well Doing (#E3111): The variation for "Be Not Weary In Well Doing" has a decal that reads "Be Not Weary <u>And</u> Well Doing."

But Love Goes On Forever (#E0202): This piece was mistakenly produced with the "dove" year mark and shipped to Canada.

Clown Figurines (set/4, #12238): The decal on the variation of this set incorrectly reads "C<u>r</u>owns."

Come Let Us Adore Him (set/11, #E2395): This set was originally released with a boy holding a lamb. Later, the boy was removed and a shepherd wearing a turban took his place. The shepherd was also sold as an individual piece, prompting some collectors to make a 12-piece set.

Faith Takes The Plunge (#111155): In the first year of this piece's production, "Faith" was seen wearing a smile instead of a frown.

Friendship Hits The Spot (#520748): This piece has two variations. The first has a decal with a misspelling: it reads "Freindship Hits The Spot." For the second variation, the table between the two girls is missing.

God Blessed Our Year Together With So Much Love And Happiness (#E2854): The decal on this anniversary piece has appeared mislabeled "God Blessed Our Years Together With So Much Love And Happiness."

Groom (#E2837): This piece from the *Bridal Party Series* was produced with either the boy's hands visible or hidden by his sleeves.

He Is Not Here For He Is Risen As He Said (#527106): The sign outside the tomb on this *Chapel Exclusive* reads "Math," instead of the intended "Matt."

HE IS NOT HERE
FOR HE IS RISEN
AS HE SAID.
MATH 28:6

I Believe In Miracles (#E7156R): To find this variation look for a figurine missing the "Sam B." signature, a blue bird and a smaller head on the boy than seen on the standard piece.

Let The Heavens Rejoice (#E5679): The variation of this ornament is missing the PRECIOUS MOMENTS decal on the bottom.

May Your Christmas Be A Happy Home (set/2, #523704): The variation of this ornament has the young boy sitting in front in a yellow shirt instead of a blue one.

My Days Are Blue Without You (#520802): **This variation** has the girl smiling, instead of frowning.

Nobody's Perfect (#E9268): **Similar to the above** variation, this one features the boy smiling instead of wearing a frown.

Prayer Changes Things (#E5214): **As** opposed to the front cover, this piece has been seen with the words "Holy Bible" on the back. The variation appeared on pieces without a mark, as well as with the "triangle" year mark.

A Smile's The Cymbal Of Joy (#B0102): **The decal on this Charter** Member Figurine has been mislabeled "A Smile's The Symbol Of Joy."

There's A Christian Welcome Here (#523011): **On** the variation for this *Chapel Exclusive* piece the angel's right eyebrow is hidden from view.

You Are My Main Event (#115231): **The** variation of this *Special Event Figurine* has pink strings instead of white strings attached to the balloons.

The following is a list of well-known variations that have yet to achieve significant secondary market value.

Baby's First Christmas (#E2372): **Prior to this ornament's suspen-**sion, an inscription was added. The piece without the caption was available for a shorter period of time and is, therefore, considered to be the variation.

Dropping In For The Holidays (#531952): **The cup in which the little angel sits in this** ornament has been seen in painted both pink and blue. Which one do you have?

He Careth For You (#E1377B) and *He Leadeth Me (#E1377A):* **These two pieces have** caused a good deal of confusion through the years as they have been found with their inspirations reversed.

I'm Falling For Somebunny/Our Love Is Heaven-scent (#E9266): Both of these pieces, which were sold as a set, have appeared as "Somebunny Cares."

Isn't He Precious (#E5379): This piece has been seen completely devoid of paint, which is considered to be very rare.

O Worship The Lord (#102229): Many pieces have appeared missing the "O" in the title "O Worship The Lord."

Praise The Lord Anyhow (#E1374B): The dog on this piece has been seen with either a black or brown nose.

Rejoicing With You (#E4724): In this piece, the "e" in the word "Bible" can either be seen or is being covered by the little girl's hand.

Sending My Love Your Way (#528609): "Sending My Love Your Way" has been produced with several variations. The figurine can be found missing the kitten at the girl's feet and also without stripes painted on the kite.

Smile, God Loves You (#E1373B): Pieces produced in the 1980s sometimes have the boy's black eye shaded brown.

Twenty Years And The Vision's Still The Same (#306843): Don't worry, you don't need glasses. On rare instances both the "sword" and the "eyeglass" year marks have been stamped on the bottom of the figurine at once.

Wishing You A Season Filled With Joy (#E2805): The dog should have only one of its eyes painted, though in the variation, both will appear painted black. The variation has been found on pieces produced with the "dove" mark.

Insuring Your Collection

*W*hen looking to insure your PRECIOUS MOMENTS collection, there are three major points you should consider:

1. Know your coverage. Collectibles are typically included in homeowner's or renter's insurance policies. Ask your agent if your policy covers fire, theft, floods, hurricanes, earthquakes and damage or breakage through routine handling. Also, ask if your policy covers claims at "current replacement value" – the amount it would cost to replace items if they were damaged, lost or stolen. This is extremely important since the secondary market value of a piece may well exceed its original retail price.

2. Document your collection. In the event of a loss, your insurance company will need proof of your collection and its value. Ask your insurance agent what information is acceptable. Keep receipts and an inventory of your collection in a different location, such as a safe deposit box, to protect them in case of emergency. Include the purchase date, price paid, size, issue year, edition limit, special markings and secondary market value for each piece.

3. Weigh the risk. To determine the coverage you need, calculate how much it would cost to replace your collection and compare it to the total amount your current policy would pay. If the amount of insurance does not cover your collection, ask your agent about adding a Personal Articles Floater or a Fine Arts Floater or "rider" to your policy, or insuring your collection under a separate policy. As with all insurance, you must weigh the risk of loss against the cost of additional coverage.

Many companies will accept a reputable secondary market price guide – such as the Collector's Value Guide™ – as a valid source for determining your collection's value.

From Paper To Porcelain – How A Figurine Is Created

*E*ach PRECIOUS MOMENTS piece begins as a drawing by artist Sam Butcher. Once he is satisfied with the way his idea looks on paper, the illustration is photographed and sent to a design studio in Nagoya, Japan. There, Master Sculptor Yasuhei Fujioka oversees its transformation into a figurine.

In the first stage of production, an artisan shapes a model of the illustration out of clay. After this is completed, the model goes through the first of many inspections to ensure Enesco's high standards of quality.

Next, the model is broken apart and molds are made from the pieces as it is easier to work on a smaller scale. Once the molds have been made, wet clay (known as "slip") is poured in them and allowed to air dry. The solid piece of porcelain that results is called "greenware."

This process is repeated until all the pieces that make up the figurine are complete. The pieces are then joined together with slip and the artisans smooth out the edges so that the figurine looks like one uniform piece. The fully assembled piece is left to air dry and then is put into the kiln to bake at 2,300° F for 14 hours.

When the figurine is taken out of the kiln, it is immersed in a mixture of pumice and water, which gives the figurine a smooth texture. Next the piece is polished and painted. The signature "tear-drop eyes" are the most difficult part of the figurine to paint – it can take an artisan three years to master the process!

Lastly, the piece goes in to the kiln for another four hours to adhere the paint to the porcelain. After a final inspection, the piece is ready for shipping to stores where it will make its public debut!

Tour The PRECIOUS MOMENTS® Chapel

*P*RECIOUS MOMENTS artist Samuel J. Butcher had a long-held ambition to build a chapel to honor the Lord. The only problem was that he wasn't sure where to build it. He knew it had to be a perfect location.

It was in 1984, while traveling by car from Arizona to Michigan, that Butcher found that elusive spot. More than 17 acres in Carthage, a town in the Ozark Mountains of Missouri, called out to

him. The land had rolling hills, a stream and even a cave; exactly what he had been looking for! Butcher bought the land and, in 1989, after four long years of construction, The PRECIOUS MOMENTS Chapel Complex welcomed its first visitors.

Today, Sam Butcher's PRECIOUS MOMENTS® Chapel Complex encompasses approximately 3000 acres of land. Visitors can tour not only The PRECIOUS MOMENTS Chapel, the focal point of the attraction, but also the Fountain of Angels and the PRECIOUS MOMENTS® Wedding Island.

THE CHAPEL

The PRECIOUS MOMENTS Chapel covers nearly 10,000 square feet and has 32-foot high ceilings. It features more than 50

biblical murals painted by Butcher. He is constantly adding to the murals and improving upon them, ensuring that every visit to The Chapel is new and different. There are more than 30 stained-glass windows featuring biblical scenes, as well as beautifully carved wooden doors (carved by Butcher and his understudy, Nelson Lete), fine bronze details, beautiful marble

floors and elaborate crystal chandeliers throughout the structure.

Visitors are sure to be moved by two rooms within The Chapel dedicated to special people who were close to Butcher during their lifetimes. One room is dedicated to the memory of Butcher's second son, Philip, who died in a car accident in 1990. The other is dedicated to Butcher's friend, Tim Ryan, who lost a courageous battle with cancer.

THE FOUNTAIN OF ANGELS®

The Fountain of Angels is an extravaganza for the senses: a water and light show choreographed to music performed by members of the London Philharmonic Symphony Orchestra. The beautiful music blasts from 42 speakers located above and around the amphitheater, making you feel as if the orchestra were right in the theater with you; while the action takes place among 250 hand-carved bronze PRECIOUS MOMENTS statues. Live shows and musical performances also take place in

the theater as well. The Fountain of Angels was remodeled in 1999 and is now enclosed in a covered 9-story theater, allowing for performances during both the day and evening, rain or shine.

THE WEDDING ISLAND

The PRECIOUS MOMENTS Chapel Complex also features a 40-acre lake that is fully stocked for fishing enthusiasts. The lake has several islands, one of which is the PRECIOUS MOMENTS Wedding Island, a romantic spot for couples. Weddings are performed on the island, which boasts its own wedding chapel with a PRECIOUS MOMENTS wedding mural and stained-glass windows; a Bride's House with pre-ceremony preparation rooms and a

Victorian mansion complete with a marble-floored ballroom and honeymoon suites. Both the chapel and the mansion were relocated to the island from other parts of Missouri.

AND MORE!

There are acres and acres of beautifully manicured lawns and landscaped gardens for you to wander through and meditate in, as well as a gallery which serves as a museum for original PRECIOUS MOMENTS artwork and awards. The Visitor's Center resembles a European city, complete with animated PRECIOUS MOMENTS characters, a castle, a moat, a waterfall – and a gift shop, of course! The Chapel gift shop was expanded and redesigned in 1999 to offer even more PRECIOUS MOMENTS products, including highly sought-after *Chapel Exclusives*.

The PRECIOUS MOMENTS Chapel Complex offers two different kinds of sleeping accommodations. You can stay at either  Cubby Bear's® RV Park, which features top-notch recreational-vehicle facilities, or at the Best Western PRECIOUS MOMENTS® Hotel. Both facilities are located close to The PRECIOUS MOMENTS Chapel Complex grounds.

The PRECIOUS MOMENTS Chapel Complex is open year-round and is free to the public, although fees are charged for tours of the PRECIOUS MOMENTS Wedding Island and performances at The Fountain of Angels. Millions of visitors from around the world have made a point of visiting Carthage, Missouri and the world's PRECIOUS MOMENTS headquarters. Why don't you?

10 YEARS OF THE PRECIOUS MOMENTS CHAPEL!

Last year was an exciting year at The Precious Moments Chapel Complex as the attraction celebrated its 10-year anniversary. Here's a look back at some of The Chapel's milestones.

1984: Samuel Butcher purchases land in Carthage, Missouri.

1985: Construction begins!

1989: The Chapel opens to the public.

1991: The museum opens to the public.

1994: The PRECIOUS MOMENTS hotel opens.

1996: Cubby Bear's RV Park opens for business.

1997: The Fountain of Angels and Wedding Island debut.

1998: A generous donation is made by Enesco to upgrade the landscaping of the grounds and renovations to the murals begin.

1999: A 9-story, theater-style enclosure to the Fountain of Angels is completed.

Let the Chapel Come To You!

Can't get enough of the PRECIOUS MOMENTS Chapel? Now you don't have to travel all the way to Carthage, Missouri to get the latest news and information. You can have it sent right to your home through a subscription to Chapel Bells Magazine! The magazine is issued quarterly and is filled with information on upcoming events, new PRECIOUS MOMENTS products and stories from collectors. For more information please contact:

CHAPEL BELLS MAGAZINE
P.O. Box 802
Carthage, MO 64836
or call
(800) 543-7975 ext. 3000
or visit their website at
www.preciousmoments.com

2000 CALENDAR OF EVENTS

The following is a list of events at The Chapel (and beyond)!

April

23 Easter Service at The Chapel

28 – May 13 Victorian Festival at The Chapel

May

4 – 7 International Collectibles Exposition in Atlanta, GA

June

22 – 25 International Collectibles Exposition in Rosemont, IL

25 – July 1 PRECIOUS MOMENTS Week at The Chapel

July

27 – 28 Licensee Event at The Chapel

September

22 – October 21 Gospel Music Month at The Chapel

December

1 – 3 Collectors' Christmas Weekend at The Chapel

Local Events:

Behind Those
PRECIOUS MOMENTS®

*E*ver wonder how Sam Butcher comes up with ideas for his artwork? He has said in the past that his ideas come from the Bible, songs and interaction with family, friends and collectors. Often, he is so touched by something he has seen or heard that he creates a figurine about the situation. Here are a few examples of pieces that have been inspired by real-life situations:

Hello Lord, It's Me Again – As a boy, Sam's oldest son Jon had his heart broken by a girlfriend who lost interest. Depressed and unsure of himself, Jon went to his father for advice. Sam suggested that the boy "call on the Lord" and soon after appeared the image of a boy on the telephone.

His Eye Is On The Sparrow – This figurine is based on a card Sam drew for a couple in need. The couple's son took his own life after coming home from the war. The family was heartbroken and, despite the support they received from friends, could not cope with the loss. Sam's card touched them so deeply that they were able to put the incident behind them and move on with their lives, knowing that their son was at peace.

I'm Following Jesus – Sam modeled this piece after his friend Carlito, who trusted that his faith in God would help him through anything. Carlito, an unemployed taxi driver, kept his faith and was rewarded with his own cab, in which he carried a sign that read "I'm Following Jesus" to help spread the word to others.

No Tears Past The Gate – Sam created this figurine for his friend Levi. Levi was despondent at the loss of his sister Lea, who passed away at the age of 18. Sam painted this picture to remind Levi that the joy of knowing that his sister is with God would come after the sadness of losing her.

Smile, God Loves You – This piece was inspired by a shopping spree! Shortly after his figurines became successful, Sam met his longtime friend Bill Biel at a men's clothing store. Bill was dressed very nicely and received prompt service, while Sam, who was dressed rather shabbily, was treated rudely and ignored. When Sam finally did find a clerk to help him, he bought a large amount of merchandise, which he paid for in cash. Sam reminded the shocked clerk never to judge a book by its cover. God loves us no matter what we look like.

The Year Of The Egg

Enesco has announced that the yearmark for 2000 pieces will be an egg. Sam Butcher explains in his own words why he chose this symbol to represent the first year of the new millennium:

"I have chosen the egg as a symbol of the coming millennium because it connotes a new beginning. And as just as we know little of what the 21st century will bring, no one knows what is taking place inside an egg. Nor will they completely understand until it is hatched and God's wonderful plan is revealed. The egg speaks of birth, of new things to come – things known only to God alone.

The egg, while it is a single object, is divided into three individual parts: the shell, the white and the yolk. In man, there are also three distinct divisions: the heart, the mind and the body. The heart speaks of our emotions. The mind, our intellect. While the body is the machine that puts into motion the actions of both the heart and mind. As we look toward a new millennium, we, too, must convey the emotions of a loving heart with a concern for those who are far less privileged. With our minds, we must assimilate the things that are important in order to face those uncertainties and build for a better tomorrow. This can only be achieved by a body that uses its mind to create, and its heart to reach out with the gift of loving, caring and sharing."

"Loving, Caring And Sharing" Around The Country

Want to make new friends, help out local charities and have a lot of fun at the same time? Want to meet fellow collectors in your immediate area? A local PRECIOUS MOMENTS club may be the answer for you!

In addition to the official *Collectors' Club* and *Fun Club* that are sponsored by Enesco, there are over 400 local PRECIOUS MOMENTS club chapters throughout the United States and Canada. The clubs usually hold 6-12 meetings annually, which are filled with PRECIOUS MOMENTS news and fun activities such as secret pals or guest speakers. "Wee Friends" in Irvine, California also holds annual craft workshops and dinner meetings for its members.

Another important aspect of club life is carrying out the messages of "loving, caring and sharing" through donations to various causes and charities. "You Have Touched So Many Hearts," an Illinois chapter, collects items for the Ronald McDonald Wish List at each club meeting. The club also makes donations to CAUSES, a children's abuse unit and Enlight Corporation, a children's camp.

Twenty members of the "Fifth Avenue Friends" chapter in Lancaster, Pennsylvania had a busy day on September 25th, 1999, when the PRECIOUS MOMENTS Care-A-Van came to town. In addition to raising almost $800 for a women's shelter, the club collected donations for the Second Harvest Food Bank, sold refreshments and raffled off gift baskets, the proceeds of which went to various local charities.

Many clubs collect soda can "pop tops" for those in need of dialysis and soup labels for local schools as well. Fundraisers and blood drives are additional ways that clubs give back to their communities. Clubs such as "Precious Moments 2x2" in Missouri also actively sponsor disabled children.

Enesco is proud of the work that the local clubs do each year and recognizes their efforts through exclusive club events. The PRECIOUS MOMENTS Cruise, one of the most eagerly anticipated events, has sailed three times since the line's 15th anniversary in 1993. Each time, thousands of collectors gather on a Royal Caribbean cruise ship for a week of PRECIOUS MOMENTS games, gifts and gossip! The fourth voyage, which is scheduled for June 2000, will sail from Canada to Alaska and is sure to be the best cruise yet!

The company also holds a Local Club Chapter Convention each October. The 1999 event, which was held October 15-16 in Arlington Heights, Illinois, drew nearly 500 club members. Seminars consisted of a new product preview, a club development program, a game show and speeches – including one by television celebrity Marshall Wallace. Attendees were also treated to a tour of the PRECIOUS MOMENTS showroom, a costume party and a "Works of the Heart" dinner and awards ceremony.

A Collectors' Christmas Weekend is held each December at The Chapel, during which the grounds are festively decorated. Collectors are welcome to explore The Chapel grounds throughout the weekend, while raffles, seminars and signings are also popular activities. This year's event will be particularly special, as it occurs during The Chapel's 10th Anniversary celebration.

If you would like more information on joining a local club, but don't know if there are any in your area, or are interested in starting your own PRECIOUS MOMENTS local club, contact Enesco's Collectors' Club Line at (877) 4-YOURCLUB.

From candles to cross-stitch, you can find nearly any thing you need with a PRECIOUS MOMENTS design. The line boasts more than 60 top-quality licensees, each of which is regulated by PRECIOUS MOMENTS Inc., the company established to assure that only the finest quality products feature PRECIOUS MOMENTS images. Here are a few of the products that can enhance your collection:

Books – Decorated Bibles and inspirational books can be found in retail stores for those who want to explore more of the comforting messages portrayed by the PRECIOUS MOMENTS pieces. For younger children, specially produced children's Bibles are also available, as well as story, coloring and activity books.

Children's Items – Mobiles, musical pull toys and soft-cloth characters make perfect gifts for infants and toddlers, while PRECIOUS MOMENTS themed games and activities will keep preschool-aged children entertained for hours! Start your infant collecting early with a PRECIOUS MOMENTS themed room, filled with decorated bedding, curtains and pillows.

Clothing – Make PRECIOUS MOMENTS a part of your wardrobe year round with T-shirts, sweatshirts, footwear and sleepwear for both the young and the young at heart. Lines of infant apparel and medical uniforms are also available. Both sterling silver and costume jewelry are sure to add a little pizzazz to your style, while beautifully decorated watches, knapsacks and handbags complete the look.

Crafts – For sewing enthusiasts, a wide assortment of embroidery and cross-stitch kits, books and pamphlets are available through licensees. Celebrate your own "precious moments" with a scrapbook kit featuring the images of all your favorite teardrop-eyed figurines!

Dolls – Dolls licensed through the PRECIOUS MOMENTS Company are one of the most popular products on the market. The dolls are collectible in and of themselves, with retirements, suspensions and limited editions within the line.

Giftware – Looking for a gift for that PRECIOUS MOMENTS collector who already has it all? A large selection of giftware is available in many categories. From ornaments and plaques to teapots and dishware sets, there is sure to be something for everyone in this category!

Home Decor – Accent your home with one of several PRECIOUS MOMENTS pieces. Themed curio cabinets are a great place to store your collection, while woven throws and linens help to dress up your furniture. Strategically placed PRECIOUS MOMENTS candles complete the look. Yard decorations, garden statues and planters spread the message of "loving, caring and sharing" to the whole neighborhood.

Party Goods – Invite PRECIOUS MOMENTS to your next party or wedding! A wide variety of stationery and invitations are available for all occasions, as well as wrapping paper, balloons, tableware and even cake decorations!

This is by no means a complete list of licensed products. And with more licensees being added every year, there are sure to be plenty of new products to come!

Extra! Extra!

The PRECIOUS MOMENTS Company recently introduced "Maggie Zene," the first Chapel Bells exclusive doll. The 16" beauty, who is dressed in a newspaper print-patterned dress and signed by Sam Butcher, is available only to subscribers of *Chapel Bells Magazine*. Produced in a limited edition of 750, "Maggie Zene" is sure to be a coveted item for years to come!

Collectors' Club News

*T*hree years after Enesco's PRECIOUS MOMENTS figurines entered the world of collectibles, fans were invited to join together to share their love of the line, meet other collectors and stay informed of events surrounding the line by becoming members of the Enesco PRECIOUS MOMENTS *Collectors' Club*. The club, which was established in 1981, was an immediate success with a membership of nearly 70,000 in its charter year. Since then, it has continued to be one of the largest collectors' clubs in the country and has been named "Collector's Club of the Year" by the National Association of Limited Edition Dealers (NALED).

A one year membership to the club costs only $28 and runs from January 1 until December 31 each year. Members joining in 2000 will receive "Thanks a Bunch," which features a lovable young girl carrying a bouquet of flowers, as their *Symbol of Membership Figurine*. In addition, club members will have the opportunity to purchase exclusive *Members Only Figurines*. For 2000, these pieces include "My Collection" and the adorable "Collecting Friends Along The Way."

A free subscription to the club's official quarterly publication, the "GOODNEWSLETTER," is another benefit of joining the club. This newsletter is filled with articles about the line, the company and collectors, as well as information on the latest releases, retirements and suspensions. Club members who join in 2000 will also receive a decorative box and journal book for recording their favorite PRECIOUS MOMENTS memories, a membership card, a gift registry that lists all of the PRECIOUS MOMENTS figurines, access to the club's exclusive web site and special mailings throughout the year.

Established in early 1999, the PRECIOUS MOMENTS *Fun Club* is great for families with younger children. The *Fun Club*, which replaced the Enesco PRECIOUS MOMENTS *Birthday Club*, provides contests, family activities, special stories for children and much more!

A one year membership to the *Fun Club* costs $22.50 and runs from January 1 until December 31. Along with a welcome letter, new members will receive the 2000 *Symbol of Membership Figurine*, "Don't Fret, We'll Get There Yet," as well as a reversible TENDER TAILS piece that turns from a caterpillar to a butterfly and a TENDER TAILS attachable caterpillar that also comes with detachable wings (both pieces are named "Iris"). Members also have the opportunity to purchase three exclusive *Members Only* pieces: "Ronnie The Rhino Beetle," "Reed The Centipede" and "Hold On To The Moment."

And that's not all! Members will also receive an illustrated storybook and a quarterly *Fun Club* newsletter that contains contests, games and stories about people and animals from around the world. In addition, *Fun Club* members will have access to the *Fun Club's* exclusive web site, which is full of games and activities that the whole family is sure to enjoy throughout the year.

Interested in joining the fun? Contact your local retailer for information on how to join the Enesco PRECIOUS MOMENTS *Collectors' Club* or the PRECIOUS MOMENTS *Fun Club*, or visit the Enesco web site at *www.enescoclubs.com*.

Easy Ways To Display!

*W*hile collecting PRECIOUS MOMENTS pieces is a lot of fun in itself, many collectors have discovered that finding new and different ways of displaying their pieces is an even greater adventure! While curio cabinets are a great way to protect, store and display your figurines, the PRECIOUS MOMENTS collection is so diverse that it lends itself to almost any decorating idea! Let your imagination take over and keep in mind that there is no right or wrong way to display your pieces. For those who still aren't convinced that they can create an eye-catching display, here are a few tips:

1. Include elements from the great outdoors! Blue painted plexiglass can serve as a lake, while some carefully created grassy banks can make the perfect fishing spot for your PRECIOUS MOMENTS anglers. Aquarium gravel can double as the real thing, while flat cookies or crackers make a convincing sidewalk! Never use real water in your displays, however, as it may damage your figurines.

2. Keep upcoming seasons and holidays in mind, as these occasions present perfect opportunities for displays. In the fall, cover a piece of red or orange fabric with some colorful dried leaves. Add your favorite Thanksgiving-themed figurines and decorate with some gourds or a cornucopia for the perfect autumn display!

A winter playland is a fun scene for when the weather gets cold. Place your favorite Christmas and winter pieces in a scene; perhaps creating multiple scenes in different areas of your home. Sledding and skating figurines look great on a frozen pond, created by covering a sheet of glass with aluminum foil. Complete the look with "snow" made from cotton.

Welcome in the spring with a festive Easter display! Add some of your favorite "bunny" pieces (don't forget to include the TENDER TAILS) to candy-filled Easter baskets. Or place fake grass on a table or shelf and incorporate Easter eggs, fresh flowers and your favorite PRECIOUS MOMENTS pieces.

3. Expand on series and themed pieces. Collections such as the *Nativity* series can easily be arranged into a holiday display by adding a stable and some hay. Christmas lights (either white or colored will work) finish the look and put the spotlight on your special collection. The COUNTRY LANE collection is another series which is easy to display. With some appropriately placed hay, the pieces take on a whole new look. A children's toy barn, some shrubs and a few fences in the background also helps give the scene an authentic feel.

4. Incorporate existing items into your displays, such as framed photographs or pictures. For instance, pictures of your child at different ages can be highlighted by pieces from the *Growing In Grace* series. Or create a dedication to your favorite pet by incorporating pictures of your pooch, some of its favorite toys and a variety of puppy-themed pieces, such as "Loving Is Sharing" and "Puppy Love."

5. Do you have an old dollhouse which has been stored away in the attic for years? Clean it out and make it part of your display! The pint-sized LITTLE MOMENTS pieces will look right at home in this environment. Also, try adding pieces to more "unusual" places for a fun display. When your guests find "Lettuce Pray" mixed in with your salad bowls in the china cabinet, they are sure to be surprised!

6. For inspiration, plan a visit to a craft shop. Craft and hobby shops are ideal places to discover ideas for new displays. Here you will find anything that you need to create the perfect display; from snow-capped trees to silk flowers to miniature accessories for your figurines. Take your time as you walk through the aisles of the store, paying extra attention to anything and everything that catches your eye!

7. Don't limit your displays to one room; spread them throughout the house! A single, strategically-placed figurine can liven up an entire room. For instance, pieces such as "Sweeter As The Years Go By" or "Eggs Over Easy" placed on a shelf near the oven will help to warm up your kitchen; while "The Story Of God's Love" is the perfect accessory for your library or bookshelf. If you have a home office, add a work-themed figurine, such as "You Are The Type I Love" to help you get through your day.

8. Give your displays a personal touch by making use of your hobbies and occupation, or those of your friends and family. If a loved one is a soccer enthusiast, add the LITTLE MOMENTS piece "You Will Always Be A Winner To Me" to a display of trophies and photographs of your loved one in action. Likewise, recognize professional achievements through PRECIOUS MOMENTS displays featuring awards, work-related photographs and items. From police officers to tailors, there is a piece for a wide variety of professions within the PRECIOUS MOMENTS collection. Plus, you can place a display in a wicker basket for a great gift idea anyone would be sure to treasure for years to come!

9. No matter how you choose to display your PRECIOUS MOMENTS collection, relax, get creative and have fun!

Glossary

bottomstamp – any identifying marks on the underside of a piece such as the title or copyright year.

closed – a piece whose production is limited by either time or quantity which is no longer available from the manufacturer.

Century Circle – a select group of retailers (40 nationwide) who receive early shipments of new pieces and exclusive products. This is the highest dealer level.

Chapel Exclusives – special pieces only available from the The PRECIOUS MOMENTS Chapel Complex in Carthage, Missouri or through their retail catalog.

collectibles – everything that is "able to be collected" can be considered a "collectible," but it is generally recognized that a true collectible should increase in value over time.

damaged box (DB) – a secondary market term used when a collectible's box is in poor condition, often times diminishing the value of the item.

Distinguished Service Retailers (DSR) – the second highest dealer level designation, these retailers also receive early shipments of new pieces and exclusive products.

exchange – a secondary market service which lists pieces that collectors wish to buy, sell or trade. The exchange works as a middleman and usually requires a commission.

limited edition (LE) – a piece scheduled for a predetermined production quantity or time. Some pieces have been limited to a specific number or limited by year of production.

markings – any of the various identifying features found on a collectible. It can be information found on bottomstamps or backstamps, an artist's signature or a production mark.

mint in box (MIB) – a secondary market term used when a collectible's original box is "good as new," which usually adds to the value of the item.

no box (NB) – a secondary market term used when a collectible's original box is missing. For most collectibles, having the original box is a factor in the value.

no mark (NM) – since 1981, PRECIOUS MOMENTS pieces have had a production mark incised on the back or bottom of the piece, which indicates the year it was produced. Pieces produced prior to 1981 are classified as having "no mark" (see also *unmarked*).

open – a PRECIOUS MOMENTS piece which is currently in production and available in stores.

porcelain bisque – the hard, nonabsorbent material used to make PRECIOUS MOMENTS figurines; ceramic made primarily with kaolin (a pure form of clay).

retired – a piece which is taken out of production, never to be made again, usually followed by a scarcity of the piece and a rise in value on the secondary market.

secondary market – the source for buying, selling and trading collectibles according to basic supply-and-demand principles

("pay what the market will bear"). Popular pieces which have retired or pieces with low edition numbers can appreciate in value far above the original issue price.

suspended – a piece that has been removed from production by Enesco but may return in the future, possibly with slight design modifications.

unmarked – term for PRECIOUS MOMENTS pieces produced after 1981, which are either missing the annual production mark or were produced intentionally without the mark (see also *no mark*).

variations – pieces that have color, design or printed text changes from the "original" piece. Some of these changes are minor, while some are important enough to affect the value of a piece on the secondary market.

year mark – also called a "production mark." Each PRECIOUS MOMENTS piece has a production mark incised on the bottom or back which indicates the year the piece was produced. These marks have been used since 1981 and change yearly.

All PRECIOUS MOMENTS pieces are listed below in alphabetical order. Following each piece in parentheses is an abbreviation for the type of item (see key) and the stock number. The first number in the page and picture column refers to the piece's location within the Value Guide section and the second to the box in which it is pictured on that page.

ABBREVIATION KEY

A	Accessories
B	Bells
CB	Covered Boxes
CC	Candle Climbers
DI	Displays
DM . . .	Die-Cast Metal
DO . . .	Dolls
E	Eggs
F	Figurines
FR	Frames
H	TENDER TAILS Hugs For You
HB . . .	Hinged Boxes
J	Jack-In-The-Boxes
LM . . .	LITTLE MOMENTS
ME . . .	Medallions
MU . . .	Musicals
N	Night Lights
O	Ornaments
P	Plates
PL	Plush
TH	Thimbles
TR	Tree Toppers
TO	TENDER TAILS Ornaments
TT	TENDER TAILS

	Page	Pic.

	Page	Pic.

	Page	Pic.

Alphabetical Index

Numerical Index

300

Numerical Index

ACKNOWLEDGEMENTS

CheckerBee Publishing would like to extend a special thanks to Dori Dimmig, Jean Jensen, Ovada Ousley, Janet Roth, Nancy Schowalter, Kristi Schult and Dianne Van Dyke. Many thanks to the great people at Enesco Corporation, The PRECIOUS MOMENTS Chapel and PRECIOUS MOMENTS Inc.